R. H. HUTTON
Critic and Theologian

R. H. Hutton reading with fading eyesight in his later years as editor of the *Spectator*.

R. H. HUTTON
Critic and Theologian

===

*The Writings of R. H. Hutton on
Newman, Arnold, Tennyson,
Wordsworth, and George Eliot*

MALCOLM WOODFIELD

CLARENDON PRESS · OXFORD
1986

Oxford University Press, Walton Street, Oxford OX2 6DP

Oxford New York Toronto
Delhi Bombay Calcutta Madras Karachi
Kuala Lumpur Singapore Hong Kong Tokyo
Nairobi Dar es Salaam Cape Town
Melbourne Auckland

and associated companies in
Beirut Berlin Ibadan Nicosia

Oxford is a trade mark of Oxford University Press

Published in the United States
by Oxford University Press, New York

British Library Cataloguing in Publication Data
Woodfield, Malcolm
R. H. Hutton, critic and theologian: the
writings of R. H. Hutton on Newman, Arnold,
Tennyson, Wordsworth and George Eliot.
1. Hutton, R. H.
I. Title
801' .95' 0924 PN75.H/
ISBN 0-19-818564-2

Library of Congress Cataloging in Publication Data
Woodfield, Malcolm.
R. H. Hutton, critic and theologian.
'R. H. Hutton: manuscript and published writings': p.
Bibliography: p.
Includes index.
1. Hutton, Richard Holt, 1826-1897. 2. Criticism—
Great Britain—19th century. 3. English literature—
19th century—History and criticism. 4. Religion
and literature. 5. Theology in literature. I. Hutton,
Richard Holt, 1826-1897. II. Title.
PR29.H8W6 1986 820' .9' 008 86-8478
ISBN 0-19-818564-2

Set by Downdell Ltd., Oxford
Printed in Great Britain
at the University Printing House, Oxford
by David Stanford
Printer to the University

For Laura

ACKNOWLEDGEMENTS

I AM glad of the opportunity to record my gratitude to a number of people who have helped and judiciously hindered this project: I am thankful in innumerable ways for the generous and unselfish support of my parents, Kathleen and Maurice Woodfield; I shall always be indebted to the teaching and the rigorous demands of Philip Davis; J. H. Prynne gave unstintingly of his time and learning; Gillian Beer gave encouragement and advice as my research supervisor; Wilbur Sanders gave me an example of humane scholarship which this book does not live up to. Ronald Hindmarsh of Heidelberg University has been generous and supportive; and I have benefited enormously from the conversation, criticism, and friendship of Richard Kerridge. I also thank Professor David Carroll, Professor Ian Jack, and Professor Christopher Ricks for their criticisms, their close reading, and their questions. I am very grateful to Kim Scott Walwyn of Oxford University Press for her care and patience. Laura Karran devoted much time and tolerance to editorial work on final drafts of the book, and the result is more readable for her pains. For the errors from which such friends and scholars have saved me I am grateful, for those which remain I am responsible.

A book of this sort is particularly indebted to the work of other scholars, and I am especially grateful to Professor Robert Tener of Calgary University. He is a selfless and painstakingly careful scholar whose knowledge of this field is unrivalled and who has, in his quiet way, cultivated a clearing in a Victorian jungle.

Finally I can sincerely thank the Master and Fellows of Sidney Sussex College, Cambridge, for the financial and social support of their institution and fellowship.

M.W.

CONTENTS

x CONTENTS

1
R. H. Hutton: 1826-1897

'THE finest and bravest critic of this generation' is how John Morley described Richard Holt Hutton in 1897.[1] The critics of this generation included such writers as Matthew Arnold, Leslie Stephen, Walter Bagehot, G. H. Lewes, and Walter Pater, yet Hutton remains the only one of these without a biographer or expositor. In fact it was Hutton's express wish that no memoir be written in his own day—although one of his colleagues did publish a brief one— but previous accounts would in any case now be inadequate since it is only in very recent years that authorship has been attributed to many thousands of important pieces of Victorian periodical writing amongst which much of Hutton's work lies.[2]

Hutton was a prolific essayist and journalist whose writing career spanned precisely half a century—he published his first article in 1847 and his last in 1897. During that time he worked as editor and contributor for a series of journals, most importantly the *Spectator*, which he edited from 1861 until his death. It is no exaggeration to say that he wrote on virtually all the major writers and thinkers of the second half of the nineteenth century, as well as many of those now regarded as minor ones. His particular interest was the relationship of literature to life and thought, especially to morality and secular society. Highly regarded in his own day, Hutton's work is not only intrinsically valuable as criticism but also one of the most reliable and consistent guides to the temper of the Victorian mind.

Although drawing on the prodigious range of Hutton's writing, this study concentrates on his work on five writers in particular, in an effort to bring out the intrinsic value of his criticism as well as showing how their writing met in the mind of one of their

[1] Letter of 14 Sept. 1897 to Meredith Townsend, in the possession of Michael Graham-Jones.

[2] See John Hogben, *Richard Holt Hutton of the 'Spectator'* (London, 1899), and accounts in a number of journals, especially *Academy*, 52 (1897), 221–2; *Contemporary Review*, 72 (1897), 457–69; the *Critic*, 37 (1900), 269–73; *Inquirer*, 56 (1897), 601–8, 641–55; *Westminster Review*, 151 (1899), 579–83. On the question of attribution, see the *Wellesley Index to Victorian Periodicals* and the *Victorian Periodicals Newsletter*, especially R. H. Tener, 'The Writings of R. H. Hutton', *VPN* 17 (Sept. 1972), 1–183, and 20 (June 1973), 14–40. See also Appendix to this volume.

contemporaries. This is not a biographical study, but some account of his life and background is necessary to indicate the particular direction his work took.

Hutton was born in Leeds in 1826. His father and grandfather were Unitarian ministers. His father, Joseph Hutton, was the minister of Mill Hill Chapel in Leeds and later, from 1835, of Carter Lane Chapel in London. His grandfather, also Joseph Hutton, was a minister in Dublin who was said to have 'wept easily in the pulpit' and who had the young James Martineau as an assistant.[3] It was clearly intended that Hutton should follow the family tradition, whose values he certainly shared, and become a Unitarian minister. The fact that he instead became a journalist and cultural critic, a religious man in a secular profession, must be explained partly by the changing and growing role and acceptability of the journalist, and partly by the significant changes in the Unitarian Church itself. These latter changes were represented and even led by James Martineau, of whom Hutton became a close follower.

The Unitarian Church had grown steadily in the eighteenth century and had become associated, especially under the leadership of Joseph Priestly, with free thought and radicalism in politics. Indeed until the passing of the 1813 Trinity Act, the Unitarian had to practise illegally (as the Toleration Act of 1689 did not apply to Catholics or Anti-Trinitarians) and a great divide separated the Unitarian Church from other Dissenters (such as Baptists, Methodists, and Presbyterians). The 1820s and 1830s were, for Unitarians, years of struggle in their efforts to change the remaining laws disqualifying Dissenters from worship, public office, and education.[4] Hutton inherited this commitment to freedom and dissent, but joined the group of progressive Unitarians dissenting from Priestley's theology and taking positive action in secular branches of politics, education, and publishing. They addressed their public by writing rather than preaching and appealed to the intellect rather than the emotions: they were not, it might be said, inclined to weep easily in the pulpit.

The fundamental character of Unitarianism lies in its belief in the Unity of God—the Unitarian denies the Trinity, and repudiates original sin and the necessity of Atonement. Many of the active characteristics of Unitarianism are shared with Victorian Liberal-

---

[3] W. R. Nicoll, *The Key to the Blue Closet* (London, 1907), 252.
[4] E. M. Wilbur, *A History of Unitarianism* (Cambridge, Mass., 1952), 353–68.

ism: it is unusually tolerant and optimistic, committed to contributions to social progress and the diligent discharge of social duties. The theological aspects of Unitarianism, however, underwent significant changes in the 1830s and 1840s as the movement of Priestley was eclipsed by that of Martineau and his colleagues. In 1835 Martineau undertook to explore the true foundation of religious belief in a series of sermons published as *The Rationale of Religious Inquiry or, the question stated of Reason, the Bible, and the Church* (London, 1836). Martineau attacked both the Roman Catholic reliance on Church authority and Protestant reliance on scriptural authority. 'Reason', he wrote, 'is the ultimate appeal, the supreme tribunal, to the test of which even Scripture must be brought'.[5] Martineau was not the first to insist that scripture should satisfy the demands of reason, but he was one of the first Englishmen to bring German biblical criticism and its fruits before an English public, and one of the first of a growing rationalist movement in higher criticism. In 1838 Charles Hennell, a Unitarian layman, published his *Inquiry Concerning the Origin of Christianity* which, by its very nature as an 'inquiry', was implicitly sceptical of biblical infallibility, though it supported the truth of the Christian faith. George Eliot studied Hennell's book closely when it was first published and although it cannot be said that it was even partially responsible for undermining her religious faith, such works were clearly part of a movement which tested the basis of Christian belief and which was supported by German scholarship. As a critic of George Eliot, Hutton was particularly sensitive to the importance to her work of her translation of Ludwig Feuerbach, and although he retained his Christian faith he retained also an intellectual sympathy with the roots of George Eliot's scepticism which makes him a peculiarly acute critic of her novels.

Although Hennell's book and similar inquiries were not necessarily atheistical, they tended to reproduce the Bible as evidence on which the reader could choose to base, or not to base, religious faith. They were a secularizing form of literature which left the individual alone with his conscience and reason: John Morley called it a 'dissolvent literature'.[6] Such biblical criticism, however, gradually became accepted in Anglican theology as part of that movement known as the Broad Church, whose milestone was the publication

---

[5] Wilbur, *A History of Unitarianism*, 367-8.
[6] John Morley, *Critical Miscellanies* (London, 1886), iii. 242.

in 1861 of *Essays and Reviews.* The acceptance of biblical criticism by the orthodoxy was slow, partly because of ignorance of German and German scholarship in the clergy and laity, but Hutton's professional career and religious affiliations show him to be in the forefront of this movement from Unitarianism to Broad Church.[7] Thus his education and early career are distinctly Unitarian, under the personal influence of James Martineau, but by 1861 he had been persuaded by the Broad Churchman F. D. Maurice of the truth of the Incarnation and thus left both the Unitarian Church and the journals associated with it. The first article he wrote for the *Spectator*, which he joined in 1861, was, significantly, a review of *Essays and Reviews.* Hutton, however, was impatient with Maurice's figurative interpretation of the language of the Bible, especially of its teaching on atonement and eternal punishment. The Unitarian and Broad Church theologies shared an appeal to the intellectual, 'scientific' Christian, but although Hutton wanted to believe as an intellectual, he also wanted the certainty represented by an external authority. It was in search of such an external source of certainty that Hutton turned to the personal authority of Cardinal Newman. This relationship never led Hutton to become a Roman Catholic (although that was rumoured) but it did lead him to the High Church. This movement from Unitarian dissenter to High Churchman demonstrates the struggle of an intellectual with religious beliefs which his own intellectual loyalties undermine and cast doubt upon.

Hutton came under the influence of his first mentor, Martineau, when he entered University College, London, as a student in 1841. The College had been established in 1828 after pressure from Radicals and Nonconformists who were still excluded from Oxbridge; it was based on the model of German professorial, non-collegiate universities such as those at Bonn and Berlin. Although this link with Germany was to become important for theology and for Hutton's religious ideas, the Council of the College deliberately omitted theology from its course, creating lasting controversy and setting up a precedent which secularized higher education in the nineteenth century.[8] From these earliest days Hutton was part of

---

[7] D. G. Wigmore-Beddoes, *Yesterday's Radicals: A Study of the Affinity Between Unitarianism and Broad Church Anglicanism in the Nineteenth Century* (Cambridge, 1971).

[8] H. H. Bellot, *University College, London, 1826-1926* (London, 1929), 1-61; J. W. Adamson, *English Education, 1789-1902* (Cambridge, 1930), 89-94.

movements which threatened to undermine the beliefs of their progenitors: liberal elements in devout enquiry threatened to foster an atmosphere of secular scepticism which worked against the interests of organized religion.

The years of Hutton's attendance were times of struggle for recognition and funding at the College, but in his memoir of Walter Bagehot, a life-long close friend, Hutton wrote warmly of his time there and praised its intellectual standards.[9] The curriculum, in keeping with a recommendation for a 'course of liberal education for civil and active life' by the now 'conservative' Joseph Priestley in his 1788 *Lectures on History and General Policy*, included 'languages, mathematics, physics, the mental and moral sciences, the laws of England, history and political economy'. By Hutton's time there was a preponderance of students in medicine and the law, and it was here that he felt the necessity of combining the religion he professed with a profession he could live by.

Hutton took his BA in 1845, winning a medal in philosophy and a distinction in mathematics. He had resolved to read for the Bar, but first took the significant and still unusual step of continuing his studies at the University of Bonn, the very university whose establishment in 1818 had moved Thomas Campbell to first put forward the idea of an English equivalent in London. It was as if Hutton were exploring the roots of his new and growing allegiance to progressive Unitarianism. Although German educational theory was beginning to exercise influence in England, a German education was still a rarity.[10] Hutton studied under Theodor Mommsen in Bonn before going on to the University of Heidelberg where he became tutor to none other than James Martineau's son, Russell.[11] Despite Hutton's intention to read for the Bar, his combined interest in German theology and Martineau's Unitarianism led him to return in 1847 to prepare for the Unitarian ministry at Manchester New College, regarded as a stronghold of the liberal Unitarians and staffed by James Martineau, John James Tayler, and F. W. Newman, among others. Hutton also produced what is probably his first published piece, an essay for the Unitarian *Prospective Review*

[9] 'Walter Bagehot', *Fortnightly Review*, NS 22 (Oct. 1877), 453–84.

[10] W. H. G. Armytage, *The German Influence on English Education* (London, 1969); G. Haines, *The German Influence on English Education and Science, 1800–1866* (London, 1957). See also W. Hamilton, 'On the State of the English Universities', *Edinburgh Review*, 53 (1831), No. 106.

[11] A. W. Jackson, *James Martineau* (London, 1900), 105.

on the state of Protestantism in Germany.[12] He did not, however, follow his course at Manchester, but returned to Germany with the Martineaus, to study theology in Berlin.[13]

The Unitarians had always been regarded as something of an intellectual élite amongst Dissenters, being more interested in publishing than in preaching the word, unlike the Methodists and Evangelicals.[14] The new breed of Unitarian was, however, regarded as élitist even by Unitarian standards, especially in Manchester, Liverpool, and Sheffield, where they were involved in reform and local government.[15] When Hutton returned to look for a ministry his welcome was far from friendly: he was the product of a London education (even Manchester New College was to move, after his time, to London in 1853), and his German education was an exotic acquisition more usually associated with the privileged and glittering likes of Monkton Milnes. In fact, Hutton did not return with a self-conscious 'European' bias like that of Matthew Arnold. Indeed, although Hutton witnessed, like Clough whom he came to know well, the stirrings of revolution in 1847 and 1848, he seems, unlike Clough, to have been virtually unaffected by political and educational radicalism in Europe.[16] Nevertheless, Hutton was regarded as a progressive élitist when he returned. This was an accusation he found particularly painful, and he was later to spend much of his life attacking notions of the pre-eminence of an intellectual 'clerisy', such as that propounded by Arnold. Hutton complained to Martineau of his treatment by a clergy and laity who did not understand Hegel, and he was advised:

I quite understand, my dear Richard, your mortification at being called too profound in your teaching . . . I faithfully believe we must bear up against this reproach, and speak faithfully what is given us to say, without much regard to that standard of usage which regulates 'unintelligibilities'.[17]

---

[12] *Prospective Review*, 3 (May 1847), 254–89.

[13] Jackson, *James Martineau*, p. 105.

[14] H. McLachlan, *The Unitarian Movement in the Religious Life of England: Its Contribution to Thought and Learning, 1700–1900* (London, 1934).

[15] Monica Fryckstedt, *Elizabeth Gaskell's 'Mary Barton' and 'Ruth': A Challenge to Christian England* (Uppsala, 1982), 145.

[16] Priscilla Robertson, 'Students on the Barricades: Germany and Austria, 1848', *Political Science Quarterly*, 84 (June 1969), 367–79; Thomas Hinton, 'German Intellectuals on the Eve of 1848', *German Life and Letters*, NS 2 (1948–49), 13–21.

[17] *The Life and Letters of James Martineau*, ed. J. Drummond and C. B. Upton, 2 vols. (London, 1902), i. 337 (Nov. 1849).

Hutton was later to be attacked for being 'too profound' as a literary critic, but his apprenticeship in contributing to journals taught him to regulate his writing to the standard of usage.

While Hutton was away in Germany in 1848, a group of Unitarians established University Hall, Gordon Square, as a religious centre for Dissenters attending University College: 'a place where instruction without reference to creed should be permitted in theology and . . . to maintain the sanctity of private judgement in matters of religion'.[18] It was thus established to supply the theological element omitted from University College's curriculum. The Hall was founded in celebration of the 1844 Dissenters' Chapels Act which settled, in the Unitarian Church's favour, disputes over claims to Nonconformist chapels and charities. The building was erected in 1850, and Arthur Hugh Clough appointed Principal with Hutton as his Assistant Principal.[19] When Clough resigned in 1852, Hutton briefly held the position before ill health forced him to resign—in 1853 the Hall was taken over by Manchester New College.

The position found for Hutton in the academic world was intended to provide him with some security while he established himself as a writer and editor. Having written occasional articles for the Unitarian quarterly, the *Prospective Review*, in 1847 and 1849, he began to write regularly for them in 1850.[20] In 1851 he was invited by the proprietor of the weekly *Inquirer*, Richard Kinder, to join the editorial staff of the journal which was established as the organ of the Unitarian Church.[21] Hutton, however, joined an editorial team which was already familiar to him since its members, Walter Bagehot, William Roscoe, Timothy Ostler, and John Sandford, had all been students at University College.

Hutton was now able to marry Anne Roscoe, the sister of one of his colleagues, after a long courtship. In May 1852, however, he was taken seriously ill with inflammation of the lungs and towards the end of October, after resigning as Principal of University Hall, he sailed for the West Indies and a healthier climate.[22] Far from

---

[18] Bellot, *University College, London*, 298–301.

[19] Wilbur, *A History of Unitarianism*, 359–65.

[20] Drummond and Upton, *Life and Letters of Martineau*, ii. 340.

[21] Roger Thomas, 'The *Inquirer*', *Inquirer*, 25 July 1942, 211, and McLachlan, *The Unitarian Movement in the Religious Life of England*, pp. 216–17.

[22] University Hall Council 'Records of Minutes', 21 May, 1 June, 3 June, 11 June, 16 June 1852.

discovering a beneficial climate there, he and his new wife found an epidemic of yellow fever raging and were both immediately victims of it. When Hutton recovered consciousness after a week in a coma he discovered that his wife had not survived. He had to be brought home by his brother-in-law, as he records in his memoir of Roscoe.[23] Hutton married for a second time in 1854.

On his return home Hutton worked for the War Office and took up his law studies again, though he did not continue in public service, nor was he called to the Bar. He returned to the editorial office of the *Inquirer*, to which he contributed regularly from mid-1853 to the end of 1855. Also in mid-1853 he took over a second editorial chair as a member of the staff of the *Prospective Review*. Hutton and the other editors of the *Inquirer* had become increasingly associated with the progressive Unitarianism of James Martineau and J. J. Tayler, and Hutton himself recorded the unease of their readership:

Our regime was, I imagine, a time of great desolation for the very tolerant and thoughtful constituency for whom we wrote; and many of them, I am confident, yearned, and were fully justified in yearning, for those better days when this tyranny of ours should be overpast . . . Only a denomination of 'just men' trained in tolerance for generations and in that respect, at least, made all but 'perfect', would have endured it at all.[24]

The orthodox members of his readership were particularly horrified by Hutton's editorials, in which he drew limits on the authority of scripture, and by his appeals to a wider audience and the authority of common men. He wrote that as theologians 'we must judge of God's nature by our own, when taken in its highest mood', and that the 'cut and dried form of Christianity' offered by Unitarianism was 'wholly outside the sphere of popular want'.[25] This appeal to the authority and needs of common men is central to Hutton's work and to this study. It explains his energetic defence of complacency, his criticism of Arnoldian exclusivity, and his admiration for George Eliot's 'provincialism' and Wordsworth's concentration on common experience. In retrospect we can see that in the 'judging of God's nature by our own' Hutton is absorbing and adapting

[23] *Poems and Essays by the Late William Caldwell Roscoe*, ed. R. H. Hutton, 2 vols. (London, 1860), i, p. xci.

[24] *Fortnightly Review*, NS 22 (Oct. 1877), 469–70.

[25] 'The Course of Theology', *Inquirer*, 10 June 1854, 353, and 'Religious Intelligence', *Inquirer*, 2 Dec. 1854, 757.

contemporary humanistic thought—especially the products of German idealism—and considering its application to 'popular want', a phrase which was to become particularly important in his discussion of the writing of Matthew Arnold. Having failed to enter the ministry, Hutton used the *Inquirer* as a pulpit from which to preach to the preachers: one of his earliest articles had been on 'The Position and Claims of the Unitarian Ministry' (*Inquirer*, 28 February 1852, pp. 129–30), and he went on to write about the Church's ministers, their sermons, their backgrounds, and their training. Though he wrote as much on literature and politics, his writing on theology has the most personal, even autobiographical element in it.[26]

At the annual meeting of the London District Unitarian Society on 1 June 1855, the young reactionary clergyman T. L. Marshall and older, dissident orthodox ministers joined with dissident laymen in passing a motion condemning the *Inquirer*'s tone and content. Hutton and his colleagues resigned at the end of 1855, probably much to the relief of Richard Kinder, who faced financial collapse as circulation dropped and the orthodoxy planned to establish an alternative journal. T. L. Marshall, it is no surprise to see, was appointed the new editor in 1856.[27]

Hutton was still at this time an editor of the *Prospective Review*. The first number of this journal had been published in 1845 by the liberal Unitarians, Martineau, J. J. Tayler, J. H. Thom, and Charles Wicksteed. By July 1852 they had been joined by W. C. Roscoe who was followed by Hutton.[28] Hutton, though, seems to have done almost all the editorial work and, according to the MS *Diary* of Henry Crabb Robinson, to whose coterie Hutton belonged, several numbers of the journal were written entirely by Hutton.[29] This seems unlikely, though Hutton certainly did now have the opportunity to write lengthy essays on contemporary theology and literature, especially on the novel.

The circulation of the *Prospective Review* was low; it probably rarely sold more than 1,000 copies, since it was regarded as a sec-

---

[26] See 'Manchester New College and University Hall', *Inquirer*, 9 July 1853, 433–4; 'Our Church Quiescent', *Inquirer*, 19 Nov. 1853, 737–8; 'Sermons', *Inquirer*, 10 Dec. 1853, 785–6, and 17 Dec. 1853, 801–2; 'Priests and Ministers', *Inquirer*, 28 Oct. 1854, 673; 'The Dynasty of Newspapers', *Inquirer*, 5 May 1855, 273.

[27] Thomas, *Inquirer*, p. 213.

[28] See Bagehot's letter to Crabb Robinson of 8 Feb. 1855 (Henry Crabb Robinson Correspondence, Dr Williams's Library).

[29] Crabb Robinson MS *Diary*, 11 Nov. 1854 (Dr Williams's Library).

tarian organ of the Unitarian Church but was distrusted by Unitarians themselves. In mid-1854 George Chapman, owner and editor of the *Westminster Review*, faced bankruptcy and the need to sell off the journal, which was anonymously edited by George Eliot.[30] In consequence James Martineau was involved in negotiations to buy it in order to establish a broader base for the views of himself and his colleagues. He was frustrated in this attempt, however, by the financial help afforded to Chapman by a 'Comptist coterie', including Martineau's estranged sister Harriet who is thought to have contributed five hundred pounds. The editors of the *Prospective Review* therefore decided, in 1855, to establish a new quarterly, as Martineau recorded:

So next, having both staff and funds in readiness, and in the opinion of experienced publishers, an open field of unrepresented opinion between heavy Whiggism and the decorous Church latitude of the *Edinburgh* on the one hand, and the atheistic tendency and refugee politics of the *Westminster* on the other, we proposed to start the *National Review*.[31]

This statement, in fact, understates in its excitement the difficulties the founders had in finding backers and staff for the *National Review*. Hutton and Bagehot agreed to become joint editors, though poorly paid and reluctant: 'Hutton and myself are sure of the blame if we fail, and not sure of the credit if it succeeds', wrote Bagehot.[32] Under their editorship, however, the *National Review* became the vehicle for some of the finest criticism of the mid-century, in which Hutton could write not only on Mill and George Eliot at length, but also on Darwin and Hegel. Bagehot also praises Hutton for his ability to extract the maximum potential out of his contributors. The journal was not only an intellectual but was also a financial success: the journal needed a circulation of 1,250 to make a profit, and had an average circulation of 1,500.[33] Hutton, however, deeply influenced by the Anglicanism of F. D. Maurice, found it impossible to reconcile his religious profession with a

---

[30] G. S. Haight, *George Eliot: A Biography* (London, 1969), 98, 140–1.

[31] Drummond and Upton, *Life and Letters of James Martineau*, i. 269.

[32] Bagehot to Crabb Robinson, 5 Apr. 1855. Bagehot received fifty pounds per annum and Hutton, who undertook to manage the journal and correct the proofs, received one hundred pounds.

[33] See William Stebbing, *Charles Henry Pearson* (London, 1900), 78–9, and Drummond and Upton, *Life and Letters of James Martineau*, i. 269. For Bagehot on Hutton's editorship, see Mrs Russell Barrington, *The Life of Walter Bagehot* (London, 1914), 221.

career associated with a journal whose loyalties remained, in spite of everything, Unitarian, and he resigned as editor in June 1862.[34] Meanwhile the Civil War in America brought circulation there to a halt, a blow from which the *National Review* never entirely recovered: the journal folded in 1864 (and should not be confused with the later *National Review*, published from 1883 until 1960).

Hutton's editorial position at the *National Review* from 1855 to 1862 was not his only commitment during this period. Late in 1856 James Wilson, the founder, owner, and editor of the *Economist*, needed a replacement for his literary editor, William Delafield Arnold. Through the intervention of W. R. Greg, a contributor to both the *National Review* and the *Economist*, Wilson appointed Hutton in May 1857.[35] In 1859 Wilson went to India as Minister of Finance, appointing Bagehot, who had married Wilson's daughter, editor and manager in 1860, a post he held until his death in 1877.

Although Hutton contributed literary reviews and political leaders to the *Economist* between 1857 and 1861, the appointment of his friend and colleague ended, as he confided to Clough, his ambition of commanding his own readership through that weekly journal.[36] His opportunity came, however, when in 1861 he became joint editor and proprietor of the weekly *Spectator*, a post he held until his death in 1897.

A brief summary of Hutton's writing until 1861, shows that he wrote for the quarterly *Prospective Review* and the weekly *Inquirer* from the late 1840s to the mid-1850s, and then for the quarterly *National Review* and the weekly *Economist*. He also contributed to the quarterly *North British Review* and the weekly *Saturday Review*. The progress of Hutton's editorial career shows him moving from journals which are explicitly linked to religious movements, to one which has more tenuous religious affiliations, to journals which are apparently secular both in terms of their editorial bias and their readership. Hutton's own writing, however, was always evenly divided between theology, literature, and politics, and of all the contributions to these journals, Hutton's were the least doctrinal, the most liberal. His writing is marked by a concentration, not only

---

34 Barrington, *Life of Walter Bagehot*, pp. 364–5.

35 E. I. Barrington, *The Servant of All: Pages from the Life of James Wilson*, 2 vols. (London, 1927), i. 135, 149.

36 *Correspondence of Arthur Hugh Clough*, ed. F. L. Mulhauser, 2 vols. (London, 1957), ii. 582.

in the weekly journal, on contemporary issues and recent publications. In strong contrast to most other literary critics, like Arnold or Richard Simpson, for instance, Hutton hardly ever wrote retrospective or historical essays. He rarely more than mentions Shakespeare, Homer, or Milton, but wrote extensively on Tennyson, Arnold, Mill, Charlotte Yonge, Browning, and later on George Eliot, Pater, and Newman.

Of this relatively early period, Hutton's writing for the *National Review*, some of which he republished in *Essays Theological and Literary* (1871), is particularly interesting. The readership of this journal was much wider than anything Hutton had previously written for and its contributors, who included Arnold and his 'Functions of Criticism at the Present Time', were free from editorial control. Hutton was able to write a great deal on contemporary fiction, show considerable interest in the work of historical and scientific critics such as Strauss, Renan, and Feuerbach, and produce long studies on Wordsworth and Goethe. Though the reception of this work is hard to gauge, Henry Sidgwick thought that his collected essays from the journal 'must rank among the most instructive studies in recent literature that have been published'.[37] Sidgwick's very word 'instructive', however, suggests that although Hutton no longer wrote for journals of dogmatic religion, his writing remains didactic in tone. Indeed, not only in tone, since his position at the *Economist*, for which he wrote two leaders a week, promised to allow him practical, political influence. It was this hope which was destroyed by Bagehot's appointment as chief editor; as Hutton confided to Clough, it would clearly 'prevent any chance of improving my position at the *Economist*, and perhaps curtail my general *influence* in politics, which I should not like'.[38] It was precisely this improvement and the promise of such influence which took Hutton to the *Spectator* in 1861.

Hutton of the Spectator

In 1893 the *Spectator*'s political rival, the Tory *Speaker*, carried a series of articles on the British press in the course of which the writer grudgingly admitted that 'bit by bit the conviction has been forced upon us that if English journalism has a chief he is to be found

[37] *Academy*, 1 July 1871, 326.
[38] Mulhauser, *Correspondence of Arthur Hugh Clough*, ii. 582.

in Mr. Hutton'.[39] Though Hutton might be said to have served an apprenticeship in journalism before 1861, and in the course of it done good and lasting work, the basis for the *Speaker*'s judgement must be found in Hutton's work for the *Spectator* and his contributions to a number of periodicals between 1861 and 1897.

The weekly *Spectator* had been founded by R. S. Rintoul in 1828 and bought by Meredith Townsend in 1861.[40] After only a few months Townsend realized that he needed both financial and editorial help, and he offered a half share to Hutton who had been recommended to him by Wilson whilst Townsend was editor of *The Friend of India*.[41] The fact that the *Spectator* had always been edited by its owners was regarded as a great strength, and subsequent owners claimed to be preserving its 'spiritual continuity'. Complaints in our time that newspapers can be bought like consumer goods were anticipated by Evelyn Wrench, who succeeded St Loe Strachey as editor–proprietor in 1925, and who wrote: 'We hope to ensure, as *The Times* has done, that the *Spectator* shall never be sold on the open market to the highest bidder.'[42] More modern and recent attempts to safeguard editorial freedom from proprietorial influence have often been supported by arguments claiming that moral absolutes are under threat, but which are really derived from a fear that potential new owners are not worthy. This fear has its origins in a time when it was voiced openly. So in 1928, W. B. Thomas, historian of the Victorian *Spectator*, wrote of a scheme to provide a trusteeship for the newspaper to ensure that it did not 'fall into unworthy hands' and commented that the proprietor of the time 'feels himself in apostolic succession to a great tradition'.[43]

Hutton was regarded as having been the first in this line; indeed it was his journal that established the tone and vocabulary which makes that comment possible without irony. Townsend, however, initially put his personal stamp on the journal by changing its format—adding four pages to its established twenty-four, using regular subleaders, and presenting the opening 'News of the Week' section in a connected, narrative form which suggested by its very

[39] 'The Modern Press: *The Spectator*', *Speaker*, 4 Mar. 1893, 242.
[40] *The Journal of Benjamin Moran*, ed. S. A. Wallace and F. E. Gillespie, 2 vols. (Chicago, 1948), i. 771–2.
[41] Barrington, *Life of Walter Bagehot*, p. 348.
[42] W. B. Thomas, *The Story of The Spectator* (London, 1928), 2.
[43] Ibid., pp. 3–4.

nature that this was one man's version of the week's events.[44] After Hutton had joined Townsend the 'News of the Week' section occupied only the first three pages, changing the newspaper into something more like a weekly review. Moreover, the title page was changed from one announcing a journal of 'News, Politics, Literature and Science' to one announcing a weekly review of 'Politics, Literature, Theology and Art'. Although the journal did cover movements in science, its replacement on the title-page must be put down to Hutton's interest.

Hutton and Townsend both wrote on political events, though generally Hutton wrote on home affairs and Townsend on foreign policy, while literature and theology were mainly Hutton's province. As D. C. Lathbury wrote in the *Dictionary of National Biography* (which is not, on the whole, accurate in its chronology of Hutton's life), 'while it would be idle to regard [Hutton] as standing in the first rank of theologians, it may be questioned whether any of his contemporaries influenced public opinion more widely'.[45] The implication of this rather ambiguous assertion is that Hutton's influence was exercised primarily as a writer on theology, but it was also a 'religious' influence, in the most general sense, in its own right. If Hutton had found a pulpit in the *Inquirer*, he found a larger congregation through the pages of the *Spectator*. Indeed, as a contemporary remarked: 'Religion had never been prominent in the journal, but Hutton at once began to preach, and he preached to a great and listening and picked audience until he died.'[46]

The audience of Rintoul's *Spectator*, so his obituary suggested in that journal in 1858, read it for its 'reliable record of events'. And, as it went on:

By far the greater part of the regular readers of the *Spectator* have always been of a class that is not affected by partisan spleen: its circulation being chiefly, as it must always aim to be, among men of culture, who like to listen to all sides of controversies, provided the argument is conducted with fairness and moderation.

The distinction here between 'class' and 'party' is important: a journal which is aimed at a specific class can afford to be confident, even smug, about its lack of 'party' bias. These men of culture, ex-

44 *Spectator*, 9 Feb. 1861, 130.
45 *Dictionary of National Biography Supplement*, ed. Sidney Lee, 3 vols. (London, 1901), iii. 21.
46 W. R. Nicoll, *The Day Book of Claudius Clear* (London, 1905), 303–4.

ercising the free play of their intellects, sound like members of the Arnoldian clerisy (though Arnold was badly received by Rintoul's *Spectator*);[47] and this was a flexibility of mind Hutton discarded. Under Hutton's guidance the *Spectator* was not exactly partisan, but it always took sides. In his very first year as editor, Hutton threw the weight of the journal behind the cause of the North in the American Civil War. Townsend supported him in this stance, though from a different point of view—where Townsend was afraid of the political implications if the republic of States disintegrated, Hutton persistently argued that the issue was a moral one, about slavery—even when its position took the journal close to bankruptcy. Again, during Kingsley's public dispute with Newman, Hutton played the arbiter and gave the judgement to Newman, whose biographer wrote of Hutton's intervention:

At this juncture there intervened a man who was already becoming a power, by force of intellect and character, in the world of letters. It was to his intervention that Mr. G. L. Craik used confidently to ascribe the direction which public opinion, in many instances trembling in the balance, took at this moment and ultimately with overwhelming force. All Hutton's antecedents seemed to be against any unfair partiality on Newman's behalf.[48]

Ward's phrase 'unfair partiality' is significant, seeming to suggest that fairness and partiality are not incompatible: certainly, Hutton seems to aim for what we might call a 'fair partiality'.[49]

Any attempt to gauge the reaction of the public to Hutton's new *Spectator* has to be selective. We might take as an example the reaction of William Cory, the educational reformer and a contributor to Farrar's *Essays on a Liberal Education*, who described himself as benumbed by the lack of any antidote to *The Times* and the *Saturday Review* until this was supplied by Hutton's *Spectator*: 'Now', he wrote in 1862, 'I read the *Spectator*, which is edited by Hutton, who used to edit the *Economist*, and I find myself once

---

[47] See J. D. Jump, 'Matthew Arnold and the *Spectator*', *Review of English Studies*, 25 (1949), 61–4.

[48] Wilfred Ward, *The Life of Cardinal Newman*, 2 vols. (London, 1913), ii. 4.

[49] There were, of course, those who dissented from this view. Edwin Abbott, for instance, attacks Hutton's account of Newman in his *Philomythus* (1891), accuses Hutton of idolatry and comments: 'Is it not within the limits of possibility that, for once, a human being should be right, and the editor of the *Spectator* wrong?' (E. A. Abbott, *Newmanianism: A Preface to Philomythus*, second edition (London, 1891), p. ix). The anti-Catholicism of this is implicit in its references to idolatry and infallibility.

more heart and hand with true lovers of freedom.'[50] The *Spectator* clearly appealed to Liberals in religion and politics. Yet when Lord Grey asserted in the following year, according to Crabb Robinson, that the *Spectator* and the *Economist* were 'producing a greater effect upon public opinion than any other periodicals', he must be understood to be thinking of a quite specific 'public'.[51] This public is vaguely suggested by Hugh Walker in a series of essays on 'Living Critics' published in *Bookman* in 1896. When Walker writes, 'there is probably no English journal that wields a stronger influence over thoughtful men than the *Spectator*', he suggests the limitations as well as the strengths of the journal.[52] Several of these later assessments, however, are less tactful and generous: the *Spectator* readership was an easy target for the *fin-de-siècle* journalist anxious to dissociate himself from Victorian complacency. So the readership was 'a public sheltered in leafy rectories and in snug villas from the headlong decisions and rowdy activity of the world'. Another writer describes the members of this readership as 'gentle souls, fond of flowers and birds . . . middle-aged and declining gracefully to a future existence for which they were fully prepared' and who 'looked askance at a Huxley travelling rough-shod over their dearest orthodoxies'. Several writers describe how this flock of simpletons would look forward to the 'repose and refreshment of Saturday evening' when Hutton would make everything all right again.[53]

These are the extreme groupings of Hutton's clerisy. Such accounts do not suggest that Hutton was a representative of the type which was his readership, though he 'represented' them in that he fought for them and voiced explicit wants and principles of which they themselves may not have been aware. In this sense Hutton has the same kind of relationship to his readers as George Eliot has to her characters: they are half perceived and half created. The caricatured gentility of his readers stands in sharp contrast to the embattled Hutton portrayed in letters and articles. Yet this very difference between his position and that of his sheltered audience

---

[50] *Extracts from the Letters and Journals of William Cory*, ed. F. W. Cornish (Oxford, 1897), 86.

[51] Crabb Robinson, MS *Diary*, 13 Oct. 1864.

[52] 'Living Critics IV: Mr R. H. Hutton', *Bookman*, 9 (Jan. 1896), 118–20 (p. 118).

[53] See Hogben, *Richard Holt Hutton*, p. 39; *Academy*, 56 (22 Apr. 1899), 451; and *Bookman*, 6 (June 1894), 85–6 [by Marcus Dodds].

does not seem remarkable to observers of his life and work, even though it is in the interest of some writers to point out the absurdity of an energetic defence of complacency. The *Academy* described Hutton as 'the Invisible David of the *Spectator*', but in spite of considerable admiration for his personal qualities, writers at the end of the century saw his writing, inevitably, as defensive and reactionary.[54] The *Dial*, reviewing Hutton's collected essays, described him as 'entrenched behind a barricade of prejudices' from which he conducted a 'skilfully defensive campaign' against the forces of secularization.[55]

There are, however, accounts to contradict this view—praise for Hutton's 'clear vision' above 'the perplexities of life', and claims that he 'taught tolerance to a class'[56]—but it is perhaps more significant to read what Hutton's intentions were when he took over as literary editor. One of his first articles, published in June 1861, was on 'The Abuses of Newspaper Criticism' and might be read as the manifesto of the new editor. He wrote:

Criticism . . . must have at least enough of the creative power it deals with to feel completely its spell and fascination. And this is not got by critical habits: it is got by a long apprenticeship to uncritical habits; by readiness of sympathy and flexibility of taste.[57]

Hutton's 'flexibility of taste' is not, of course, matched by flexibility of belief, so that while the subject matter of his writing is broad and diverse, his interests and convictions are consistent and even narrow. Hutton's idea of 'flexibility' is quite different from Arnold's notion of flexibility, and it is the limitations of the Arnoldian canon and clerisy which Hutton claims to be going beyond:

The only criticism which is really likely to be useful on the minor works of everyday literature is that which has been trained and disciplined in worthier studies. Here is the mistake of the cut-and-dried man of culture. He goes about with the secret of having learned to appreciate the 'grand style'. He has lived in Homer till he can recall the roll of that many-sounding sea. . . . When first fortune compels him to deal with the daily literary efforts of ordinary Englishmen he chooses such as are more-or-less connected with his real admirations . . . No doubt it is a trial to men steeped in the culture of the noblest literature in the world, to appreciate fairly the ephemeral

54 *Academy*, 56 (22 Apr. 1899), 451.
55 *Dial*, 17 (1 July 1894), 17.
56 Hogben, *Richard Holt Hutton*, p. 20; *Academy*, 52 (18 Sept. 1897), 221.
57 *Spectator*, 29 June 1861, 697.

productions of a busy generation. It seems beneath them, and the more they trample it beneath them, the less are they competent to detect its higher tendencies. But still the critic who allows this feeling to grow upon him abdicates his true office. Unless he can enter into the wants of his generation, he has no business to pretend to direct its thoughts.[58]

Hutton clearly saw his editorial apprenticeship in 'worthier studies' more applicable than it might seem to his literary work because it enabled him to detect the 'higher tendencies' of writing. He takes it for granted that his task is to write on 'everyday literature', major or minor, to 'deal with the daily literary efforts of ordinary Englishmen' whatever his own personal admirations may be, and to direct the attention of his readers to what he believes is permanent in the ephemeral. He announces that his concern will be with the contemporary in writing, indeed the contemporary and the English, and the present needs of his readers. In spite of Hutton's replacement of 'Science' with 'Theology', his concern is to avoid anachronism, to avoid measuring the present in literature by the 'classics', and to avoid the creation of his own clerisy. His natural opposite is Matthew Arnold and the Arnoldian view of the modern element in literature. Arnold's 'On Translating Homer' had just been published when Hutton was writing this 'manifesto'—Hutton would have denied its portentousness—and Arnold is clearly the type behind Hutton's 'cut-and-dried' man of culture, Arnold's leisured criticism contrasting with 'the ephemeral productions of a busy generation'.[59] Hutton's notion of 'entering into' the wants of his generation almost ensures his own disappearance, while Arnold's critical pose ensures the inflation of the 'office' of the critic.[60]

The first function of criticism, says Hutton, is 'to apprehend that which lies above its own sphere', where 'above' is used both qualitatively and ethically, and its second, 'to translate for others what the few teach or conceive'.[61] He takes his subject matter to be mainly the contemporary, but aims also to 'see deeper into the infinite beauty of Homer, or Chaucer, or Shakespeare' and if

---

[58] *Spectator*, 29 June 1861, 697.

[59] Compare also Hutton's criticism of Unitarianism as a 'cut-and-dried form of Christianity' which was also 'wholly outside the sphere of popular want' (above, p. 8).

[60] John Woolford, 'Periodicals and the Practice of Literary Criticism', in *The Victorian Periodical Press: Samplings and Soundings*, ed. Joanne Shattock and Michael Wolff (Leicester University Press, 1982), 109–42 (p. 134).

[61] *Spectator*, 29 June 1861, 697.

necessary to insist on the directions in which they 'fail to satisfy the wants of the many'. It was, indeed, this 'seeing deeper' which his Unitarian congregation, those whom Martineau had described as maintaining a system of unintelligibilities, had thought 'too profound'. When Leslie Stephen reviews Hutton's essays in 1871, he accuses Hutton of trying to 'squeeze more out of a metaphor' of Shelley's 'than it will naturally produce', and concludes: 'if all other men see less than they ought, Mr. Hutton is inclined to see more than really exists.'[62] Similarly, Matthew Arnold, commenting on an article on himself by Hutton, thought that the piece had Hutton's 'fault of seeing so very far into a millstone'.[63] Arnold's publisher, Alexander Macmillan, wrote to him on the reception of *Essays in Criticism*: 'the article has Hutton's fault of seeing round and over you too much. The parallel between Newman and yourself is to me somewhat fanciful.'[64] That 'creative power' which Hutton thought criticism should share with its object could clearly appear to be mere invention. Arnold, in fact, thought very highly of Hutton's writing on his poetry—he had a copy of his 1867 *Poems* sent to Hutton before any other review copies were sent out, and considered Hutton's 1872 essay on his poetry 'far more careful, abler and graver than any which has yet appeared'.[65] When Hutton wrote on poetry he was evidently less likely to appear 'fanciful' and more confined to comments on the text before him. When he wrote on prose, however, such as Arnold's *Essays in Criticism*, he was able to expand on what he saw 'round and over' the text. It is this writing about more than the text offers, and discussing its general context, direction, and intention—what *The Times*'s obituary of Hutton described as his 'rare faculty for delineating with fine, oftrepeated strokes the moral atmosphere wherein a writer moved and dwelt'[66]—that provides the greatest source of interest for the present work.

Hutton wrote several thousand articles for the *Spectator* and it is impossible to give a brief account of their scope, although a survey of his work shows that he devoted most space to Newman, Arnold,

---

[62] *Saturday Review*, 18 Feb. 1871, 214.

[63] *Letters of Matthew Arnold 1844–1888*, ed. G. W. E. Russell, 2 vols. (London, 1889), i. 248.

[64] *Letters of Alexander Macmillan*, ed. G. A. Macmillan (London, 1908), 187.

[65] *Letters to a Victorian Editor, Henry Allon*, ed. Albert Peel (London, 1929), 171.

[66] *The Times*, 11 Sept. 1897, 6.

Tennyson, Wordsworth, and George Eliot, and Browning, Clough, Carlyle, Huxley, Mill, Ruskin, and Trollope.[67] He also contributed a large number of essays to quarterlies like *Macmillan's Magazine*, the *Contemporary Review*, and *Fraser's Magazine*. The format of these gave him space to expand an argument, and it freed him from the occasional nature of weekly reviewing, though the subject matter and even the readership was similar to that of his weekly newspaper. Hutton wrote for journals whose bias was liberal in religion and politics. A number of these journals were owned or controlled by James Knowles with whom, amongst others, Hutton founded the Metaphysical Society as neutral ground on which opposing arguments could be fought out. Both Hutton and Knowles, whose *Nineteenth Century* was founded as a published and public version of the Metaphysical Society, believed that all periodicals should provide such a neutral ground. Hutton shared with Knowles a belief in the peculiar importance of the periodical to the age in which they lived, an age not 'propitious for books' since, said Knowles, 'so much was happening, so many facts cast before us every day, that interpretation was fast becoming the peculiar role of periodicals.'[68]

Hutton produced twelve books, but six were collections of periodical essays (his niece was responsible for publishing two further posthumous collections), and four were editions of the writings of his closest friends, W. C. Roscoe and Walter Bagehot (of whose work Hutton edited three collections). He did, however, write two critical biographies as books, one on Scott (1878) and one on Newman (1891).

The very crowded nature of the world described by Knowles partly explains why Hutton was prepared to risk the occasional and potentially ephemeral nature of periodical writing. It also partly explains why Hutton had very little life outside that of writer and editor. He not only edited the *Spectator*, he also managed it, signed the cheques, and corrected the proofs—so that towards the end of his life he was almost blind. Bagehot was doing much the same thing at the *Economist*, and the two would retire to the Athenaeum every Friday, their newspapers put to bed, to play chess.

---

[67] See Appendix.
[68] Priscilla Metcalf, *James Knowles: Victorian Editor and Architect* (London, 1980), 362.

Hutton did play some part in public life while editor of the *Spectator*. He served on the Board of the London Library, sat on the Senate of the University of London, was deeply committed to the anti-vivisectionist movement, acted as President of the Surrey Liberal Associaton, and late in life took a rather bizarre interest in psychical research.[69] Yet on the whole Hutton's public service was carried on from behind his desk, and although his writing has the stamp of personal conviction, it is very rarely of an emotional or autobiographical kind. Hutton, for example, corresponded with Gladstone, whom he described as 'a great moral and spiritual friend', for twenty years from 1876 to 1896; yet a reader of the *Spectator* would never know this from his writing. Much of this correspondence is concerned with literary and theological issues, but in the 1880s the *Spectator* attacked Gladstone and helped to divide the Liberal party over Home Rule. In his letters Hutton repeatedly and very emotionally expresses his regret at being unable to follow Gladstone: 'I cannot tell you how much I feel it', he wrote, and 'I can hardly tell you how difficult my work as a journalist has become to me, since I felt compelled to take a different view from yours on the Irish question. Instead of enjoying it as I used to, it has become all duty work ever since.'[70] This change of tone is quite unnoticeable in the *Spectator*. Similarly, Hutton corresponded with Newman over a period of some twenty-one years, if intermittently, yet the emotional and even desperate Hutton revealed in those letters is virtually contradicted by the Hutton who analyses Newman in a series of reviews and a book.

Hutton, it must be remembered, was one of the breed of preachers-turned-writers who did not weep easily in the pulpit. He always owed to Martineau the belief that Reason was the supreme tribunal. At the same time Hutton made no secret of the fact that he was deeply moved by literature and by political causes, such as the fight against slavery in the Southern States. Hutton did not want to be regarded as merely a personal authority, imposing *ex cathedra* views upon his readership in the manner of Carlyle, Ruskin, and Arnold. He passionately believed that man should exercise his private judgement, that he should be free. He felt, paradoxically

---

[69] See Hutton's letter to Herbert Gladstone, 5 Oct. 1883 (Viscount Gladstone Papers, BL Add. MS 46048/281).

[70] See Hutton's letters to Gladstone, 15 Nov. 1887 and 22 May 1886 (W. E. Gladstone Papers, BL Add. MS 44215/340 and 44215/332).

perhaps, that he had no choice but to defend this freedom to choose—hence his words to Gladstone: 'I felt compelled'. Hutton's life's work, in content and in tone, is a continual cry against the erosion of real convictions freely arrived at, and the decline of rational exchange into subjectivity. He saw these as the deep, non-theological dangers of secularization.

2
Literature and Secularization

THE Hutton who was thought a powerful and influential fighter for his beliefs must be looked for in his published writings. Yet what, if he was the 'Invisible David of the *Spectator*', was Hutton fighting against, and if he was 'entrenched behind a barricade', who was the enemy? The *Nation* described him as 'a stout foe of materialism, necessarianism and agnosticism', while the *Athenaeum*, no particular friend to Hutton, said:

Throughout a period of great intellectual ferment, Mr. Hutton stood forward as the champion of spirit against the assaults of Materialism, and as the champion of Christianity against Agnosticism and Scepticism. . . . Mr. Hutton was one of those who faced the first onslaughts; he protested that spirit was an element in the universe at least as real and at least as potent as matter.[1]

This portrait threatens to overreach itself in suggesting Hutton's heroism and risks bathos in pitching his 'protest' against an 'onslaught'. Yet it is true that the single common element in Hutton's work on every subject is his concern with the relation of that subject to the beliefs of the age and to the decline of religious belief.

Hutton addresses himself directly to this issue several times, in fact he is credited with having first used 'agnostic' in print, and he admits the reality of secularization in discussing its consequences. Hutton returns most frequently to the question much discussed in recent studies of the issue, namely the effect of secularization on the language of moral transactions and definitions, and on language in general, but also discusses the effect on human character and on our notions of what lies behind everyday words like 'truth' and 'life'.[2] In 1877 Hutton contributed an essay to a 'Modern Symposium' in the *Nineteenth Century*, a symposium intended as a printed version of a Metaphysical Society debate and to which contributions were made by James Stephen (who chose the subject),

[1] *Nation* 60 (17 Jan. 1895) 57; *Athenaeum*, 22 Apr. 1899, 489.
[2] Alasdair MacIntyre, *After Virtue: A Study in Moral Theory* (London, 1981); Owen Chadwick, *The Secularization of the European Mind in the Nineteenth Century* (London, 1975).

Lord Selbourne, James Martineau, Frederick Harrison, Dean Church, the Duke of Argyll, Henry Clifford, Thomas Huxley, and William Ward.[3] These, commented the *Saturday Review*, were 'the chosen illuminati', and it is to the general debate with such figures that Hutton's essays must all be seen as contributions.

In an 1856 essay on 'The Moral Significance of Atheism', Hutton wrote: 'Atheism shakes the authority of the moral faculties of man, by doing away with all adequate means of *expressing* the infinite distinction between right and wrong.'[4] This, to Hutton, is the real change brought about by the questioning of religious belief. The decline in belief itself is, in a sense, of no consequence since as Hutton says at the beginning of the essay and was to repeat, in almost identical terms, in an essay on 'The Atheistic View of Life' in 1880, 'the facts are not altered by our belief or disbelief in God' and 'there is no teaching more mischievous in its effects than that which makes human belief in God the *first* regenerative power in human society.'[5] In this later essay he argues that atheism 'degrades the meaning of the greatest words in every language', and in the following year he says that it will no longer be possible 'to define for yourself what you are to love and what to hate'.[6] It is this definition of the '*infinite* distinction between right and wrong' which Hutton fears will be lost, the conscience's guide for 'its sense of the absolutely boundless significance it sees in every moral choice'.[7] But this sense is itself a feature of the secularized mind and found expression in literature in the novel—for which reason, I suggest, Hutton thought the novel an implicitly secular form and took great interest in it.

It was what Hutton saw as the loss of the point of view of the eternal which would alter human character or what he calls 'the scenery of the inner life', because as he wrote in 1880: 'the new Agnosticism or Atheism teaches that the form of man's character is itself nothing but a transient circumstance'.[8] Although Hutton does not see them as causes, he naturally reaches for illustration to the

[3] *Nineteenth Century*, i (1887), 331–58, 531–46.

[4] Reprinted in *Theological Essays* (1871), p. 18.

[5] *Fraser's Magazine*, NS 21 (May 1880), 652–67 (p. 652); *Theological Essays* (1871), p. 5.

[6] *Fraser's Magazine*, loc. cit., p. 665; 'Secularism', *Expositor*, NS 1 (1881), 1–12 (p. 9).

[7] *Theological Essays* (1871), p. 19.

[8] *Fraser's Magazine*, loc. cit., pp. 659–60.

growth of the social sciences—the formative influences of transient circumstances—and to natural science:

If the agnostics are right . . . we must find in persons more and more of the insignificance of mere things, in the brightest eye only a development of nervous function and a crystalline lens; in the sweetest smile only animal complacency lighted up by transitory sympathy, or the partial re-excitation of some faded current of parental instinct.[9]

Science seems to provide emotive analogies though not causative influences. Yet Hutton is clearly using terms which would be familiar to followers of the Darwinian debate when he argues that in giving up Christianity, society is giving up its moral inheritance, giving up the roots of the sanctions for the very values upheld by secular morality. He applies the analogy to character: 'by long dwelling on the Christian type of character men have learnt to imagine that that type of character could stand alone'.[10] He fears a general change in the meaning of 'character' itself. This is the change expressed by Arnold and Pater: the identification of character with *temperament*. He fears the growth of the belief that men 'stand alone', or in moral terms the growth of subjectivism—the doctrine that all evaluative judgements are expressions of preference, attitude, or feeling. He consequently criticizes Arnold for being both 'too intellectual' and 'too emotional', in a way which to us might seem paradoxical at first sight. He does not see this subjectivism as a source of freedom for the individual but the opposite, that the necessary effect of secularization 'must be to diminish incalculably the sacredness of the individual and personal to the advantage of the general and the impersonal'.[11]

The lines of Arnold's poetry with which Hutton seems almost obsessed are those which refer to the solitude created by the power which:

> bade betwixt our shores to be
> The unplumb'd, salt, estranging sea!

The expression of this sentiment in poetry seems to move Hutton in a way it would not in prose. I suggest that in the novel, on the other

9 *Fraser's Magazine*, loc. cit., p. 664.
10 *Expositor*, loc. cit., p. 11; *Nineteenth Century*, loc. cit., pp. 544–5.
11 *Expositor*, loc. cit., p. 10.

hand, Hutton saw a resistance to the secularization of character, that his appreciation of the novel in these terms is uniquely important, and that this provides an explanation of and counter to Arnold's neglect of the novel form.

The sort of selfhood provided by the novel, the 'novelistic' character, as it were, seems to reclaim for Hutton what Alasdair MacIntyre describes as the lost, in the secular world, 'conception of a whole human life as the primary subject of objective and impersonal evaluation'.[12] The novel seems to remind Hutton of an order he *felt* was passing away, one in which a man had a function in life by the fulfilment of which he could be judged and in which the adjectives 'right' and 'wrong' were indices of facts. He felt that function itself was a changing concept, that character was becoming 'a development of nervous function', and that according to the secular view of life character was not able to 'resist' circumstance but was itself a mere circumstance.

It could be argued, indeed, that Hutton's own character is one which resists secularization yet also reflects it. I am not referring to the content of his work but to his position as an Editor: he combines as such the functional concept of selfhood, by fulfilling a role impersonally evaluated by his readers and readership, with the subjective sense of selfhood, of judging issues by his own standards. Victorian culture might partially be defined by its 'characters', like the Editor, the Explorer, and the Engineer, who combined function and personality. This combination is a product of secularization, and Hutton seems to have been peculiarly aware of his historical position: he defends 'old' values but insists on remaining contemporary, and attacks those writers (such as Arnold, Tennyson, and Pater) whose contemporaneity exhibits itself, paradoxically, in nostalgia. Indeed, in an age of periodicals Hutton has an old-fashioned respect for 'the book'.

Hutton did not waver from his views on the influence of secularization expressed in 1856: they were not only repeated in the later accounts but also, in retrospect, laid the foundation for his appreciation of the most non-secular Victorian, Cardinal Newman. Indeed Hutton's suggestion then that 'the Atheist has no infinite calculus applicable to human actions' foreshadows Newman's comparison of the operation of the Implicit Reason with the oper-

---

[12] Alasdair MacIntyre, *After Virtue* (London, 1981), 32.

ation of the calculus.[13] From 1856 it is the empirical bias of secular thought which Hutton distrusts: he denies that 'life' contains 'truth' at all, and suggests that to the secular mind truth is reduced to 'information' about the world such that the future 'highest truth' would be 'an account of the observed and quite momentary influences of human minds upon each other'.[14] Hutton's interest in secular literature seems to be based on the belief that it is the highest truth for the world he lives in: an account of that world, but an account which he takes as an *occasion* for inquiry and not the source of it. Such is his view of life itself, in the same essay:

The awkward and constrained intercourse of human beings, so rarely interchanging the real secrets of the heart, and often most frigid when covering the intensest life, is not adequate to sustain the growth of deep affections. It supplies the occasions, not the sources of that growth.[15]

For Hutton as for Newman, life provides the occasion for belief but not its cause. Similarly, literature provides occasions but not sources of belief and emotion: Hutton frequently regards writers as providing occasions for beliefs in spite of their own profession of belief or non-belief. Scott, in particular, was the occasion for beliefs which he could not be said to have caused. This view of the status of literature is like Hardy's view of love: the object of affection is the occasion not the source of the feeling.

Materialism and literature

The term 'materialism' was widely used in the second half of the nineteenth century to denote those tendencies which serve the physical rather than the intellectual or spiritual life of man, so that popularly it referred to a practical bias rather than a set of beliefs.[16] Hutton, however, felt that the tendencies of his own day were materialistic in a more specific sense, that they reflected the belief that every moral and spiritual fact has its basis wholly contained in

[13] J. H. Newman, *An Essay in Aid of a Grammar of Assent*, new edition (London, 1973), 278. Hutton may have known Newman's 'On the Analogous Nature of the Difficulties in Mathematics and those in Religion', *Christian Observer*, 6 Mar. 1821.

[14] *Theological Essays* (1871), p. 24.

[15] Ibid., p. 20.

[16] 'What is Modern Materialism?', *Spectator*, 19 July 1873, 919; Leslie Stephen, *What is Materialism? A Discourse Delivered in South Place Chapel, Finsbury, March 21 1886* (London, 1886).

a material fact, and that the 'lower' organization is the whole and sufficient cause of the 'higher'.[17] Hutton did not see his age as more 'carnal' than previous ages, nor did he feel it was less concerned with 'spiritual life' than other epochs. The age, he felt, was specifically materialistic in its inversion of causality in matters of moral experience and, by extension, in all experience. Hutton was interested, for example, in the debate in the early 1870s, perhaps originating in Douglas Spalding's paper on the instincts of birds in *Macmillan's Magazine* in February 1872, about the imagined state of mind of a duplicate human organization physiologically identical in every respect with that of a man who had experienced several years of life. Hutton argued that the materialist would believe that the reproduction of every nerve and every brain cell would produce a man with hopes and affections identical with those of the man of experience. This was for Hutton the model of Victorian materialism: 'if you could only forge', he wrote, 'the material fact without going through the usual moral and spiritual antecedents for producing it, you would find that you had arrived by a short cut at the moral and spiritual fact.'[18]

In his writings on secularization which I have already cited, Hutton argues that secular morality takes linguistic short cuts in not 'going through the usual antecedents'. More specifically, all the five writers treated in the following chapters are studied by Hutton for how they dealt with experience and how it dealt with them: his only books which were not collections of essays were, significantly, biographies, almost hagiographies, aimed at telling what Newman and Scott 'went through'. Of the five it is Arnold who tried to take the short cut signposted by Hutton. He argues that Arnold wants the products of belief without the spiritual antecedents, that he appeals to experience as if it is always something past and always something that happens to other people: 'but you cannot', Hutton wrote, 'found on mere experience *without* the experience'.[19] For Hutton literature is a means, in a secular world, of passing on experience when belief in teaching by *example* is dead.

[17] See 'Materialism and its Lessons' (1879), and 'Professor Tyndall on Physical and Moral Necessity' (1877), both in *Contemporary Thought and Thinkers*, i. 310–18, 235–45.

[18] 'What is Modern Materialism?' p. 919; 'Materialism and its Lessons', pp. 310–18.

[19] *Essays on Some of the Modern Guides of English Thought in Matters of Faith* (1887), 124. All subsequent references are to this edition.

The field of experience is for Hutton not the area where you put your spiritual beliefs to the test, but where you defend them. Even then your success in defending them is not a measure of their truth —the consequent confidence in being right is what made Newman seem arrogant when defending his beliefs in public dispute with Kingsley. This may seem, indeed, like a rationalization of prejudice, but for Newman and Hutton the facts of belief *were* prejudged, they did not follow the causal logic of experience. Arnold, on the other hand, concluded that the advantage of his view of the Bible was that 'experience, as it increases, constantly confirms it', and 'that though it cannot *command* assent, it will be found to *win* assent more and more'.[20] This claim seemed to Hutton the result of Victorian materialism: experience was appealed to as proof of beliefs which it also produced, so that experience was both the ground and the verification of belief. The most important anti-materialist text in this debate, as contemporary commentators realized, is Newman's *Essay in Aid of a Grammar of Assent* (1870). Here Newman argued forcefully that the word 'assent' employed as Arnold employs it is superfluous since such an assent is merely the repetition of the act of inference from experience.[21] Newman, that is, attempted to free assent from experience and to give it a commanding authority which the believer could exercise himself in what Newman calls 'a living act of the mind'.

Hutton consistently describes the writer as if he were involved in an almost heroic struggle with experience, and as if writing were itself the exercise of the free 'living act of the mind'. Hutton wrote:

In acts of freewill the sense of human solitude is always at its height; for in them we distinguish *ourselves* from all things else. And in the world of imagination this spiritual freedom is especially remarkable.[22]

The 'world' of the imagination is to Hutton a real world and one in which the writer encounters real choices. In asserting that literature is an expression of freedom and will, Hutton is reacting against Romantic notions of genius and inspiration—against, for example, the idea that Wordsworth and Tennyson were 'poets of reverie' and 'lost themselves' in their writing. Hutton argues that they found

---

[20] 'Literature and Dogma', *Dissent and Dogma*, ed. R. H. Super, *Prose Works of Matthew Arnold*, vi (Ann Arbor, 1968), 378.
[21] Newman, *Grammar of Assent*, p. 165.
[22] *Literary Essays* (1871), p. 108.

themselves in their writing, that they imposed influences on themselves which were stronger than those imposed by circumstance.

The writer, to Hutton, seems always solitary and always struggling to resist the influences of the world, or of his or her own tendencies. He seems to see literature almost entirely in terms of this struggle even if the literary product is not commensurate with it: 'it is the resistance to cherished purposes', he wrote, 'which accumulates these purposes into something capable of striking the eye and the imagination'.[23] This notion that moral purpose can be stored up in a sort of ethical bank account until one wants to conduct a substantial transaction is immediately translated by Hutton into literary terms, in the belief that 'what is true of moral purpose is equally true of literary impressions'. Hutton is, then, an appropriate critic of writers who might be seen as having struggled to combine moral purpose and literary impression—as he thought of Newman, Arnold, George Eliot, Tennyson, and Wordsworth. His language will not, though, do justice to those writers who were not, in his view, joined in the struggle—the case with Keats, Dickens, or Jane Austen. Thus the latter is described as 'not grappling with any of the great problems of duty or faith', and he classes her with Mrs Gaskell, Trollope, and Thackeray as writers who 'never exhibit characters in any direct contact with the ultimate realities of life' and whose characters are 'never seen grasping at the truth by which they seek to live, or struggling with a single deadly temptation'.[24]

The greatest 'old struggler' in literature was, Hutton believed, Walter Scott, who, though limited by his indifference to the spiritual life, illustrates the highest moral and literary virtues. Scott was Hutton's hero as man of letters, and he describes his *Journal* as:

the story of a great intellectual and moral struggle ending in defeat, but in defeat in which there is absolutely no personal failure, no conscious yielding of a single inch of ground, no concession to weakness, no self-deception, no shrinking from the truth, no despondency, and no ostentation of pretended indifference. Everywhere you see the same large, clear insight, the same large, genial nature, the same indomitable resolution, the same sober suffering, the same calm fortitude, the same frank determination to face the worst and do the best . . . the magnanimity, the habit of endurance.[25]

---

[23] *Brief Literary Criticisms*, pp. 16–17.
[24] *Brief Literary Criticisms*, p. 172; *Modern Guides*, p. 150.
[25] *Brief Literary Criticisms*, pp. 150–1.

Scott's magnanimous determination is implicitly set against materialist determinism, he is for Hutton an illustration of the survival of
individuality, he is always 'the same'. He gives Scott the status of a
tragic figure without making any such claims for Scott's literary
productions. Moreover, Scott becomes so much the type that
Hutton wants to set against Jane Austen or Trollope that his rhetoric
carries him away. Hutton himself quotes Scott's comment to
Skene, 'Do you know, I experience a sort of determined pleasure in
confronting the very worst aspect of this reverse and saying, Here I
stand, at least an honest man', which seems full of the ostentation
of pretended indifference.[26] Scott's experience seems to be so
powerful to Hutton, powerful out of proportion to the ends Scott
strove for, because it represents an occasion not a cause, and a
struggle against those influences which the materialist would grant
authority to: Scott's life represents the struggle for freedom against
determinism, of personality and individuality against impersonal
forces, of magnanimity against scepticism.

Scott's intellectual and moral struggle is admired by Hutton in
spite of his 'entire unconsciousness of spiritual efforts'; his is a
physical effort reflected in an heroic literature. Yet it is this very
unconsciousness which makes him comparable with later Victorians,
his *Marmion* expressing the efforts of a physical will which has
forgotten its spiritual basis: his secularization of virtue makes him
contemporary. It is significant that, however seriously, George
Eliot named Scott as the first unsettling influence on her early
orthodoxy.

None of these writers, Scott, Newman, Arnold, Tennyson,
Wordsworth, or George Eliot, is admired for a religious belief
shared by Hutton, yet the language in which their 'struggles' are
described is remarkably similar in each case. Similarly he takes
them to be struggling for a single thing, for 'real' knowledge which
is not worldly, not cynical. He characterizes Newman's work as 'a
permanent effort to face the facts of the world as they are' without
'sinking into that cynical and despondent honesty which acknowledges the evil of the world only as an excuse for giving up the
struggle with it'.[27] In each case Hutton finds a resistance which is

---

[26] Ibid., p. 156.
[27] *Cardinal Newman*, p. 115, p. 5. See also 'Cardinal Newman', *Contemporary
Review*, 45 (May 1884), 642–65 (p. 657), and 'Modern Cynicism', *Spectator*,
20 Dec. 1890, 899–900.

not mere intransigence but is the effort to transmute 'the cruel pressure of human limitations' into creative energy.[28] On these grounds Wordsworth is the most successful of these writers, one who, wrote Hutton, 'has the power to transmute the greatest apparent obstacles into the very substance of his own visionary energy'.[29] Yet though Hutton brings this common discussion to each of these writers, the *givens* of the discussion, that is the very notion that, say, religious difficulties are not insuperable, derive from Hutton's liberalism in religion and politics.

Liberalism and literature

The essential Liberalism, its faith in the human capacity to judge and change the external world, must be seen as the inversion of Materialism. We might sum up the principles of liberal religion as a faith in the unhindered capacity of human nature to fulfil its potential, a belief that nature is inherently beneficial, that man is not only capable of but bound to exercise 'private judgement', that the Deity is discoverable through evidence of the external world, and that a revelation of the Deity is a complete manifestation, not merely a mystery or an addition to a set of mysterious specific givens.[30] This is much more precise than the popular use of the term 'liberal' in, for example, discussion of education—as Newman uses the word in *The Idea of a University*, which he distrusted as an easy source of satisfaction, to mean that which is without sequel or end. Newman's ambiguous and ironic account of 'Useful Knowledge' almost represents what Hutton saw as the use of literature:

It is the parent of virtue, the nurse of religion, it rouses, exalts, transports, enlarges, tranquilises and satisfies the mind . . . It makes us know our duty, and thereby enables us to do it; by taking the mind out of itself, it destroys

---

[28] *Aspects of Religious and Scientific Thought*, p. 292.

[29] *Brief Literary Criticisms*, p. 114.

[30] See 'The Liberal Movement in English Literature', *Spectator*, 21 Nov. 1885, 1150–1; 'Liberalism and Culture', *Spectator*, 16 Dec. 1882, 1607–8; 'Liberalism and Ritualism', *Spectator*, 2 Sept. 1882, 1131–2; 'The Rival Liberalisms', *Spectator*, 15 Dec. 1888, 1756–7; 'The Nobler Liberalism', *Spectator*, 7 Nov. 1891, 632; 'The Liberal Clergy and the Liberal Party', *Spectator*, 16 Jan. 1897, 77; 'Liberalism or Reaction?', *Spectator*, 26 Dec. 1896, 298–9; 'The Future of Liberalism', *Spectator*, 2 Jan. 1897, 4. See also H. L. Weatherby, 'Newman and Victorian Liberalism: A Study in the Failure of Influence', *Critical Quarterly*, 13, No. 3 (Autumn 1971), 205–15, and *Aspects of Religious and Scientific Thought*, pp. 78–9, where Hutton studies the ethical implications of the work of the physicist Tyndall.

anxiety. And in addition, it is a kind of neutral ground, on which men of every shade of politics and religion may meet together, disabuse each other of their prejudices, form intimacies, and secure cooperation.[31]

Hutton shared only that distrust of the tranquilizing effect of knowledge, and saw the discussion of literature and physical science as carried out on what Newman called 'a kind of neutral ground'. Hutton felt that the press as a whole provided the kind of arena which Newman disparaged, indeed later journals tried to encompass such discussion in each publication, as the *Illustrated London News* announced in 1877: 'The event of the month in the magazine world is, of course, the appearance of the *Nineteenth Century*, an event to be hailed by all who discern the importance of maintaining a perfectly neutral ground for the free expression of contemporary thought.'[32] This neutral ground was made real and institutional by Hutton and Knowles in the Metaphysical Society, which Hutton unsuccessfully tried to get Newman to join.

The opposite to Hutton's liberalism in matters of human learning is the position taken by Newman and Arnold: though differing in almost every other way, they are the spokesmen for two kinds of clerisy. Hutton barely considers Newman's opposition to Liberalism, though Newman voices it in the early Oxford sermons, in which he attacks 'the schools of the World' where 'the ways towards Truth are considered highroads open to all men' and 'everyone is considered on a level with his neighbour'.[33] Similarly, the *Grammar of Assent* is an attack on Liberalism's collapsing of faith into a limited sort of Reason which sees Christian Evidence as the ground for belief and not, as Newman saw it, as the reward for belief. Though Hutton is aware and critical of Newman's monopoly on truth and Roman Catholicism's putting religion in the hands of a qualified priesthood answering to an infallible Pope, he is much more consistently critical of the Arnoldian clerisy. Arnold, he wrote, 'regards the power of seeing things as they are as the monopoly of a class; and, indeed, arrived at as he arrived at it, it must always be regarded as the monopoly of a class.'[34] That is to say, the

[31] C. F. Harold, *John Henry Newman: An Expository Study of His Mind, Thought and Art* (London, 1948), 174.

[32] *Illustrated London News*, 10 Mar. 1877, 227.

[33] L. H. Yearly, *The Ideas of Newman: Christianity and Human Religiosity* (Pennsylvania, 1978), 108.

[34] 'An Intellectual Angel', *Spectator*, 3 Feb. 1866, 125–6, (p. 126).

Arnoldian clerisy seems far more dangerous to Hutton, since it attempts to monopolize the perception of the real while denying the spiritual.

If the liberal function of literature is opposed to these class monopolies its positive aims and efforts remain, inevitably, rather vague, though they might be summarized as a process of 'enlargement', be it in terms of class, of readership, or of the moral state of the individual—the reason for the repeated use of 'magnanimous' in Hutton's vocabulary of approval. Literature is to Hutton an outward appeal to inward nature, to an inner life which is the proper source of faith, and he has no hesitation in identifying the inner life of the author with the effect of the writing.

The novel seems to Hutton the form most likely to 'enlarge' the feelings of the reader, as well as the form most likely to reveal narrowness. So he finds in Forster's comment that Dickens had no 'city of the mind' evidence for his view that Dickens demonstrated 'an absolute deficiency of an inner life, and the want of magnanimity it entails'.[35] Again, comparing the novels of Jane Austen and Trollope with those of Scott: 'The domestic novel, when really of the highest kind, is no doubt a perfect work of art, and an unfailing source of amusement; but it has nothing of the tonic influence, the large instructiveness, the stimulating intellectual air, of Scott's historic tales.'[36] The terms of this description are familiar but inexact: it is not clear what 'the highest kind' refers to or what a 'tonic influence' is. The latter is a particularly common phrase in Hutton's work and refers to the effect of writing in spite of its intention, so that he can write of George Eliot: 'The total effect of her books is altogether ennobling, though the profoundly sceptical reflections with which they are penetrated may, to some extent, counteract the tonic effect of the high moral feeling with which they are coloured.'[37] Her novels seem to enlarge the feelings Hutton already possesses and wishes to cultivate, and these are the 'higher' feelings.

[35] *Contemporary Thought and Thinkers*, i. 99.
[36] *Sir Walter Scott*, p. 104.
[37] *Brief Literary Criticisms*, p. 179. See also the use of the word 'tonic' and its connection with resistance in Hutton on Arnold: 'Arnold is never quite at his best except when he is delineating a mood of regret, and then his best consists not in yielding to it, but in the resistance he makes to it . . . He is always one who finds a secret of joy in the midst of pain, who discovers a tonic for the suffering nerve' (*Modern Guides*, pp. 134-5).

In a concluding review of Trollope's essay on the moral effects of novel reading, Hutton wrote of the author's novels: 'You do not feel the more manly for reading him, as you do for reading Scott; nor the more free, as you do for reading Miss Brontë; nor the more just, as you do for reading George Eliot'.[38] These all seem to be writings of the 'higher' kind, where 'higher' means, as it does in Martineau's *Types of Ethical Theory*, an alternative to the Utilitarian and Materialist notion of the 'outer': the very vagueness of Hutton's notion of the use of knowledge and of literature must be seen as specifically anti-Utilitarian.[39] At the same time this use of 'higher' is specifically Christian and though related to Hutton's interest in modes of thought and writing which resist antagonistic modes this sense of 'higher' must be distinguished from later nineteenth-century statements of heroic resistance which are generally agnostic—such as those we find in Arnold, Henley, Newbolt, Housman, Kipling, and Conrad.

There is some connection between the poetry of 'relished melancholy', which expressed a kind of aimless stoicism, and the aesthetic values recommended by Pater, although this idea of beauty as ultimately objectless and deriving from an inner consistency can also be seen as a debased form of liberalism in its popular sense (the sense Newman employs: DeLaura is right in connecting Newman, Arnold, and Pater).[40] So we find in the well-known conclusion to *The Renaissance*, Pater ending with: 'For art comes to you proposing frankly to give nothing but the highest quality to your moments as they pass, and simply for those moments' sake'. Here the word 'highest' has moral overtones which are inappropriate except in so far as Pater is countering Utilitarian ethics in emphasizing 'the moment': for implicit in the Utilitarian ethic, as Hutton points out, is a heavy sense of responsibility for the future.[41]

Hutton's use of the word 'higher' is that of the anti-Utilitarian Liberal Christian. It is no exaggeration to say that the fundamental cause and aim of all Hutton's writing is religious, aiming to give a religious explanation to motives or events which might also be explained in secular terms. So he would argue that a Utilitarian

---

[38] 'Mr. Trollope on the Moral Effect of Novel Reading', *Spectator*, 4 Jan. 1879, 10.

[39] *Contemporary Thought and Thinkers*, ii. 45.

[40] David Daiches, *Some Late Victorian Attitudes* (London, 1969), 39–40.

[41] 'The Prevalence of Melancholy', *Spectator*, 17 Jan. 1885, 78–9. See also 'The Melancholy of Our Modern Culture', *Spectator*, 22 Aug. 1863, 2398–400.

principle of equal *rights* might be translated into a religious impulse of self-sacrifice: 'theology transfigures', he writes, 'the haggling acquisitive motive of the man who demands his fair share of the happiness of the world into the generous motive of the man who demands the right to give himself up to the service of those who are most miserable and helpless.'[42] Theology would seem to be the study of and revelation of higher intentions behind phenomena which might be seen as the mere manifestation of social tendencies. Literature seems to be to Hutton a secular theology, revealing and generating higher, magnanimous motives for actions which could be explained in terms of secular cynicism.

What Hutton called the *literary* interest both included and enlarged the *moral* interest. There is a crucial passage in Hutton's 1876 Preface to the second edition of his *Theological Essays*:

Is not the deed or sign, the action or the smile or frown by which a moral or spiritual truth is illustrated, an essential element in the truth itself? Might not our Lord's own sentence on the woman taken in adultery—'Let him that is without sin amongst you cast the first stone'—if uttered by a cynic, by a disbeliever in human virtue, have been turned into a sneer at the radical rottenness of human nature—an argument for universal tolerance of sin founded on universal despair—instead of what it was, an argument for universal tenderness and sympathy, with self-abhorrence, founded on the universal consciousness of weakness and temptation?[43]

In his essay on Maurice, Hutton says: 'Maurice's interest in man was moral and not properly literary. He writes as if man were a moral being and nothing else'.[44] I am suggesting that the function performed by theology in Hutton's Preface is a *literary* one, giving a sense, in his words, 'of the absolutely boundless significance in every moral choice'. And, conversely, the 'highest' function of literature is to provide explanations for motives which the world might see in cynical terms. Moreover, literature's resistance to communicating truth as mere information is better suited to distinguishing between persons than is the treatise. Hence also, as that quotation makes clear, Hutton's close attention in his literary essays to the *language* of literary production as an essential element of the truth itself.

[42] *Aspects of Religious and Scientific Thought*, p. 37. See also Hutton's 'The Service of Man', *Contemporary Review*, 51 (Apr. 1887), 480–93.
[43] *Theological Essays*, second edition (London, 1877), p. xii.
[44] 'Cardinal Newman', *Contemporary Review*, 45 (May 1884), 642–65 (p. 642).

Utilitarianism and literature

The function of literature was for Hutton a moral one: the enlargement of the reader's understanding of the 'higher' springs of human conduct, possibly in resistance to the intention of a specific literary work. The most important and consistent alternative attempt to describe and circumscribe the inward springs of conduct was carried out by the Utilitarian writers against whom Hutton, in seeing literature as an expression of liberty, set himself.

Hutton addresses himself to the argument directly in answering Mill's essays on Liberty and Utilitarianism in the 1850s. Refusing to sanction any inward standard of right and wrong, Mill proposes to judge actions by their results, hence he argues that those actions which affect only the agents, which are 'self-regarding', can never be called immoralities, though they may be proofs of folly or of lack of self-respect. Hutton argues that this notion of the 'self-regarding' action suggests a false distinction *in kind* between the inward conditions of self-reproach attending the disposition which affects only the agent and that which attends dispositions or actions which primarily affect others. Hutton argues that Mill's distinction is a political and not a 'literary' one.[45] Hutton finds the power of reproach an entirely inward matter.

It is difficult to arbitrate between Mill and Hutton because their respective notions of the nature of the operation of the mind and the nature of human society are in such opposition. Mill puts beyond the range of social criticism those actions which are purely individual, whereas Hutton does not believe in the possibility of the purely individual as a category of a different range of moral actions. Hutton thinks of moral reproach almost entirely in terms of self-reproach authorized by a standard which is divinely implanted: even if he admitted the possibility of the 'purely individual' he would deny that the agent himself judges his own actions by their consequences. The language used by Mill to describe moral transgression implies that agents can be conceived of as outside the social body, invading it. Hutton's language suggests that he sees transgression as rebellion from the inside. That is to say, Hutton's

---

[45] 'Mill on Liberty', *National Review*, 8 (Apr. 1859), 393–425. See also 'Utilitarianism and the *Saturday Review*', *Spectator*, 19 Oct. 1861, 1144–6; 'Utilitarianism', *Spectator*, 11 Apr. 1863, 1868–9; 'The Latest Phase of the Utilitarian Controversy', *British Quarterly Review*, 1 (July 1869), 68–91.

belief in inward life is such that he attributes it both to men and to society. For Mill, society is a kind of arbiter between the members of it, and this arbitration the best judgement of its own best external interests. However, Hutton's positive notion of the nature of society is very close to George Eliot's idealistic humanism. Moreover, he seems to see the function of writing as rendering intelligible this inner life of society and thereby enlarging it.

George Eliot becomes for Hutton the example and later the authority for the consideration of human will and purpose which he opposed to Mill's consideration of consequences. Indeed the novel in general seems to Hutton capable of producing moral spaciousness in spite of a lack of faith. He wrote of Browning: 'he conceives men in their relation to each other, and in mental collision with each other; but, after all, he does not care which way the battle goes, except so far as that is involved in his interpretation. There is no *narrative* force in him at all.'[46] The emphasis on narrative is Hutton's, as if the word and the action naturally implied some commitment of personal sympathy, a sense that there is something at stake. That something is staked on the judgement of character, which 'tends to enlarge the moral field of view'. The moral value of the novel for Hutton attaches to the importance of character and motive: the difference between the judgements of Mill and of Hutton and George Eliot is that for Mill the adjectives 'right' and 'wrong' are attached to actions, which is a 'moral' judgement, while for Hutton and George Eliot the adjectives are applied to persons and form the 'literary' judgement.

Hutton's emphasis on narrative seems to have combined with his interest in strength of character to produce his belief in the moral and aesthetic qualities of the realistic novel.

The progressive secularization of Victorian society provoked widely expressed fears that individual lives would be rendered meaningless. W. H. Mallock, whose criticism of George Eliot I shall discuss later, argued in his *Is Life Worth Living?* that the fear was based on the loss of an object in life: the loss of a function, and the loss of an object of veneration. Mill was his obvious example, and we could write the history of Victorian ideas as an account of attempts to defend or replace objects of activity or veneration. The Christian concept, however, of man's functional status is not that

---

[46] *Literary Essays* (1896), p. 197.

of a static function, rather it is typically represented in the depiction of man engaged on a journey or quest to some known end (the depiction which Tennyson tried to secularize). It is this *narrative sense of selfhood* which is supplied for Hutton, as I have already suggested, by the novel.

As Barbara Hardy has argued, narrative is vital to our attempts to make ourselves understood.[47] It denies that life is a series of episodes, as Pater would have it seen. I have already indicated that for this reason Hutton and Townsend tried to make their newspaper read like a narrative. More importantly, the narrative of the realistic novel seems to have been to him a defence against secularization in that, first it depicted characters taken by others to be living out stories which ran from birth to death, and second it depicted characters who were the subjects of histories that were essentially their own and no one else's, with their own peculiar meaning. This combination Hutton called the 'double view' of life which only the novel could provide, and which retained for Hutton the disappearing sense of a 'whole life'.

The nearest literary form to the novel which could provide this sense of a 'whole life' was the biography, and in this sense all Hutton's writing is 'biographical', not only his critical biographies of Newman and Scott, in taking into account the whole life and work of his subjects. It is important, though it may seem incidental, that Hutton was a leading member of the society formed to produce a complete works of Wordsworth, while Arnold produced a selection from Wordsworth, a version of the poet 'relieved of poetical baggage' recommended by Pater in his essay on Wordsworth four years before Arnold's book was published. To Hutton a selection, as he was to remark of a selected 'Wit and Wisdom' of Matthew Arnold, deprived the reader of the writer's intention and the wholeness of his argument. A selection was materialistic in the sense I have discussed: its reader aimed to reach experience by a short cut and to deprive language of its roots. For Arnold and Pater, the selection freed the reader from the tyranny of the writer's intention and left him with his own personal touchstones. Indeed, selectivity (of subject, of audience) was Hutton's ground of disagreement with Arnold.

---

[47] Barbara Hardy, 'Towards a Poetics of Fiction: An Approach Through Narrative', *Novel*, 2 (1968), 5–14 (p. 5).

The 'double view' which provided for Hutton a narrative sense of selfhood would suggest to me that *David Copperfield* might have been his archetypal novel. Yet he wanted a novelist whose deliberate intention was to produce this double view: George Eliot was the novelist he was waiting for. As I try to show in my final chapter, Hutton's studies of the novel from the 1850s can be seen to imply that George Eliot will be his ideal novelist. She remained, however, only an ideal since she lacked the belief in religion he thought implicit in the novels. In *Middlemarch* he found secular characters struggling against their environment, and while his criticism of *Romola* (acknowledged by George Eliot) was that in spite of the historical setting the characters had obviously read Feuerbach, he saw that *Middlemarch* was specifically addressed to the question of man's function in society, to the need for an object in life. George Eliot describes Dorothea as searching for some object 'which would reconcile self-despair with the rapturous consciousness of life beyond self'.

Hutton felt Dorothea's character showed that a nature which is not self-regarding is more likely to err than one which is self-seeking, but finds it 'impossible to believe that this rare nature does not find any satisfying inward life to compensate these blunders, and turn them into the conditions of purer strength and less accidental happiness.'[48] Hutton even suggests that Mary Garth is the real 'heroine' of the novel because her spiritual strength defeats the 'meanness of opportunity' which the rest of the novel is limited by. This distortion of the novel by Hutton shows the extent to which he identifies moral criticism with literary criticism. Yet he also identifies a distortion of George Eliot's when he points out that in the 'Finale' to *Middlemarch* she tries silently to change an agent of omission ('meanness of opportunity') to an agent of commission ('the society into which she was born'). Hutton sees this as a tendency, not restricted to George Eliot, to aggravate the faults of society: 'a frequent tendency in those who find no anchor for faith, to throw upon some abstract offender like "society" the faults they see in those who most satisfy their longing for perfection.'[49] This looks at first like a precursor of the modern parody of liberalism ('society is to blame'), but what puzzles Hutton is the extent of George Eliot's idealism without faith: to him she is magnanimous

[48] *Modern Guides*, p. 206.
[49] Ibid., p. 212.

in excess of the evidence for magnanimity which she herself presents. Though Hutton does not articulate the personal disappointment, he is clearly saddened to find that the pre-eminent artist in, what is to him, the most important form, could share what he took to be the Christian ideals but not the Christian reality.

Conclusion

In the chapters which follow I shall go on to elaborate and illustrate the issues raised by this general discussion of Hutton's life and work.

I have suggested that all Hutton's work has a 'religious' basis and intention, and my next chapter comprises a detailed account of his spiritual progress, as charted through his relationship with Newman. This relationship had, as I hope to show, contrasting public and private sides. The use of 'literary' to which I have already alluded, and the status of 'realism' afforded to products of the imagination, was largely authorized by Newman, especially in his *Essay in Aid of a Grammar of Assent*. I shall concentrate on Hutton's reaction to this book and on his sense that its argument was implicit in all Newman's work, including the much earlier 'Oxford Sermons'.

The status of religious and imaginative assent is the subject of Hutton's critique of Arnold as recounted in my third chapter. To Hutton, Arnold's paraphrase of God ('a tendency not ourselves which makes for righteousness') seems to have implied a theory of meaning, intention, creation, and character: an implicit *literary* theory. His critique of Arnold also focuses on Arnold's notion of 'character' and the exclusivity of Arnoldian culture and audience, in contrast to Hutton's aim of 'enlargement'. I suggest that the work of Hutton and Arnold might be characterized as contrasting responses to Newman, beginning with the comparison by Hutton of Arnold and Newman which Macmillan thought fanciful. I hope to conclude by showing how Hutton admired Arnold's poetry at the expense of his prose, and how Hutton wrote in terms of which Arnold could not have approved: Arnold, like Leslie Stephen, thought that Hutton saw more in poetry than really existed.

In the chapter following the account of Arnold, I shall analyse Hutton's 'reading' of the poetry of Wordsworth and Tennyson. His 'Wordsworth' belongs to a critical movement, which also includes Leslie Stephen, Edward Caird, and the members of the Wordsworth Society, which saw the poet as an ethical teacher. This movement stands in contra-distinction to that to which the 'Wordsworth' of Arnold and Pater belongs. I hope to show that Hutton's view of Wordsworth was a seminal one. As the occasion for a perception 'into the life of things', Hutton contrasts Wordsworth with Tennyson: to him Wordsworth demonstrates a resistance to influences with which he saw Tennyson colluding.

The 'real' which Hutton took Wordsworth as having perceived is, however, unlike the perceived real behind the flux of appearance which Arnold and Pater found in Wordsworth. Hutton's interest in Wordsworth was founded on the poet's respect for the everyday: Hutton's reading of Wordsworth was what I have called 'novelistic', and what Arnold called 'provincial'. My final chapter is an account of Hutton's anticipation of the ideal novel, represented by George Eliot, in his early writings on Charlotte Yonge, Elizabeth Sewall, and Jane Austen. I shall conclude with his defence of George Eliot, concentrating on his unique perception of all her work as a 'translation' of her version of Feuerbach.

The terms of these accounts, especially those referring to such concepts as 'intentions', 'character', 'author', and 'text', have been the subject of debate in current criticism and my own uses of them are, consciously or not, bound to have been influenced by these debates. Indeed, many of the oppositions in these accounts, such as Hutton's criticism of Arnold paraphrase of 'God', which opposes intentionality to historical determinism, prefigure current oppositions. However, I have attempted to isolate and recreate the terms of Victorian criticism, even when that terminology seems to be inadequate in the eyes of its users. This terminology and this inadequacy are, to some extent, the indirect subjects of this study.

3
J. H. Newman

Introduction

R. H. HUTTON was Newman's defender, critic, 'translator', and
to some extent his follower. The account of their relationship,
particularly of the private exchanges and arguments which lay
behind Hutton's public writing, constitutes a history of Hutton's
mental life and of the complex reception of Newman's work.

Hutton first wrote about Newman in 1850 ('Newman's *Discourses Addressed to Mixed Congregations*', *Inquirer*, 16 February
1850) and he went on to write some thirty-six articles, including
long essays, and a book on Newman. His last piece on him was a
comparison of Newman and Tennyson for the *Spectator* in 1896.
Hutton's *Spectator* writing on Newman virtually began and ended
in controversy: his first *Spectator* article on him was a contribution
to the public argument with Kingsley ('Newman's Sarcasm', 20
February 1864) which Newman's biographer thought crucially influential, and in the 1890s Hutton wrote a series of articles defending him against the attacks of E. A. Abbott.

The article on the Newman–Kingsley row prompted Newman to
write to Hutton, thus beginning a correspondence which continued
until 1873. At this point, however, the correspondence apparently
ceased for ten years, only to be resumed in 1883. They met,
though, only once, when Newman called at the *Spectator* office
unexpectedly in 1866. The gap of ten years is not explained in the
correspondence: their letters were usually occasioned, though their
contents not caused, by an article of Hutton's or by a question,
often of a very technical theological nature, posed by Hutton.
Perhaps such questions did not arise during the apparent ten year
gap (I say 'apparent' since letters may simply not have survived or
been discovered), so the silence implies not a rift, but a measure of
agreement. It is, though, odd that Hutton should not have written
when Newman was made a cardinal, and his *Spectator* articles do
show some anti-Catholic feeling during those years.

However, Hutton's writing for the public often had a quite different emphasis from that of his private correspondence. He did

not *quite* contradict himself, but the confident tone of the *Spectator* editor is often belied by the questioning correspondent. At his most extreme point of difference between the public role and the personal, Hutton is critical of Roman Catholic theology in his newspaper while considering following Newman into the Church.

In this chapter I hope to follow the course of the correspondence and set it beside Hutton's published work. I shall concentrate, therefore, on the period after Hutton became editor of the *Spectator*. I shall begin with his first impressions of Newman and his contribution to the Kingsley argument, then discuss Hutton's reviews of the 'Oxford Sermons', reprinted in 1868, and of the *Essay in Aid of a Grammar of Assent* (1870). I shall go on to look at his long retrospective studies of Newman published in book form and in the *Contemporary Review* and in *Good Words* during the second part of the correspondence in the 1880s. I shall conclude with his defence of Newman against E. A. Abbott and his final evaluation of Newman.

The Influence of Newman

I attempted in my first chapter to suggest how Hutton's interest in literature was 'religious', how literature was to him a kind of secular theology, providing insights into motive and producing moral enlargement. I cited his comment that F. D. Maurice's interest in man was 'moral and not properly literary', and in that comment Hutton is contrasting Maurice and Newman: the latter being 'properly literary' in his interests. This is not meant to suggest that Newman is more interested in literature, indeed Hutton quotes with approval Newman's attack on the leisurely man of letters. Hutton's meaning is that he finds in Newman the authority for a belief in the 'reality' of products of the imagination. While the account given in this chapter is intended to provide a representative example of Hutton's theological work and to be a record of his mental life, it is also intended to show how his notions of 'realism' and the literary have a theological basis.

In a well-known passage in the *Grammar of Assent*, Newman quotes from Elizabeth Gaskell's *North and South* the avowal of faith of a 'poor dying factory girl'. He asserts, virtually without comment: 'Here is an argument for the immortality of the soul.'[1]

[1] J. H. Newman, *An Essay in Aid of a Grammar of Assent*, new edition (London, 1973), 312. All subsequent references are to this edition.

The *Grammar of Assent* is an argument for the status of the imagination and its products as 'real', as able to produce real belief. Indeed, the book is tacitly *the* Victorian philosophical defence of the
literary mind and the imagination. Technically, the book is an investigation of belief as a state of mind, of what the mind does when
it makes an act of faith. Newman does not set forth arguments for
belief, but tries to describe what it is to believe them or to assent to
them. Assent to a proposition which deals with the abstract he calls
'notional', and assent to a proposition which deals with the individual or singular he calls 'real': in the first draft of the book this
latter category was called 'imaginative'.

Very simply, Newman's *Grammar of Assent* equated the imagination with the real, and he calls the faculty which sanctions real or
imaginative assent the 'Illative Sense'. In earlier work he calls this
faculty the 'Implicit Reason'. When he comes to look back on
Newman's work, Hutton judges his most important contribution to
thought to have been the account of Implicit Reason, what Hutton
translates as 'Literary Reason'. Hutton saw that this account not
only bears fruit in the *Grammar of Assent*, but has its roots in the
'Oxford Sermons', especially those on 'Implicit and Explicit
Reason' and on 'Unreal Words'. As a novel, *Loss and Gain* might
also be seen as a product of belief in the rational effect of a literary
text.

These texts—the 'Oxford Sermons', *Loss and Gain* and the
Essay in Aid of a Grammar of Assent—are the most important to
Hutton and the ones on which I shall concentrate.

Hutton once wrote that if he ever had to suffer a period of solitary confinement and was given the chance to choose one or two
books to accompany him, he would take some of Newman's
because they show 'the comparative indifference to outward circumstances in a world ruled by God'.[2] I do not think that Hutton is
there referring to what Newman wrote as a source of Christian
Stoicism, but rather that he is expressing his belief that Newman's
account of the Illative Sense provided an inner equivalent of external life. That is to say, Newman's account might seem like a
justification of subjectivity, and was appropriated as such by
Arnold and Pater, but Hutton sees that he was trying to describe a
mental counterpart to practical life. The Illative Sense as Hutton
sees it in retrospect is the same sense which justifies the assumptions

² *Contemporary Review*, 45 (May 1884), 643.

and unrecognized 'acts of faith' which make everyday life possible. I would suggest that literature in general provides Hutton with an alternative to everyday life which is its counterpart and not an escape from it.

In applying the Illative Sense to everyday life Hutton is, however, in danger of secularizing Newman, which in many ways is just what Arnold did. In Newman's thought the resistance to secularization is provided by his anti-Liberalism, his notion that only a few are capable of exercising reason. Hutton, as I noted earlier, opposes the notion of the clerisy, secular or sacred, and continually struggles with this problem of the privacy of Newman's thought.

This problem is related to the general one of attributing 'influence' to Newman. In defining what 'materialism' meant to Hutton, I suggested that he saw as 'materialist' the attribution of spiritual effects to secular causes. Similarly, Newman would have thought it 'materialist' to attempt to play a causative part in Hutton's spiritual life. Hence Hutton's requests for guidance repeatedly met with oblique refusals. When I take Newman's writing to be the occasion for Hutton's thought and not the cause of it I am trying to take into account Newman's own intention and obliquity. Nevertheless my own method implicitly contradicts Newman's teaching by using a chronological sequence and implying causal development. Newman complained in 1847 of our confusing the *ordos chronologicus* with the *ordos logicus*, or attributing the status of *causae* to acts which are merely prior in time to their supposed effects.[3] Over thirty years later, in an important letter to William Froude, he set down as his most important *dictum* the following: 'It is to me a perplexity that grave authors seem to enunciate as an intuitive truth, that everything must have a cause.'[4] The words are from the *Grammar of Assent*.

Hutton's desire to find an impetus and a guide in Newman is doomed to failure in the sense that Newman does not believe that actions have worldly causes: this disbelief is not temperamental but reasoned. Indeed the point about the Implicit Reason is that it cannot be followed in its movements. So Hutton can accept Newman's

[3] *Letters and Diaries of John Henry Newman*, xii, ed. C. S. Dessain (London, 1962), 31 (8 Feb. 1847).

[4] *Letters and Diaries of John Henry Newman*, xxix, ed. C. S. Dessain and T. Gornald (London, 1976), 113 (29 Apr. 1879). See also *Cardinal Newman and William Froude: A Correspondence*, ed. C. Harper (Baltimore, 1933), and *Grammar of Assent*, p. 31.

account of this faculty but is not obliged, according to Newman himself, to accept the conclusions reached by another's exercise of that faculty. Newman wrote of the Implicit Reason in 1840:

The mind . . . makes progress not unlike a clamberer on a steep cliff, who, by quick eye, prompt hand and firm foot, ascends how he knows not himself, by personal endowments and by practice, rather than by rule, leaving no track behind him, and unable to teach another. It is not too much to say that the stepping by which great geniuses scale the mountains of truth is as unsafe and precarious to men in general, as the ascent of a skilful mountaineer up a literal crag. It is a way which they alone can take; and its justification lies in their success. And such mainly is the way in which all men, gifted or not gifted, commonly reason,—not by rule, but by an inward faculty.[5]

Newman's later work is a consistent effort to scale this mountain of truth without recommending that anyone follow him: we might describe his total output as 'A Grammar of Ascent'.

It is to the operation of the Explicit Reason, says Newman, that the words 'analysis, criticism, rules' and the like belong. We can see that Hutton's work as a literary critic and cultural guide is both authorized and undermined by Newman, and he partly avoids the problem by splitting his work between the public and the private spheres. The difference was, though, never reconciled: at the root of it is Hutton's defence of the authority of common men in opposition to Newman's reliance on an infallible ecclesiastical institution.

Newman's sense that each man is his own centre has something in common with the secular and relative notion that each man is alone in a moral jungle. Where they differ is that Newman believed that all men found eventual unity in God. Hutton would, however, have agreed with Leslie Stephen's opening words in his essay on 'Dr. Newman's Theory of Belief':

Some persons, it is said, still cherish the pleasant illusion that to write a history of thought is not on the face of it a chimerical undertaking. Their opinion implies the assumption that all contemporary thought has certain common characteristics, and that the various prophets inspired by the spirit of our own as of every age utter complementary rather than contradictory doctrines. Could we attain the vantage ground which will be occupied by

5 *Parochial and Plain Sermons*, new edition, 8 vols. (London, 1868), viii. 257. See also Nicholas Lash, 'The Notion of Implicit and Explicit Reason in Newman's University Sermons', *Heythrop Journal*, 11 (1970), 48–54.

our posterity, we might of course detect an underlying unity of purpose in the perplexing labyrinth of divergent intellectual parts.[6]

Hutton is one of those who is continually trying to find a unity underlying the divergent intellectual movements of his day, and the Metaphysical Society institutionalized the attempt. His was an attempt to see with the eyes of posterity. Newman, on the other hand, positively resisted attempts to be defined in terms of his contemporaries—he was not so much independent of contemporary thought as ignorant of it. He also resisted Hutton's repeated attempts to entice him into the Metaphysical Society.[7]

From our vantage ground we can see connections where Stephen saw only perplexity. But Hutton was not satisfied with resting on perplexity and waiting for posterity to write the history of thought in the nineteenth century. I would suggest that he saw the danger of Newman's position, his refusal to teach others how to follow, as being that it would leave the disbeliever in a moral labyrinth. He foresaw, and lived just long enough to read Hardy's Jude telling the crowd at the Commemoration: 'I am in a chaos of principles, acting by instinct and not after example.'[8] Hutton wrote to Newman of his looking for 'gleams of light', and seems to feel responsible to his readership for shedding some light on the perplexities of thought. Ironically, he often uses Newman for the purpose of creating common ground, as the occasion for consensus but not its cause. The text he most often returns to is Newman's 'Oxford Sermon' on 'Unreal Words'. He wrote in 1886:

If any one idea has been common to the religious and to the sceptical thinkers on religious subjects in this curious century of ours . . . that common idea has been the duty of not using 'unreal words' on religious subjects. Cardinal Newman was the first to inculcate this, in one of the earliest and finest of his Oxford sermons.[9]

Under this head Hutton draws together Carlyle, Ruskin, James Stephen, Martineau, Huxley, Spencer, Frederic Harrison, and Wilfred Ward, but markedly excludes Matthew Arnold. Leslie

---

[6] Fortnightly Review, NS 22 (Nov. 1877), 680.

[7] On Newman's limited knowledge of contemporary thought, see D. A. Pailin, The Way to Faith: An Examination of Newman's 'Grammar of Assent' (London, 1969), 62.

[8] Thomas Hardy, Jude the Obscure, new Wessex edition (London, 1974), 346.

[9] Spectator, 24 July 1886, 982.

Stephen wrote of a lack of an underlying unity of *purpose*, and Hutton seems to attempt to replace this with a unity of choice of means and thus create a sense of unity of purpose. The unity, we might say, is to Hutton God's purpose, for otherwise his would be simply a more specific version of Arnold's attempt to define the spirit of the age.

All of Hutton's work shows the struggle between incommensurate desires for unity of vision and for knowledge of the divergent. His reaction to Newman concentrates and dramatizes the struggle into its more recognizable religious mode: the attempt to unify the desire for religious belief with the perception of truth. Hutton privately expresses the desire for emotional religion, and publicly argues the need for rational argument. He never succeeded in reconciling the two divergent claims, and, as I have said, his relationship with Newman provides the occasion for the expression of the problem but simultaneously preempts its solution.

Loss and Gain

In a letter of 1865 Hutton gave Newman this brief summary of the course of his mental life to that date:

> Mr. Martineau first made me to see that the old Unitarianism was as weak as it was unsuccessful. Mr. Maurice first taught me that the Incarnation could be held on a Protestant basis, and all your books, *Loss and Gain* especially, have given me gleams of light which I have not found elsewhere. But since the last step I have stood still.[10]

The last sentence of this is a barely disguised plea for a guide and impetus to spiritual development, but Hutton's 'last step' is in painful contrast to the agile 'stepping by which the great geniuses scale the mountains of truth' and who cannot teach others the way. His phrase suggests that where Hutton stands is not the final or secure position of his development. It has to be remembered that this was written the year after Hutton had confidently defended Newman in the pages of the *Spectator* as if quite assured of his position. On the basis of that letter we must look to his reading of *Loss and Gain* for the source of both the confident defence and the cry for help.

[10] *Letters and Diaries of John Henry Newman*, xxv. 29 (12 Sept. 1865).

Hutton first wrote about Newman in 1850 and first heard him preach in the same year.[11] The 'private' importance of Newman to Hutton must be dated from his reading *Loss and Gain*, Newman's first publication as a Roman Catholic in 1848. It is from this time that Hutton, writing in 1865, felt he had stood still in terms of spiritual progress. In his 1891 biography of Newman, Hutton wrote that he thought the book admirable 'for the fidelity with which it sketches young men's thoughts and difficulties, partly for its happy irony, partly for its perfect representation of the academical life and tone at Oxford'.[12] This retrospective and public account does not suggest the profound effect the book actually had on him as a thoughtful young man in difficulties.

This was an effect he only confessed to Newman, who became a sort of unofficial Father figure. In his first letter to him Hutton described *Loss and Gain* as nothing less than 'in some sense an era in my life'.[13] As a literary critic Hutton was used to describing the effects of books and despite the careful 'in some sense' the impression he leaves is that the effect was a deep one. The phrase 'an era in my life' may not be deliberately chosen and certainly it and phrases like it are extremely common in descriptions of dramatic reactions to books. Hutton's associate James Knowles, for example, uses an analogous term when he describes the effect on him of first reading *In Memoriam*: 'opening it haphazard at the Geological Stanzas I could not put the book down until I had read it all through . . . It made an epoch in my life.'[14] These reactions, one to a novel and the other to a poem or series of poems, do not apologize for attributing strong reactions to works of literature. Though the phrases may be used without much conscious thought, the descriptions of epoch-making books seem to be used to mark periods in personal histories of thought in exactly the same way that they are used to mark milestones in the history of thought in general. In the case of both Hutton and Knowles the books are markers rather than influences or simple causes. To repeat Newman's point, their chronological place is not necessarily their logical one: these books did not *cause* the reactions to them.

[11] Ibid., xxi. 86 (28 Feb. 1864).

[12] *Cardinal Newman* (London, 1891), 194. See also C. Crawford, 'The Novel that Occasioned *Loss and Gain*', *MLN* 65 (1950), 414–18.

[13] *Letters and Diaries of John Henry Newman*, xxv. 60 (25 Feb. 1864).

[14] James Knowles, 'Tennyson and Aldworth', in *Tennyson and his Friends*, ed. Hallam Tennyson (London, 1911), 245.

Nevertheless, when Hutton enlarges on his reaction to the novel in a letter to Newman later in 1864, he comes close to attributing a causative effect to the novel which must have made Newman very uncomfortable. Hutton wrote:

When I was eighteen the passage in which Willis describes the Mass in *Loss and Gain* very nearly made a Willis of me,—I mean a man who *dives* experimentally into the Church in the hope of faith rather than one who goes into it because he sees it to be true. But since then I have got a growing conviction that faith however mysterious ought to prove itself to the mind and has the power to do so. Still that passage about the Mass has a strange fascination for me which I cannot quite analyse.[15]

This letter states the problem which was to remain intractable, namely the relation of faith to proof, or the relation of the religious emotion to the mind. This was, indeed, the problem to which Newman addressed himself in the *Grammar of Assent*, where he argues that instinctive faith can prove itself to the mind. If Hutton had believed this he might have been sufficiently moved by the novel to become a Catholic.

Though Hutton tells Newman he was eighteen when he read *Loss and Gain*, in actual fact he was twenty-two when the book was first published. However unwittingly, he seems to make himself younger in order to *almost* dismiss the early enthusiasm as the excess of an impressionable and callow youth. Yet he expressly clings to the 'strange fascination' of the book while confessing an inability to analyse it, or to expose it to what Newman would have called the operations of the Explicit Reason. The overall effect is to make him seem younger now, in 1864, than his thirty-eight years, in spite of his 'growing conviction'.

In private Hutton might have been content to rest on his non-analytical assertion of the power of certain passages or words, but he criticized Arnold for his blunt refusal to analyse the Arnoldian 'touchstones' and in public print Hutton felt bound to account for his reactions and fascinations.

Hutton's public writing on Newman in the 1850s, that is between the publication of *Loss and Gain* and *Apologia Pro Vita Sua*, shows an argued resistance to the impulses confessed to in the letter. His most important essay on Newman and Catholicism during this period was probably one titled 'Romanism, Anglicanism and

[15] *Letters and Diaries of John Henry Newman*, xxi. 120–1 (15 June 1864).

Protestantism' published in the *National Review* in 1855 and re-published in book form in 1871 and subsequent editions (1877, 1880, and 1888). This would suggest a continuing belief in its arguments and conclusions.

In this essay Hutton quotes the passage from the Mass which he cited in the letter, in the course of which Willis says: ' "I could attend masses for ever and not be tired. It is not a mere form of words,—it is a great action, the greatest action that can be on earth".'[16] Hutton's quotation from the long passage in which these words occur implies his admiration for it, but he does not mention his fascination with it. I would suggest that Hutton is deeply moved as a literary man by the notion of words which have the status of acts. For although he concurred with Newman in his condemnation of the man of literature who, perhaps like Arnold, found his 'true dignity and honour' in literature's unreality, its 'saying without doing', Hutton admired words which expressed beliefs sincerely held. He considered these words to be actions. Conversely, Hutton had a great admiration for reticence in literature and in society, as it carried for him 'a deep sense of responsibility for all those words which are pregnant with action'.[17] Those words of Willis's seem to move Hutton because they validate Hutton's general feeling that language may be the index of forces beyond the reader or listener and yet may be no less moving for that. Just as Dorothea wanted an object in life which would 'never justify weariness', so Hutton is drawn to a form of words which he could attend to 'for ever and not be tired'. This is how Hutton treats literature: he describes a line of Arnold's as 'inexhaustible'. Both Hutton and Dorothea are looking for means of resisting *ennui* and the prevalent world-weariness, and Hutton was clearly once prepared to find these means in the language of the Catholic Mass. This must be seen as, in the general sense, a 'literary' reaction.[18]

In the essay in which he quotes Willis's words, however, Hutton does not make clear any sympathy for the Mass or the beliefs behind it. After a long critical history of the Catholic Church conducted partly as psychological analysis of the 'Roman character', Hutton cites those words as evidence of the *institutional* conception

---

[16] J. H. Newman, *Loss and Gain* (London, 1848), 290.

[17] *Spectator*, 27 Aug. 1887, 1146.

[18] D. Mackinnon, *A Study in Ethical Theory* (London, 1957), 129; F. Townsend, 'Newman and the Problem of Critical Pose', *Victorian Notes*, 14 (May 1956), 22–5.

of Catholic worship. They illustrate the Church's 'temptation to confound a real presence with a local form'.[19] Hutton describes the 'Roman character' as devoid of 'rich inward sources of self-occupation' but obsessed with the external task of expanding its laws and institutions. He argues that the Catholic Church ignores the inward source of spiritual life and claims for her own acts 'as fixed physical *occasions* of spiritual influences, the right of being their exclusive *cause*'. He is suggesting that Catholic rites are claimed to have a causal relation to the faith they celebrate.

I hope it is clear that, paradoxically, Hutton is applying Newman's thought to Newman's Church. Tacitly, Newman is treated as an exception, and Hutton uses the secular side ('the greatest action that can be on earth') of *Loss and Gain* to attack the Church. Hutton never, anywhere, makes it explicit, but the Catholic Church Hutton describes is not one Newman would have joined. It is a Church concerned with secular influence, the Catholic Church feared by Hutton's readers. Indeed the argument Hutton elaborates, that Rome does not distinguish between absolute truth and 'truth of moral effect or, in other words, social and political *pietas*', is essentially that of Charles Kingsley: that Rome has no 'strong love for truth *as truth*'.[20]

The explanation for Hutton's defence of Newman, though he never articulates it, is his belief that Newman does have a strong desire for the absolute truth. This is what Hutton principally looks for in *all* writers. He admits, in the 1855 essay, that a reliance upon and limitation by a body of theory which provides tacit intellectual justification for the Church's power draws upon a faith in 'the affinity of human nature for pure religion and its deep love of moral excellence'. He concedes that a species of authority so powerful that it is its own evidence of being true is a source of *freedom* from the servitude of private judgement and makes us 'suspect as false that which we cannot show to be human'. Yet Hutton has to reject the source of this freedom for, as it were, the sake of his readership: not in the sense of having to satisfy their expectations or pander to their prejudices, but in the sense that to him the *vox populi* registers the influence of the *vox Dei*. He distrusts the manipulation of the laity, but trusts the 'common cry', the authority of common men: 'what the *vox populi*, rightly questioned, rejects, is

[19] R. H. Hutton, *Theological Essays*, 3rd edition (London, 1888), 382.
[20] Ibid., pp. 386–7.

not and cannot be divine truth'.[21] Newman is not excepted from
this criticism, and Hutton could never reconcile himself to the
power of the priesthood as a special class with 'more than human
influence and less than human experience'.[22] It has to be added,
though, that Hutton's parenthetical condition that the spontaneous
authority of common men is trustworthy when they are 'rightly
questioned' suggests that he does see a role for human authority in
matters of belief. He seems to see his function as asking the right
questions.

Hutton's point of disagreement with the Catholic Church was on
the role of the priesthood and the Pope, and on some points of
dogma such as the status afforded to saints and their relics. Some
of his criticism, especially that aimed at the causative claims of
ritual, are more appropriate to Puseyism and perhaps that was his
real target. He admires in the Catholic Church, so far as we can
provide the analysis he could not, its affirmation that unconscious
actions are a real sustaining power, while Protestantism taught that
pure life proceeds from conscious faith. This was Hutton's state of
mind in 1864: he implicitly excepted Newman from Catholicism's
materialism, he maintained a 'literary' admiration for Newman's
words and the Catholic trust in emotion, but could not reconcile
himself to the authority of a worldly priesthood.

Apologia Pro Vita Sua

When Hutton's literary criticism was surveyed by Hugh Walker in
1896, Walker commented, citing his work on Scott, that Hutton
seemed particularly in sympathy with writers who showed an interest in public life.[23] This seems to me to be true but in a subtle
sense: Hutton seems most interested in writers whose 'words' have
the status of 'actions'. He gives some of Wordsworth's words this
status because the poet seems to him moved by the power of his
own reflected emotion. He does the same for George Eliot because
her words imply to Hutton a source of strength greater than her
expression of it.

---

[21] Ibid., pp. 388–9. See also C. S. Dessain, 'Cardinal Newman on the Laity',
Louvain Studies, 16 (1961), 51–62, and the later, excellent discussion of Newman in
S. Femiano, *The Infallibility of the Laity* (New York, 1967).

[22] See also my later discussion of the Arnoldian secular clerisy, ch. 4.

[23] *Bookman*, NS 9 (Jan. 1896), 120.

Newman was anything but a public man, yet Hutton felt that he was grappling with real issues of experience, and this gave his words the status of action. 'Public life' has nothing to do with, say, involvement in political issues. When, through his argument with Kingsley, Newman became a public figure it merely seemed to make literal the relationship Hutton had always seen Newman as having with 'real life'.

The public row with Kingsley had its roots, on Kingsley's side, in Protestant prejudice. On Newman's side the row represented a polarized opposition to Liberalism. Attacks on the power of Rome in the second half of the century had united Catholics behind an opposition to Liberalism, and the mediating Liberal Catholic Movement under Acton had virtually disappeared with the failure of their organ, the *Home and Foreign Review*, in 1863.[24] The furore provoked by the argument can only be explained by the sudden polarizing of opinion: deep-rooted Protestant feelings came to the surface, while Catholics seemed to take the opportunity to attack Liberalism in thought, imperialism in politics, and commercialism in society.[25]

When Hutton defended Newman he ignored these issues and treated Newman's reply to Kingsley as a literary text: he subjects its language to analysis in order to ask the question, 'What is the coherent basis behind this text?'. His defence of Newman is titled 'Father Newman's Powers of Sarcasm', and he writes:

Mr. Kingsley is a choice though, perhaps, too helpless victim for the full exercise of Father Newman's powers . . . [His] weaknesses are all gauged, probed and condemned by a mind perfectly imperturbable at its basis of intellect, though vividly sensitive to the little superficial ripples of motive and emotion it scorns . . . scorn which the habit of his mind in judging all human weakness by inflexible dogma has made part of the very essence of his marvellous insight into human frailty . . . One of the greatest secrets of Dr. Newman's wonderful power is an intellectual basis for his mind of that

---

[24] For a general account of the controversy, see Robert Martin, *The Dust of Combat: A Life of Charles Kingsley* (London, 1952). See also John Holmes, *More Roman Than Rome: English Catholicism in the Nineteenth Century* (London, 1978), especially ch. 3, 'Newman and the Failure of Liberal Catholicism'; and the same writer's 'John Henry Newman: History, Liberalism and the Dogmatic Principle', *Philosophical Studies*, 23 (1974), 86–106.

[25] See J. Coulson, *Newman and the Common Tradition: A Study in the Language of Church and Society* (London, 1970), 136–43.

peculiar hardness tending to cruelty which most easily allies itself with a keen intellectual sense of the supernatural.[26]

Hutton is at pains to stress the intellectual basis of Newman's writing, to give his theology the status of reason. He does not compare Newman to a theologian but to Thackeray. Each writer exposes the vanity of human wishes but while Thackeray provides a secular source of scorn, Newman suggests that 'God's rule is one huge sarcasm on man's doings'. He calls this cruelty on Newman's part, but Hutton clearly admires and even envies the dogmatic inflexibility which his liberalism denies him.

To Hutton the debate between Kingsley and Newman was important because it represented a clash of two uses of language, the Protestant language of prejudiced first impressions and the Catholic language of casuistry, and of two exclusive bodies, the clerisy of the Protestant literary establishment and the *lingua communis* of the Catholic Church. The language of Catholicism is seen as an artificial network which adapts words to previously computed social ends and 'violates that implied understanding by which in ordinary intercourse men look rather to general emphasis, drift, and effect than to rigid definition and refined distinction.' The Catholic Church 'overreaches us by preparing herself too carefully for intercourse with the unprepared'.[27] Its language is concerned with the tactics and strategies of speech at the expense of the truthfulness of the first impression it gives. The language of the Protestant establishment is self-occupied, cares 'little for the unfair result of blurting out first impressions', and 'weighs justice to others at a trifling rate so long as there is no conscious insincerity in the language used'.[28]

The distinction implied in Hutton's discussion is: Catholic language is used with regard to its effect on the reader or listener, while Protestant language is concerned with sincerity and candidness. The perplexity we see in his letters to Newman seems to have its source in his preference as a literary man for the former while still maintaining a theological allegiance to the latter.

In the exchange of letters following Hutton's defence of Newman, there is a tacit but undiscussed distinction drawn between the

[26] *Spectator*, 20 Feb. 1864, 206–7.

[27] *Spectator*, 26 Mar. 1864, 356. See also S. Mendel, 'Metaphor and Rhetoric in Newman's *Apologia*', *Essays in Criticism*, 23 (1973), 357–71.

[28] *Spectator*, 26 Mar. 1864, 356.

'literary' effect of Newman's writing on him and its theological effect. In February 1864 Newman wrote, 'against the etiquette of the literary world', to thank Hutton. In reply Hutton called his writing 'a mere act of justice', giving his own words the status of moral acts, and acts aimed at the argument and not at the personalities. He thanks Newman for the literary effect of his writing, which had failed to persuade him of the truth of Catholic doctrine but had 'done more to enlarge and in many respects to elevate' his faith than those of any other writer.[29] Newman's response to this was to praise Hutton's writing on Catholicism as 'evidently written not at random, but critically . . . the expression of earnest and personal feeling'. Perhaps this sounded to Hutton, in spite of those words 'not at random', like praise for his Protestant sincerity. In any event, it drew from him an explanation of his motives and intentions:

It grieves me to see the unfairness with which you are treated by those whose profession is 'liberalism'. I wanted [i.e. in the article] simply to express that underlying the wide and delicately sympathetic imagination which your writings show, there seems to me to be always a deep attachment to a dogmatic and theological view of the universe, resting less on what I should call personal inspiration than on the *connected* view of a coherent body of theological truth.[30]

What appeals to Hutton in Newman is the wholeness and connectedness of his beliefs. I have already tried to show how as a literary critic it is this wholeness which Hutton both looks for and tries to supply, but he wanted a spiritual equivalent for the wholeness he could impose on his external life.

Hutton goes on in the letter to compare Newman with his early mentor, F. D. Maurice. Newman's mind, he argues, rests on 'a clear and comprehensive system' of revelation, while Maurice's theology is 'a broken cluster of deep but insulated insights' which he little cares to weave together 'and believes human intellect to be unable to weave together'. I have already cited Hutton's distinction between Newman and Maurice as that between a 'literary' and a 'moral' view of the world.[31] 'Literary' would seem here to mean referring to a whole system of thought which can be communicated to the reader. So, for example, Arnold's work is not 'literary' since,

---

[29] *Letters and Diaries of John Henry Newman*, xxi. 60 (25 Feb. 1864).
[30] Ibid., pp. 67–8 (28 Feb. 1864).
[31] See above p. 36, and *Contemporary Review*, 45 (1884), 642.

despite his stress on his own 'wholeness', it also rests on a broken cluster of insulated insights.

However, Hutton's criticism that Maurice placed a limitation on human intellect could be applied to Newman: Newman's resting on a human source of authority places a limitation on the progress of individual reason. It is the perception of this that seems to have prevented Hutton taking any more steps after leaving Unitarianism and the Broad Church of F. D. Maurice. In June 1864, in the letter which describes his strange fascination with *Loss and Gain*, Hutton tries to explain his stumbling block:

I have struggled my way out of Unitarianism to a deep belief in the Incarnation, but not by the road of 'authority' which you teach as the only road to theological truth . . . Such gleams as God puts into our hearts I glean eagerly from all sides, but I never could grasp the argument for supposing that the Church could teach us more than God can directly. I have always thought the Roman theology fuller of self-revealing truth than almost any other of the coherent *systems*, but my stumbling block has always been that a true theology ought to be (and I think is) self-revealing and does not need the organism of a visible institution to drive it home to the conscience and the heart.[32]

Newman replied to this immediately though with reluctance, considering Hutton's 'earnest and independent mind', and with care: many of the difficult parts of these letters exist in discarded versions. He gives us an example of Catholic theology subjecting language to definition within its own system:

What you designate as 'self-revealing' is surely a truth which *when told us from without*, commends itself intensely, manifoldly, intimately to our hearts. If you mean nothing more than this, I agree with your use of the word 'self-revealing'—but where I should differ from you is, that I should not consider such an internal acceptance or embrace of a doctrine a *sine qua non* condition of its being a truth.[33]

Newman has gone immediately to the question of 'authority'. He is suggesting that Hutton mistakes him in assuming that he teaches authority to be the only road to truth, and that Hutton could not himself have struggled this way without *some* authority. He translates Hutton's term 'self-revealing truth' into 'a self-revealing truth', replacing the idea of abstract truth with the idea of a solid,

---

[32] *Letters and Diaries of John Henry Newman*, xxi. 120 (15 June 1864).
[33] Ibid., p. 121 (18 June 1864).

absolute truth. Newman's final sentence is crucial: the internal acceptance of an idea is not a condition of its truth. An idea to Newman is independent of those who hold it: it does not cease to be true because people cease to believe it. Hutton seems to have shared this idea, hence his confidence, so reassuring to his readers, that secularization does not affect the facts of religion.

Newman goes on to argue that he does not consider the Church as an oracle, but as a visible authority. Indeed, the reasonings which persuade the generality of men he calls philosophy and not religion. Religion depends upon a revelation which might come from any text, 'a Greek poem, even the Koran', and the individual will be bound by this revelation 'though it creates *no obligation for any but himself'*. Newman is, though, restricting the use of the word 'revelation' to the communication of those truths which cannot be proved by reason (hence the alleged scepticism of the Catholic Church). This has the effect of making the letter an appeal to Hutton's assent but at the same time implying that Newman's belief is his own and creates no obligation on Hutton to believe it.

The implicit literary theory that texts may be the occasions for beliefs of which they are not the source was accepted by Hutton. Yet he remained sceptical of the institutionalization of literary flexibility in a Church and its dogma. He writes in his reply of his feeling that such an institution and one's allegiance to it may 'prevent by a sort of capillary repulsion' the apprehension of divine truths 'by the heart'. Hutton seems to want to leave himself open to influences from all sides, to avoid 'detachment'. He had used the scientific metaphor when writing of *Apologia Pro Vita Sua* when, having used a passage from *Loss and Gain* to illustrate Newman's 'closeness to life', he speaks of 'a certain intervening current of detaching feeling' in Newman's thought which 'acts like a capillary repulsion to separate it from actual contact'.[34]

The metaphor suggests that detachment in Newman was natural and instinctive, and that his thought was fluid and shifting. Kingsley thought it fluid and 'shifty'. Hutton is providing a summary of his association with Newman, who intervenes in his life but retreats from actual contact or influence. Significantly, Newman did not reply, it seems, to Hutton's letter mentioning the detaching effect of Catholic doctrine. Hutton continued, however, to look to Newman for some reconciliation of private judgement and authority,

[34] *Spectator*, 11 June 1864, 682–3.

and for some further justification for giving private feeling the status of 'contact with the actual'. He found such a justification in the *Essay in Aid of a Grammar of Assent* and in his re-reading of the Oxford Sermons.

The 'Oxford Sermons'

Contact between Hutton and Newman was renewed in 1865 when Newman sent him a copy of a new edition of the *Apologia*. In return, Hutton sent Newman a copy of his only theological tract, his *Incarnation and Principles of Evidence*, first published in 1862. He hoped Newman would comment on 'the relation of internal to external evidence', and asked how any man 'with his intellect unbiased' could accept all the books of the Bible as free from historical error and morally authoritative.[35]

Newman put aside the tract because, he explained much later, he was afraid it would interfere with the work on which he was engaged, the *Grammar of Assent*. He did, though, answer Hutton's question by separating 'historical fact' from 'moral authority' because 'we have not the natural ability to resolve moral questions as to ascertain facts'. Here we can see that while Hutton's mode of arguing is to try to integrate opposing forces, Newman always dismantles the argument he is dealing with and redefines its terms. The *Grammar of Assent*, which has a relatively simple central idea, is such a dismantling argument. Another difference between Hutton and Newman is the limits they place on the authority of common reason and common men. Newman's limit to 'natural ability' is a summary of his attack on Liberalism, an attack renewed and strengthened in the second edition of the *Apologia* which Newman had just sent Hutton.[36] Not surprisingly, the correspondence is subdued for the rest of the 1860s and its contents are unrelated to personal intellectual concerns.

In 1867 Hutton made an unsuccessful attempt to recruit Newman's help in Walter Bagehot's bid, also unsuccessful, to become Liberal MP for London University. In the same year Newman sent Hutton a copy of the verses which he, virtually alone among literary critics, had praised. Later in the year Hutton reported to him his

---

[35] *Letters and Diaries of John Henry Newman*, xxi. 482–3 (3 June 1865).
[36] J. Gilbert, 'Histoire de la publication de l'*Apologie* dans ses éditions successives', *Études anglaises*, 27 (1973), 262–74.

first meeting with Gladstone, when Newman's work had been the chief subject of conversation. After a lull in the correspondence, Hutton tried to recruit Newman into the Metaphysical Society in 1869 and again in 1871, when he complained, 'the physicists are almost too many for us!'.[37] Newman refused on the grounds that he was too old and not sufficiently widely read (which was probably true). Considering the quintessentially 'liberal' aims and nature of the Society, to 'obtain some basis of metaphysical science on which all metaphysicians might agree', Newman's refusal is predictable. It may be that Hutton aimed to resist the liberalizing influence of the scientists, or perhaps this is evidence of a tendency to turn a blind eye to some elements of Newman's thinking and to isolate the most palatable.

At the end of the sixties there was an important event in the progress of the relationship and Newman's reputation. This was the republication of the 'Oxford Sermons' in 1868, in *Parochial and Plain Sermons*.

Hutton devoted a long review to the sermons and was, as usual, not entirely in Newman's favour. He tries to separate the elements which would apply to the generation which now reads them from the elements which have driven Newman out of sympathy with those 'who have most cared not only to know the truth, but to live for it'.[38] As if in contrast to himself, Hutton attacks Newman for his 'misinterpretation of and comparative contempt for the new intellectual forces of our own day'. This public attack is quite different in tone and content from the correspondence, which is exchanged without reference to 'contemporary thought', as if the intellectual problems like the historical criticism of the Bible were private to the two men.[39]

The word which recurs through Hutton's review of the Sermons, and indeed through all his work on Newman, is 'realist'. His notion of Newman's realism is used to make him applicable to the age, and it provides a basis for Hutton's appreciation of the realistic in art.

---

[37] *Letters and Diaries of John Henry Newman*, xxv. 303 (21 Mar. 1871).

[38] *Spectator*, 5 Dec. 1868, 1437.

[39] In contrast, note the comment by a writer in the *Academy* reviewing Hutton's *Aspects of Religious and Scientific Thought*, a collection published two years after his death: 'There is something Titanesque in the way Mr. Hutton set himself each week to appreciate, to explain, to flout, or to annex to his own service the ripe thought of his day. None escaped him. Maurice, Clifford, Kingsley, Newman, Huxley, Tyndall, Jowett, Browning, Tennyson, Dr. Martineau, Mill, Matthew Arnold—he docketed them all.' (*Academy*, 56 (22 Apr. 1899), 451.)

Newman, he argues, has never treated revelation as the expression of the inscrutable will of God, he is 'a realist in the sense of believing that all religious distinctions are created not *by* our minds or even *for* our minds, but are deeply rooted in the moral constitution of all moral beings.' Newman is also 'a realist in treating human faith, human thought and language on religious subjects as worthless unless they mark out and point to spiritual causes and tendencies infinitely deeper and more full of meaning than any mere acts of ours'. The word *realist* is being used in such a special sense that its meaning is almost private: realism is strangely analogous to spirituality and the non-material.

Hutton's discussion of Newman's realism is focused on what for Hutton was a central text, the sermon on 'Unreal Words':

Dr. Newman points out that words may be, so to say, *more* real than those who use them are aware of. They may be the indices of powers and forces far beyond what those who use them suspect, because those who use them have only got a superficial glimpse into the action and heart of those forces. Just as 'weight' meant a great deal more than Newton himself knew when he first began to suspect what the moon's weight really meant, and as the idea of which the word was the index carried him far beyond his own meaning when he first used it, so Dr. Newman points out that moral professions often mean far more than those who make them know, and thus commit the soul to the larger meaning, not the less, embarking those who use them on enterprises far beyond their immediate intention, nay, far beyond their immediate strength.[40]

The sermon is a warning against the unmindful or diluted use of sacred terms, a warning applied by Hutton to those attempting to retain sacred concepts in secular morality. Yet he also takes from the sermon a more generally applicable stress on the responsibility of using a word, especially if the word has already been used before (see my later discussion of Arnold's 'touchstones').[41] Newman wrote in the sermon:

Words have a meaning, whether we mean that meaning or not; and they are imputed to us in their real meaning, when our not meaning it is our own fault. He who takes God's name in vain, is not counted guiltless because he means nothing by it,—he cannot frame a language for himself; and they who make professions, of whatever kind, are heard in the sense of those

---

[40] *Spectator*, 5 Dec. 1868, 1437.
[41] See below, chapter 4, 'Poetry'.

professions, and are not excused because they themselves attach no sense to them.[42]

The importance of this to Hutton as a literary critic can hardly be exaggerated. He took it to suggest that language always means more than it says and that its users are accountable to its full meaning, that whatever his intention a writer's words have tendencies which may not be under his control. To write in controlled language is to 'mean the meaning' of your words, and any disparity between the meaning of the words and the intention of the writer threatens to work to his disadvantage by inviting contrast or bathos. Hutton sees Wordsworth as being particularly open to this danger. Newman's account did not, for Hutton, free words of a writer's intention, but it did invite him to measure the distance between the writer's meaning and the autonomous movement of the language.

Newman seems to be a 'realist' in seeing human emotions, beliefs, and human language as having deeper sources than the apparent vehicle of them. Presumably this is Hutton's meaning when he calls Newman's 'realism in the truest and most modern sense of that term,—in that sense in which modern science has taught us to understand the full depth of realism'. I take it that Hutton is thinking of scientific laws which are, like realistic religious distinctions, not created by the human mind but are immanent in nature: so Newton's word 'gravity' was scientifically realistic in carrying him beyond a meaning he could comprehend, a meaning which was in the world and not in him.

This is a strange conclusion for Hutton to reach, but it is his attempt to show how Newman is unwittingly contemporary: Newman's own words have committed him to a meaning greater than his conscious intention.

Hutton manages to suggest a way in which Newman is contemporary, but he also makes clear where he feels Newman is wrong in terms quite different from the reverential pleading of his letters to him. He states that Newman has separated himself from the intellectual movements of his day by applying his notion that faith is an act of trust to the *intellectual* side of belief, such that, like real words, it is an act of whose consequences we are ignorant. This distinction of Hutton's, dividing the act of faith from the belief in creeds, is not a distinction Newman would have recognized. When

---

[42] J. H. Newman, *Parochial and Plain Sermons*, 8 vols. (London, 1868), v. 33–4.

Hutton says that Newman aims 'to risk error, in order to believe right', Newman would have replied that his belief was prior to the reflection that he might be risking error.

Hutton feels that Newman confuses belief in God with belief in evidence of God, that Newman retreats with an instinctive capillary reaction from contact with the intellectual problem. Hutton wants to know if he can believe as an *intellectual*, not in spite of that. He writes that Newman's notion of obedience is 'at the root of his errors':

Obedience is no duty except in relation to a moral claim. An intellectual conviction may come through obedience to a moral claim, but it cannot come from any act of intellectual obedience, for the words have no meaning. You may feel confident that a special authority on intellectual subjects is right, through having usually found him right, but you cannot *obey* him intellectually, you can only be convinced and persuaded by him.[43]

Though his readers could not have known it, we can see that this precisely sums up Hutton's feelings about Newman: he is convinced by him but cannot obey him.

Newman's next publication, the *Grammar of Assent*, which came out two years later, in 1870, could not have been better timed. It was addressed to just this question of the infinite distinction between being convinced and holding a conviction. The book is anti-intellectual, it attacks intellectual convictions and rational conclusions. That is to say, it ironically supports Hutton's conclusion that he could not look to Newman for support: the paradox expresses Hutton's perplexity.

An Essay in Aid of a Grammar of Assent

The book was published in April 1870 and reviewed at length by Hutton, as well as by most other leading intellectuals, and Newman addressed himself to Hutton's review in the correspondence. Two months before the book's publication, however, Newman wrote to Hutton after having read the tract he had put by five years earlier. 'For twenty years', wrote Newman of the work he had been engaged on, 'I have begun and left off an inquiry again and again, which yesterday I finished. I began it in my Oxford University Sermons, I tried it in 1850,—and at several later dates, in 1859, and in 1861.'[44]

---

[43] *Spectator*, 5 Dec. 1868, 1438.
[44] *Letters and Diaries of John Henry Newman*, xxv. 29 (13 Feb. 1870).

It is touching that Newman should write to Hutton the day after finishing the book, and Hutton seemed especially touched intellectually by the continuity stressed by Newman. Though it is obvious from the book and Newman's work, we can see from his letters that the *Grammar of Assent* was literally an expansion of the 'Oxford Sermons'. He wrote to Meynell that he would not rewrite the sermons for a new edition, but would write a work on 'the popular, practical, personal, evidence of Christianity, i.e. as contrasted with the scientific, and its object would be to show that a given individual, high or low, has as much right (has as real and rational grounds) to be certain, as a learned theologian who knows the scientific evidences.'[45] The book is implicitly addressed to Hutton's problems, especially on the use of evidence and on the power of the clergy.

Newman, however, does not recommend the book he tells Hutton he has just finished. Instead, the letters exchanged before its publication deal with the wisdom and possibility of Hutton being received into the Roman Catholic Church.

Newman's letter to him of 24 February, from the Birmingham Oratory, ends with the words: 'There is a report in this place among the Priests that "a gentleman named Hutton connected with the *Spectator* has been secretly received into the Catholic Church". I mention this to put you on your guard, what you say and to whom'. If, however, he had used the same terms when speaking of Hutton as he used when writing to him, Newman may have been the source of the rumour. His letter of 16 February speaks in terms of 'when you are in the Church':

I shall never wish you to become a Catholic merely to get rid of your painful doubts. I don't see that that is a sufficient motive—and I do see at least the danger of their reviving when you were in the Church, if you had not let them die a natural death before you came into it.[46]

Hutton's readers would have reacted with shocked disbelief at the notion that he had 'painful doubts'. It would be generous to suggest that these doubts were limited to his feelings about the Catholic

[45] A. J. Boekraad and H. Tristram, *The Argument from Conscience to the Existence of God* (Louvain, 1961), 168–9 (letter of 5 Jan. 1860). See also John Holmes, 'Newman's Relation to the Development of Scientific and Historical Criticism in England', *Clergy Review*, 64 (1979), 28–90, and G. Evans, 'Science and Mathematics in Newman's Thought', *Downside Review*, 96 (Oct. 1978), 247–66.

[46] *Letters and Diaries of John Henry Newman*, xxv. 30 (16 Feb. 1870).

Church, but the implication of Newman's first sentence is that Hutton's doubts are deeper. Hutton's letters, though, limit their discussions to the status of the Church. They do not exactly contradict what he writes in public. Yet what in public is expressed as a certainty, that Roman Catholics are in the wrong, becomes in private a doubt about the extent to which they may be right: both express doubt but from importantly different points of view.

The questions asked by Hutton in these letters are quite specific and concern matters of Church doctrine, such as its teaching on eternal punishment and on heresy, and Newman took great care over his answers. Yet, in spite of my suggestion that the book was well-timed from Hutton's point of view, when writing to Newman after its publication he said that it did not 'bear much on any of the particular worries which have taken up my mind lately'. This shows how far Hutton had moved to Newman, since the worries on his mind were concerned with matters of doctrine internal to the Church. Indeed he felt, writing on the *Grammar of Assent* in the *Spectator*, that it 'contains very little indeed that is distinctively Roman Catholic, and that only incidentally'.[47] This conclusion is in marked contrast to the view of almost every other commentator of the time, and the book drew long articles from, among others, Leslie Stephen, F. D. Maurice, J. H. Thom, J. A. Froude, Henry Sidgwick, Richard Simpson, and J. B. Mozley. Most thought the book a work of Catholic propaganda. I would suggest that Hutton had accepted so much of Catholicism's doctrine that he was no longer susceptible to such propaganda.

The book is not so important to Hutton for what he says about it as for what he does not say—his silence is a measure of his agreement. For him then, it concerned itself with 'the scope and legitimacy of the intellectual operations subsidiary to practical beliefs' by which he means 'beliefs full of complex elements, where no laws of invariable linear succession, such as those which determine the order of natural phenomena,—the laws, for instance, of gravitation and those usually called laws of nature,—are by the nature of the case discoverable.'[48] This is to Hutton the book which shows that Newman is actually above scientific thought or the advances of contemporary reason. He concludes his review with a personal statement on 'converging probability':

[47] *Spectator*, 2 Apr. 1870, 439.
[48] Ibid., p. 436.

Here, says Dr. Newman, is a solution which solves, for me at least, all these converging lines of fact, and expectation;—and is not that 'surplusage of assurance' which crowns such a belief with certitude legitimate? Indeed, may it not be taken as a finishing divine touch given to the best use of human reason?

This is an admission that he has been convinced by Newman even if he cannot obey him. Hutton sent his article to Newman who, though pleased by the account ('it is a great pleasure to me to find how exactly you have translated me'), isolated four points of difference. It is the most detailed response from a subject of Hutton's work that we have.[49]

First, Newman complains of Hutton's continual use of the word 'practical' to describe arguments which are sufficient for action. Newman asserts that practical arguments may lead to assent, not merely to action. Here Hutton has deliberately restricted Newman's teaching, perhaps because he finds Newman 'impractical' in that he does not provide arguments to which Hutton can unconditionally assent.

Second, Hutton cites Newman's use of Newton's *Principia* as an example of his argument in favour of certainty deriving from the convergence of probabilities. Newman points out that he is only using Newton as a parallel case, and suggests, rather ironically, that Hutton's mathematics are rather dated. Newman draws a parallel between the modern differential calculus and the Illative Sense.[50]

Third, Hutton speaks of the *a priori* instincts and expectations which converge as probabilities, but Newman points out that the words *a priori* do not apply to his arguments, which are merely prior in the order of investigation.

Fourth, Newman complained that the use by Hutton of the phrase 'surplusage of assurance' implied that it was Newman's while it was, in fact, Locke's. Newman takes Locke to mean that there is a degree of assent greater than the force of the reasons on which it is based. Newman, on the other hand, thinks the outcome of combined probabilities not a real proof but only an anticipation of the conclusion. Newman calls the *recognition* of this conclusion an assent (which does not admit of degrees) while the proposition

49 *Letters and Diaries of John Henry Newman*, xxv. 35–7.
50 Evans, 'Science and Mathematics', pp. 258–64.

assented to when seen as a conclusion is a mere inference and is always associated *in the mind* with the reasons which led up to it.[51]

Those words 'in the mind' are crucial. When Newman answered a letter from William Froude in 1879 on the matter of assent, he made the simple but central distinction: 'we differ in our use of the word *certain*: I use it of minds, you of propositions.'[52] Some contemporary readers realized that the *Grammar of Assent* was a natural history of the mind and, as such, belonged to the private world: Richard Simpson, for instance, saw it as a 'mental autobiography', a counterpart to *Loss and Gain* and *Apologia Pro Vita Sua*.[53] Taking up Newman's distinction as explained to Froude, we might say that Hutton remained certain of the propositions of the *Grammar of Assent* but remained in an uncertain mind. Similarly, his public work represents the certainty of his inferences, his private writing the uncertainty of his conclusions or his inability to turn his inferences into assent.

Consequently the letters from Hutton to Newman continued to be strenuously critical yet dependent. He continues to use the word 'practical' in discussing belief, as if the term denoted something he could not give up. His reply to Newman's comments on his article ends with the words: 'God give me some deeper knowledge of the truth before I die'. A year later, in March 1871, he writes almost hysterically: 'I sometimes almost despair of gaining in this life the light I crave.' Yet still to his *Spectator* readers he is calm and certain. It is no wonder that Hutton admired the realistic novel as a sort of secular theology: it represented something to fall back on. Moreover, it should be remembered that this was just the time when Hutton was reviewing *Middlemarch*, as it came out in instal-

[51] R. Naulty, 'Newman's Dispute with Locke', *Journal of the History of Philosophy*, 11 (1973), 453–7.

[52] *Letters and Diaries of John Henry Newman*, xxix. 114 (29 Apr. 1879). See also M. Olive, 'Le Problème de la *Grammaire de l'assentiment* d'après la correspondance entre Newman et William Froude', *Bulletin de littérature ecclésiastique*, 37 (1936), 217–40.

[53] 'Dr. Newman's *Grammar of Assent*', *North British Review*, NS 13 (July 1870), 428–52. Simpson wrote of the book: 'It is avowedly a history of the author's own mental processes, not, as in the *Apologia Pro Vita Sua*, in their relation with external circumstances, but in their logical relation among themselves. It is a rational autobiography in which the changes are recorded *not in the order of time; but in the order of their intelligible sequence*' (p. 428, my italics.) For a full modern discussion of the relation of the two books, see J. Robinson, 'The *Apologia* and the *Grammar of Assent*', in *Newman's Apologia: A Classic Reconsidered*, ed. V. Blehl and F. Connolly (New York, 1964), 103–59.

ments (from December 1871 to December 1872), and regretting George Eliot's disbelief in the source of the higher life she implies.

A year after the letter expressing his despair, in 1872, Hutton conveys his continuing perplexity to Newman. He is in no doubt about his beliefs, but he seems to want a source of certainty deeper than belief; he wants to know how *as an intellectual* he can be in no doubt.

> The tendency of the religion of the day to dissipate itself in the vaguest sentiment and smoke oppresses me more and more, and often makes me turn to your Church with a vague passionate yearning that I feel to be dangerous and even distrustful of God . . . I feel as if the tendencies of the day were all witnessing against the only truth I can firmly grasp . . . But when I look more narrowly at your Church I see nothing but what daunts me still more on the other side—an apparent utter disregard of evidence in fixing the Creed in the days when the Creed acquired its first hold on the mind . . . I feel heartily with you that I would prefer to see England bigoted, superstitious, gloomy, even cruel, to seeing her without faith in the supernatural, but it is the most difficult of earthly problems to combine the religious spirit with the spirit of intellectual severity as to the objective conditions of belief.[54]

Hutton's repeated 'I feel', 'I look', 'I see', is a confessional style in marked contrast to his editorial 'we . . .'. Hutton is caught between subjective yearnings which are possibly no better than vague religious sentiment, and the objective severity which questions the evidence for the object of that sentiment. In his own day, religious sentiment seemed represented by Catholicism and objective severity by scientific agnosticism: Hutton felt he had to choose.

As if to demonstrate the uneasy combination of intellectual severity and emotional sensitivity, the letter ends with an apology for bothering Newman and an explanation that 'the sight of your handwriting always unlooses something in me', but then the intellectual severity reasserts itself. For Hutton adds a post-script harking back to the old argument:

> The more I think of it the less can I understand how any accumulation of mere probabilities is to amount to certainty at all, or how moral certainty, short of mathematical, can be *in the strictest sense* certainty at all.[55]

---

[54] *Letters and Diaries of John Henry Newman*, xxvii. 38–9 (1 Mar. 1872).
[55] See the discussion of this by J. Bastable, 'The Germination of Belief within Probability According to Newman', *Philosophical Studies*, 11 (1961), 81–111.

Newman's reply to this was a kindly laying down of familiar arguments from the *Grammar of Assent.*

Judged by the arguments of his own book, Newman could hardly have done otherwise. In the *Grammar of Assent* he draws a clear and crucial distinction between an inference and an assent: to infer is to conclude and is conditional upon logical argument; to assent is to unconditionally accept the truth of a proposition. Ordinarily, Newman argues, we confuse the two but 'if a professed act can only be viewed as the necessary and immediate repetition of another act, if assent is a sort of reproduction and double of an act of inference, then I do not see what we mean by saying that there is such an act.'[56] Hutton, we might say, could never have been merely argued into the Roman Catholic Church by Newman because he would not have been assenting to the truth of its propositions. He could not be allowed to merely 'double' or 'reproduce' Newman if his belief was to be *real.* Hutton realizes this and so feels dependent yet helpless: he took from the 'Unreal Words' sermon a wariness of reproducing the words of others, but the *Grammar of Assent* provided a rigorous argument for not trusting mere repetition.

We might contrast this notion that to be the 'double' of another man is not to share his beliefs with the materialist argument cited in my previous chapter on the possibilities of reproducing a human organism which would have identical feelings and beliefs to the man of experience. Even more importantly we might contrast it with the secular morality of 'sympathy' embodied in George Eliot and deriving, as I shall discuss later, from her translation of Ludwig Feuerbach's *Essence of Christianity.* In her translation Feuerbach says: 'It is not until a man has reached an advanced stage of culture that he can double himself so as to play the part of another within himself.'[57] To George Eliot this 'doubling' *is* religion; 'God', as she says in her essay on 'The Evangelical Teaching of Dr Cumming', is 'an extension of the effects produced by human sympathy'.

Both the *Grammar of Assent* and the *Essence of Christianity* try to answer the same question: how do we gain an image of God? For Hutton the answer provided by Feuerbach and adapted by George Eliot was 'unreal' in that it explicitly argued that 'God' was identical with and not independent of our belief in Him, and by exten-

---

[56] *Grammar of Assent*, p. 165.
[57] Ludwig Feuerbach, *The Essence of Christianity*, trans. Marian Evans (i.e. George Eliot), (London, 1854), 83.

sion questioned the whole existence of absolute and independent beliefs. It was the aim of the *Grammar of Assent* to maintain the independence and, indeed, privacy of belief as distinct from inference. To Hutton, George Eliot's morality was an example of the dissipation of religion into vague sentiment of which he complained to Newman.[58]

Culture and the Illative Sense

To Feuerbach and George Eliot the advanced stage of culture was demonstrated in an ability to go out of yourself, to enter into other people's minds and hearts. To Newman such a stage was demonstrated by self-containment. In a passage which was a favourite of Hutton's, from a letter of 8 March 1843, Newman wrote:

Religious truths are reached, not by reasoning, but by an inward perception. Anyone can reason, only disciplined, educated, formal minds can perceive. Nothing, then, is more important to you than habits of self-command. You are over-flowing with feeling and impulse; all these must be restrained, ruled, brought under, converted into principles and habits or elements of character.

The inward perception is that which in the *Grammar of Assent* is called the Illative Sense. Culture seems to be for Newman the process of trusting but ruling the Illative Sense.

According to Newman's argument, what he calls 'the logic of facts' determined by life demands an inner equivalent which we also hold in common. For Locke, from whom Newman took the phrase 'the logic of facts', there were certain exceptions to his doctrine of proof: some propositions demanded assent as if they had been firmly and infallibly demonstrated. Newman argues that such assents are not exceptions:

They are to be found throughout the range of concrete matter, and that supra-logical judgement, which is the warrant for our certitude about them, is not mere common sense, but the true healthy action of our ratiocinative powers.[59]

---

[58] 'Evangelical Teaching of Dr. Cumming', *Essays of George Eliot*, ed. Thomas Pinney (London, 1963), 187. See also R. H. Hutton, 'Realism in Unbelief', *Spectator*, 7 Apr. 1877, 433–4: 'It is simply unreal sentimentalism to require the attitude of mind appropriate towards a God of love and righteousness from one who believes there is no God of love and righteousness' (p. 434).

[59] *Grammar of Assent*, p. 317.

This supra-logical judgement is the action of the Illative Sense, where 'sense' is used, says Newman, as a parallel to the use of it in 'good sense' or 'a sense of beauty'.

The Illative Sense is not mere common sense, but nor is its exercise limited to the learned. Thus it seemed to Hutton to mediate between the clerisy and the authority of common men: the Illative Sense seems to have validated Hutton's notion of a popular culture. He translates the Illative Sense as 'a sort of living act of the mind', and takes Newman to be describing a mental counterpart to practical life—despite Newman's objections to the word 'practical'. In Hutton's view Newman is trying to reverse Goethe's dictum that we must try to find an equivalent something outside for everything inside us. To Hutton the Illative Sense is an inner counterpart to the everyday. He describes all of Newman's work as an attempt to map out 'that fine and intricate middle region which connects the logic of facts with the logic of the understanding'.[60] According to this account, Newman is mediating between the demands of the mind and the claims of the everyday.

If we were to make the necessary connection which Hutton did not make for us, we might say that the 'living act of the mind', when cultivated and brought under control, expresses itself in 'real words'. That is to say, a 'real' word in this sense denotes an idea or belief which is internal to the writer or speaker. We cannot duplicate that reality merely by repeating the word. A 'real' reading would therefore be conducted on two levels: the reader would consider the internal state of the writer, and would consider the relation of those words to his own state of mind. Reading would in this sense, which is the sense Hutton seems to employ, have affinities with religious contemplation. Indeed, Arnold and Pater saw this and tried to secularize the contemplative aesthetic. In practice, Hutton combines imagination of the writer's intention with an examination of his own beliefs. We might call his literary criticism 'imaginative', bearing in mind that Newman had originally used the word 'imaginative' in place of 'real'.[61] It was this imaginative reading that Leslie Stephen and Macmillan, for example, considered to have seen more in a text than really existed.

[60] *Contemporary Thought and Thinkers*, ii, p. 274. See also the account by B. Reardon, 'Newman and the Psychology of Belief', *Church Quarterly Review*, 158 (1959), 315–32.

[61] J. Coulson, *Religion and Imagination* (London, 1981), 60, 82–3. See also W. Lamm, 'Newman on the Imagination', *MLN* 68 (1953), 73–80.

Intellectual culture demands both trust in and control of the Illative Sense. Aesthetic culture demands trust in and control of those real words which are the external equivalent of the living act of the mind. Newman is not merely being paradoxical when he says that anyone can reason but only an educated mind can perceive. To perceive is to exercise the Illative Sense, to perceive intelligently is to cultivate the Illative Sense. Similarly, to write intelligently is to be aware that your words are no more 'factual' than your assents. A 'real' writer's words are not logical, they are full of implications of which he knows he cannot be fully aware. The distinction Newman draws in the *Grammar of Assent* is one between the language of logic, which has stripped language down to its unreal, inferential sense, and that of literature, which is rich in meaning unintended by the author.

Ironically Newman is not himself a 'real' writer judged by this standard. *Loss and Gain* is not a real novel, although it refers to experiences of language, such as Willis's experience of the Mass, which are 'novelistic' and which treat language as pregnant with action. Hutton wrote of Newman's prose style:

How tender is the style in the only sense in which we can properly attribute tenderness to style, its avoidance of every harsh or violent word, its shrinking aside from anything like overstatement.[62]

Hutton gives Newman's style the attributes of the man himself. He claims that Newman's poetry 'engraves even more powerfully because with a greater reticence and severer reserve of manner, the scars and vestiges of a unique experience'.[63] A reticence which impresses by its very reserve can be imagined in life, and Hutton's impression depends upon his knowledge of Newman's character. 'Real' writing is precisely that which risks overstatement, it ventures to say more than it knows. In this sense 'real' writing is an act of faith, so for Hutton the most real writers were Wordsworth and George Eliot, who implied a faith they did not profess. Similarly, as I hope to show, Arnold's poetry is 'real' and his prose 'unreal'.

Newman in retrospect

During the last two decades of the century, Hutton wrote three long retrospective essays on Newman for the *Contemporary Review* (in 1884 and again in 1886) and for *Good Words* (in 1890). He also

---

[62] *Modern Guides*, p. 61.   [63] *Spectator*, 25 Jan. 1868, 103.

published a critical biography on Newman in 1891, in addition to
some twenty articles on him for the *Spectator*. This period saw the
revival of the correspondence between them. Their first apparent
contact after ten years was concerning a technical point of which
version of scripture to accept. Hutton wrote to Newman in May
1883 to give his reasons, after reading William Cureton's *The
Ancient Syriac Version of the Epistles of Saint Ignatius* (London,
1845), for preferring the Syriac text of the Epistles of Saint Ignatius
in the Nitrian MS to the generally accepted one in the Midicean and
other MSS.

In other words, the subject is still the reliability of scriptural
authority. In the letters of 1884 there is some warm reminiscing of
their previous contact over the Kingsley debate, but it reads like the
reminiscing of two men (Newman was now eighty-three but Hutton
only fifty-eight) whose positions are now unlikely to change. To
some extent, indeed, the relationship was reversed, with Newman
asking Hutton about trends in contemporary thought. It is like an
old father becoming dependent on the son. Most astonishing is
Newman's question: 'Have you yourself written or can you recommend to me any reliable Catholic or Anglican statement of the real
undeniable instances in which the *facts* of science are inconsistent
with the text of Scripture?'[64] Ten years or so earlier the question
might have been rhetorical, but here it seems open.

For Hutton's retrospective view of Newman we have to rely on
his published work, though treating it with some caution. In his
excellent 1884 essay he goes back to the old texts, the sermon on
'Unreal Words' and *Loss and Gain* (the same piece on the Mass),
with the teaching of the *Grammar of Assent* between the lines. The
Newman of the 1884 essay is praised for his 'literary flexibility of
mind' in combining 'insight into the realities of the human world in
all its details' with an 'unwavering inwardness of standard' in judging that world.[65] Hutton seems to be at pains to give Newman's
work the status of a scientific advance, as if by doing so he is giving
literature a 'scientific' status. We must remember his desperate cry
to Newman from the barricade against scientific materialism: 'the
physicists are almost too many for us!'

---

[64] *Letters and Diaries of John Henry Newman*, xxx. 357 (5 May 1884). See also
John Holmes, 'Newman's Attitude to Historical Criticism and Biblical Inspiration',
Downside Review, 89 (1971), 22–37.
[65] *Contemporary Review*, 45 (1884), 642.

So he describes Newman's achievement as that of having recorded 'the natural history of the emotions' and, in their relation to divine truth, 'the natural history of human infirmities'.[66] Newman's greatest 'scientific' contribution is shown to have been his account of the action of the Implicit Reason:

If it has been the special philosophical work of the last generation to show us how much of almost mechanical intelligence there is in the very structure of our bodies, to say nothing of the habits of our minds, it has been Cardinal Newman's special work to explain the operation of implicit and unconscious, as distinguished from explicit and conscious reasoning, on the higher life of men, and to vindicate the trustworthiness of that implicit reasoning wherever it is made the instrument of a constant and earnest purpose.[67]

Newman is not here seen as in opposition to scientific advances, but as having provided an *equivalent* to science, to have shown the mechanical operation of the human mind. Hutton goes so far as to claim that the advances of science were nothing 'compared with the startling mental revolution effected within thirty or forty years at most': this mental revolution is Newman's account of what Hutton calls 'the unconscious'.[68]

Newman's account of the Implicit Reason, from the Oxford Sermons to the *Grammar of Assent*, is in Hutton's view his greatest achievement. But the 'key' to this achievement and to Newman's character is, says Hutton, the sermon on 'Unreal Words':

It is a sermon which, more than any other known to me, gives the key to Dr. Newman's permanent effort to face the facts of the world as they are, to make men honest with themselves, and yet to keep them from sinking into that cynical and despondent honesty which acknowledges the evil of the world only as an excuse for giving up the struggle with it . . . The teaching of the sermon is not that we should carefully cut down our best words to the frigidity and poverty of the realities within us—that is the cynic's moral—but that, when we are in earnest in desiring to feel even more deeply than we do, we should use the great words put into our mouths by our highest teachers, almost as prayers, using them in the hope to be taught to mean what we say in its fullest and deepest significance.[69]

Hutton's final words are crucial to his work as a literary critic. Newman's teaching seems to justify Hutton's being moved by

[66] Ibid., p. 643.   [67] Ibid., p. 665.
[68] *Modern Guides*, p. 50.   [69] *Contemporary Review*, 45 (1884), 656–7.

literature which deals in emotions deeper than his own. Hutton's desire 'to feel even more deeply' than he does is an emotional equivalent to the Catholic 'wish to believe'. But he goes on to say, not that we must use great words to learn what *they* mean, but to 'mean what *we* say' in its deepest significance. His distinction between 'meaning' and 'significance' is very important: the former refers to the poverty of our intention and the latter to the depth of the language independent of our intention. As I discuss later, Arnold's use of great words as pagan prayers, 'touchstones', could be said to derive from a slightly different reading of Newman's teaching.

The sermon, says Hutton, is a key to Newman's 'permanent effort to face the facts of the world as they are'. The phrase 'permanent effort' is almost paradoxical: we expect effort to be, by its nature, temporary and relative. A permanent effort is always conscious of the temptation to rest. Hutton seems to have re-read into Newman the need to make the temporary into principles, to convert feelings into habits of character.

Having placed so much stress, in this 1884 essay, on Newman's notion of unconscious reasoning, on using great words as indices of powers beyond your own, and on Newman's character, Hutton returned to the subject two years later. As if to correct a wrong impression, Hutton insists 'it was Reason, and Reason alone, which made him a Roman Catholic'. He explains: 'the Roman Catholic is in Newman as deep as his *thought*, the High Churchman as deep as his *temperament*, and the Christian as deep as his *character*.'[70] He seems to be stripping off layers like the skins of an onion, to imply that Newman's Catholicism was the least significant part of his work, and that he was *au fond* simply a Christian. It is no mere coincidence that Hutton was by this stage a High Church Christian who could not make the intellectual step to Roman Catholicism. This autobiographical element, however, never enters into the essay.

Hutton compares Newman and Arnold in the same essay: it is the comparison which Arnold's publisher thought 'fanciful'. Hutton judges that both writers needed, intellectually, some external authority on which to lean. Arnold used the impersonal *Zeitgeist* for support, Newman the infallible authority of the Church. Each is criticized for placing a secular source above a divine one. The

[70] *Modern Guides*, p. 68.

implication that the Roman Catholic Church is a secular source indicates Hutton's final distance from it. His last vivid image of Newman is that of a doctor tending 'restless reason' by drugging it:

He has a wonderful insight into the natural history of all our morbid symptoms. His hand is ever on the feeble and rapid pulse of human impatience, his eye is keen to discern the hectic flush on the worn face. He sees in the Roman Catholic Church a great laboratory of spiritual drugs which will lower fever and arrest the growth of fungoid parasites, and he cannot help grasping at the medicaments she offers.[71]

The implication of the image is that the Catholic Church is opium for the people, that Newman treats the symptom but not the disease of rationalism.

Hutton's final view of Newman, expressed in the *Good Words* essay in 1890 and in the book the following year, is that his contribution to thought was his analysis of the mind and of language, and that he was admirable for his insight into life and his renunciation of that life. In explaining Newman's Catholicism, he admits that it is 'just' but not 'fitting' to accuse Newman of making a 'willing assent' to a doctrine he could not know was true. The accusation is not 'fitting' because 'if any man examine his real creed on any subject' he will find assumptions and unacknowledged authorities.[72]

This account finally undermines Newman because it denies his beliefs but it makes his means of holding those beliefs applicable to secular and everyday convictions, and to beliefs derived from secular literature. Hutton inevitably secularizes Newman in explaining him to a wider readership and in dissociating him from Catholicism.

Conclusion

Hutton's biography of Newman makes no mention of any sort of personal relation between the two men. He was, however, virtually forced into a final personal defence of Newman by a biography of him intended in part to answer his own, a work called *Philomythus* by Edwin Abbott.

Hutton reviewed the book very unfavourably in the *Spectator*, calling it 'one long charge of habitual insincerity' and writing of

---

[71] Ibid., p. 79.   [72] *Cardinal Newman*, pp. 80-1.

Abbott's 'disbelief in the use of words as a means to the attainment
of truth'.[73] Since Abbott accused him of falsifying facts, Hutton
was not the most objective of commentators and Abbott sprang to
his own defence in a long letter to the *Spectator* which was published with a similarly long editorial comment.

Abbot wrote again but Hutton returned his letter and pronounced
the correspondence closed. Hutton's editorial handling of the affair
and his views of Newman became associated in Abbott's mind so
he immediately, and at his own expense, published a second edition
of *Philomythus* titled *Newmanianism* in which the rejected letter
formed the Preface.

With an irony which was doubtless deliberate, Abbott accused
Hutton of setting himself up as an infallible authority and of wor-
shipping Newman as a Saint. 'Is it', he asks, 'not within the limits
of possibility that, for once, a human being shall be right and the
editor of the *Spectator* wrong?' He goes on to accuse Hutton of
'continuous (though unintentional) misrepresentation of the object
of his idolatry . . . he is almost insanely "sincere" '.[74]

Abbott means that Hutton is sincere in his idolatry, and that he
accepts Newman's words without question and thereby misrep-
resents him. He writes of Hutton's quotations from Newman:

> Let anyone read Mr. Hutton's extracts two or three times over; let him
> write them out, at least once; then let him take them to pieces, putting
> nouns for pronouns where necessary, carefully supplying latent assump-
> tions, and noting any shifting use of words—and in almost all of them it
> will be found that what seemed like a safe fabric of smoothly cogent logic
> bursts like the merest bubble of hollow rhetoric.[75]

If this sounds like 'practical criticism' it should come as no surprise
to find Abbott's breakdown of Newman cited, without comment,
in the first chapter of I. A. Richard's *The Meaning of Meaning*.
Ironically, many of Richard's psychological assumptions were
foreseen by Newman, who would also have supported Abbott's
general notion of 'latent assumption'.

Hutton did not review Abbott's *Newmanianism*, but he did
review his subsequent *The Anglican Career of Cardinal Newman*.
His defence of Newman's language implies that its 'latent assump-

[73] *Spectator*, 18 Apr. 1891, 538.
[74] E. A. Abbott, *Newmanianism* (London, 1891), pp. ix–xi.
[75] Ibid., pp. xxxvii–xxxviii.

tions' are the whole point, that it is not logic but a living act of the mind analogous to faith, and that the connecting arguments are not on the page but in the head. The defence, based on a notion of real words as analogous to real belief, seems exposed and this in the face of a new generation's idea of real words and forensic reading. Abbott accuses Newman of 'an inward and absolute contempt for words'.[76] Hutton, citing the 'real words' sermon, accuses Arnold of having a contempt for language in exactly the same terms. For the *fin de siècle* reader such as Abbott the Arnoldian aestheticism has taken priority, and although Arnold did not subject language to the sort of analysis Abbott recommends, the notion of trust in words which are indices of powers beyond you seems dated. The Arnoldian adaptation of Newman's 'inwardness' authorized this later aestheticism, the raising of the role of the critic and reader so that words did not seem beyond him, and the need to give reading the status of scientific analysis.

[76] E. A. Abbott, *Philomythus* (London, 1891), 214.

4
Matthew Arnold

ARNOLD was the most important literary and cultural critic to be studied by Hutton, who wrote about him in almost sixty essays and reviews between 1853 and 1896. However, his most substantial work on Arnold was written in the three decades from the 1860s to the 1880s, and although most of the pieces were occasioned by some publication or lecture of Arnold's, two of the longest and most considered were retrospective: 'The Poetry of Matthew Arnold' in 1862, and 'Newman and Arnold' in 1886.[1] The scale and consistency of this critical effort is quite unique among Arnold's critics.[2] I shall examine in this chapter Hutton's analysis of Arnoldian culture, religion, and poetry by drawing on the whole range of Hutton's writings, but especially the essay on the poetry and the comparative essay on Arnold and Newman.

Hutton admired Arnold's poetry and his admiration was respected by Arnold, who thought Hutton his most acute critic and instructed his publisher to send him review copies. Hutton, however, consistently attacked Arnold's position and method as a literary and cultural critic, sometimes implicitly setting himself up as the alternative source of cultural authority. It is difficult, in giving an account of Hutton's critique of Arnold, to avoid colluding with it and placing all the stress on his side of the argument. I have, therefore, attempted to suggest Hutton's limitations and misjudgements and to state Arnold's case when it is not evident or not fairly represented. Nevertheless, this chapter in particular does argue Hutton's case, though I hope it does not prejudge it.

Arnold and Newman

The Newman of the preceding chapter was, to a large extent, Hutton's Newman, whether he was writing in private or in public. Arnold's Newman was importantly different in many respects. He

---

[1] *British Quarterly Review*, 55 (Apr. 1872), 313–47, and *Contemporary Review*, 49 (Apr. 1886), 513–34.

[2] S. Coulling, *Matthew Arnold and His Critics* (Athens, Ohio, 1974); C. T. Wilkins, *The English Reputation of Matthew Arnold, 1840–1877* (Urbana, Ill., 1959). See also Patrick Creevey, 'Richard Holt Hutton on Matthew Arnold', *Victorian Poetry*, 16 (1978), 134–46.

was, as David DeLaura has documented it, the progenitor of a sort
of secular Oxford movement which included Arnold and Pater,
and whose values are exactly opposed by Hutton's.[3] This movement secularized Newman's stress on 'inwardness' as the pre-
eminent spiritual quality so that it emerged as the 'impassioned
contemplation' which Pater found in Wordsworth. The movement
took Newman's Illative Sense and produced Arnold's Imaginative
Reason and Pater's use of the same phrase. For Arnold and Pater,
Newman was an authority for an interest, in contradistinction to
Hutton's interests, in European art and mythology. Finally, and
most importantly, Newman provided an authority for the appeal to
a cultural élite, a kind of aesthetic Calvinism.

In retrospect we can see Arnold as having secularized some of the
important elements of Newman's thought, and the continuity of
Victorian ideas is firmer for our seeing this. Moreover, Arnold
himself explicitly appeals to Newman's work on occasion. Yet
Hutton was not inclined to connect the two men more than he
thought necessary. In his 1886 essay on them, reprinted in *Essays
on Some of the Modern Guides of English Thought in Matters
of Faith*, Hutton suggested that although Arnold came under
Newman's influence at Oxford in the early 1840s, while Newman
was preaching the Oxford sermons, Arnold still belonged to a later
generation. He suggests that Arnold even then belonged to the
stoical rather than the religious school, 'the school which magnifies
self-dependence, and regards serene calm, not passionate worship,
as the highest type of the moral life.'[4] He suggests that Arnold
clearly belongs to the generation after Newman, when Emerson,
Froude, and Chamber's *Vestiges of Creation* were in vogue, but
also to a generation before the limits of 'certain premature scientific assumptions' were laid down. Hutton belonged to the same
generation. He does not articulate it as a general idea, but Hutton's
argument is that Arnold's character was formed during those years
and that all his later work 'betrays the immovable prejudices' of
that time. Arnold remains for Hutton caught between two worlds,
or rather caught between the world and the other-worldliness of
Newman. Similarly T. S. Eliot—who in his essay on 'Arnold and
Pater' had looked back to 'the solitary figure of Newman in the
background'—thought Arnold's 'writing in the kind of *Literature*

---

3 D. J. DeLaura, *Hebrew and Hellene in Victorian England* (London, 1969).
4 *Modern Guides*, p. 127.

and Dogma a valiant attempt to dodge the issue, to mediate between Newman and Huxley'.[5]

What Hutton did find in common between Newman and Arnold, however, was a strong desire to rest on something beyond their own insight, 'something they can regard as independent of themselves'.[6] Elaborating on this suggestion, we might say that Newman gave his own insight the independence of generalization by defining it as the Illative Sense, and defended the authority of a Pope who was infallible and a priesthood which carried out his wishes. Arnold similarly generalized Reason, argued for the existence of an 'Eternal something not ourselves which makes for righteousness', and implicitly defended the authority of a cultural clerisy. Again, Arnold's literary criticism appeals to an external absolute, 'the absolute beauty and fitness of things', 'the best that is known and thought in the world', the canon of touchstones. Hutton did not believe in either of these sources of absolutes, not the moral absolute of Newman's Catholic Church, nor the aesthetic absolute of Arnold's clerisy. Indeed the distinction does not seem clear to Hutton in quite those terms, though the connection is, I suggest, clear to us in ways that were not accessible to him.

Writing in 1863, during the Colenso controversy, Arnold attributed to Newman the view that 'knowledge and truth are not attainable by the great mass of the human race at all' and quotes Newman's words: 'The few (those who can have a saving knowledge) can never mean the many'.[7] The words are from Newman's 1837 sermon 'Many Called, Few Chosen', a favourite text of his and of Arnold's. Hutton was to make a particular point of Arnold's 'borrowings' from other writers and from beliefs he did not share, and to attack Arnold for using, in Newman's phrase, 'unreal words'—borrowing words without their intentions. However, this cultural Calvinism is the basis for all Hutton's remarks on Arnold.

Arnoldian culture and the secular clerisy

Hutton, as I have already tried to show, wrote for a select audience, yet his intention was like George Eliot's in the novel: to expand the

[5] T. S. Eliot, *Selected Essays*, 3rd edition (London, 1951), 431; T. S. Eliot, *The Use of Poetry and the Use of Criticism* (London, 1933), 105–6.

[6] *Modern Guides*, p. 48.

[7] 'The Bishop and the Philosopher', *Lectures and Essays in Criticism*, ed. R. H. Super, *Prose Works of Matthew Arnold*, iii (Ann Arbor, 1962), 43–4.

moral sympathies of his readership. He considered himself a 'moral' critic, not an 'intellectual' or 'aesthetic' one; he thought himself like all other men even if unlike them in knowing it. Although he never actually sets himself up as an alternative personal authority to Arnold, his descriptions of what the alternative might be like are clearly autobiographical. Drawing such an implicit distinction between Arnold and himself, he wrote in 1866: 'There are two ways of getting at almost all true discriminations,—the mode of calm and leisurely intellectual survey, and the mode of upward-labouring faith,—by the clue of pure thought, and by the clue of moral sympathy'.[8] This distinction was a central one to Hutton: the 'moral' critic working up from the world and up from the text, in sympathy with both, and the 'intellectual' critic surveying from a height, looking down on the text and writing, said Hutton, 'for those who were able to look down, not for those who felt themselves looked down upon'.[9]

Those final words might be taken to mean that Hutton wrote for a readership 'looked down upon' by God, not merely by other men. That is to say, his distinction is not primarily one of social class, but one of belief and culture. Nevertheless, Hutton is also concerned for those who are 'looked down upon' in the more obvious sense, for those who are socially despised. This is evidenced by his defence of the abolitionist aims of the American Civil War, which I shall discuss later.

The key distinction between Arnold and Hutton is between the 'intellectual' and the 'faithful', and between 'pure thought' and 'moral sympathy'. Hutton believed Arnold to lack 'sympathy' with contemporary thought and forms of writing, especially the realistic novel, while being a product of a definable 'modern' spirit. Paradoxically, though Hutton still holds beliefs which Arnold feels belong to an older phase of culture, he is not reactionary in his intellectual or literary tastes. Hutton especially seemed to realize— to an extent shared by very few critics—that the realistic novel was a secular form in many ways (in its implicit relativism, in its suggesting the boundlessness of choice, for instance), but that it also resisted some of the results of secularization, particularly the subjectivity with which Arnold and Pater colluded. The novel provided, as I shall discuss in a later chapter, what Hutton called a

8 *Spectator*, 3 Feb. 1866, 126.
9 *Spectator*, 7 Dec. 1895, 815.

'double view' of life: it showed characters with inner lives, but also provided those lives with a narrative content, a function, and a meaning, which Hutton felt was lost in a secular society.[10] Though he does not discuss at any length Arnold's neglect of the novel, I would suggest that while Hutton saw the novel as the contemporary vehicle for 'moral sympathy', Arnold felt, even if only instinctively, that the realistic novel was opposed to cultural secularization as he saw it: thus his notions of 'character' and 'life' are, as it were, anti-fictive.

When we refer to the readership outside the Arnoldian clerisy we are speaking, essentially, of the general novel-reading public. When Hutton speaks of 'culture' he means every product of popular culture. In one of the first pieces he wrote for the *Spectator*, what I have called his 'critical manifesto', Hutton wrote of the need for the reviewer to break down 'the exclusiveness of genius', to cultivate 'uncritical habits' such as 'readiness of sympathy and flexibility of taste'. It is, he argues, the mistake of the 'cut and dried man of culture' to claim to direct the thoughts of his generation if he does not bother to understand its wants.[11] Less than a year later he was reviewing *On Translating Homer* by just such a cut and dried man of culture whose sympathy, he says, is anything but 'ready'. Although 'flexibility' is a key Arnoldian word, Hutton denies it to Arnold himself:

For a critic, he remains too much himself. 'The critic of poetry', he says, 'should have the finest tact, the nicest moderation, the most free, flexible, elastic spirit imaginable; he should be the "ondoyant et divers", the undulating and diverse being of Montaigne'. The definition is perfect, but Mr. Arnold is too intellectual to attain the flexibility—the undulating, elastic nature he describes. His head is too clearly lifted above his subject to permit him to enter into it with full sympathy.[12]

The very fact that Arnold defines and limits these characteristics to the critic of poetry seems to annoy Hutton. The aesthete depicted by Hutton has almost more in common with Pater than with Arnold. Pater's first essay, on Coleridge, was not published until

---

[10] R. H. Hutton, 'Puseyite Novels', *Prospective Review*, 6 (1850), 531–2; Alasdair MacIntyre, *After Virtue: A Study in Moral Theory* (London, 1981), 211.
[11] *Spectator*, 29 June 1861, 697.
[12] *Spectator*, 22 Mar. 1862, 328. See also William Robbins, *The Arnoldian Principle of Flexibility*, University of Victoria English Literary Studies, 15 (Victoria, BC, 1979).

1866, but there Hutton would have found 'elasticity' identified with the modern 'relative spirit'. Just as Pater drew out aesthetic implications in Arnold's work (as he drew on Arnold's 'Pagan and Medieval Religious Sentiment' in his essay on Winckelmann), so Hutton seems to see the future Pater in Arnold's work. Pater's essay on Wordsworth did not appear until 1874, but Hutton seems to see in Arnold the cultural spectator of that essay and in Arnold's writing the embryo of the dictum: 'to witness this spectacle with appropriate emotions is the aim of all true culture'.[13]

The first target of Hutton's criticism is Arnold's choice of subject. He implicitly criticizes Arnold's failure to accommodate the new and the everyday. His second target is Arnold's manner. Hutton attacks him, we might say, for contemplating life with inappropriate emotions or without appropriate ones. He wrote of Arnold's style:

the unquestionable truth of the matter, the condescending grace of the manner, the serene indifference to practical results, the dogmatism without faith, the didacticism without earnestness, the irony without pain, the beauty without love.[14]

The characteristics he lists are those of manners or style without 'proper' emotion. He is as much concerned with Arnold's mien as with his meaning, since the one is part of the other. To some extent Hutton is attacking the clerisy represented by Arnold: attacking its confidence, its assumed right to lead and govern, its stoicism, its classicism, its condescension. The effect of Hutton's definition by omission is to suggest that Arnold succeeded in producing a 'complete' effect but failed to find a 'wholeness' which was inclusive. The word Hutton repeatedly uses of Arnold is 'charming': it might 'charm the purely literary taste of all true culture', he wrote, 'but leave absolutely no impression on the minds of the Philistines he is criticising'.[15] The 'charm' is taken from a social class, but the

[13] Walter Pater, *Appreciations* (London, 1889), 62.

[14] *Spectator*, 3 Feb. 1866, 125.

[15] Ibid., p. 126. See also the similar comments by Henry Sidgwick in his important essay 'The Prophet of Culture', *Macmillan's Magazine*, 16 (Aug. 1867), 271–80 (p. 278): 'If any Culture really has what Mr. Arnold in his finest mood calls its noblest element, the passion for propagating itself, for making itself prevail, then let it learn "to call nothing common or unclean". It can only propagate itself by shedding the light of its sympathy liberally; by learning to love common people and common things, to feel common interests.' See also S. Coulling, *Matthew Arnold and his Critics*, pp. 189–90.

matter from an intellectual class which Arnold addresses without intending to enlarge. Hutton's intent is in stark contrast: 'to translate for the many what the few teach or conceive'.

The combination of 'grace' with cultural intent is peculiarly Arnoldian and carefully cultivated. Hence Hutton argues that Arnold is too much himself as a critic, lacking that flexibility which he would have liked to somehow borrow from Montaigne, yet at the same time not himself at all, not his 'earnest' self but a persona inhabiting a culture. We are asked not merely to consider Arnold's failure to 'get results', to impress the minds of the philistines, but to criticize his whole recommendation of cultural growth by a manner which is, both culturally, and socially, exclusive. Hutton seems to feel that Arnold's idea of culture could, in its transcendence of identity, only possibly include himself.

In 1866 Hutton summarized Arnold's work as arguing that 'the power of seeing things as they are is the monopoly of a class'. He did not deny that Arnold saw life steadily, but he denied that he saw it whole. Yet by 'whole life', Arnold would have replied, he meant the wholeness of his own life, a concern for which was Culture. Hutton, however, felt that Arnold paid for his 'steadiness' by the sacrifice of his 'wholeness'. He wrote:

Mr. Arnold himself only sees life steadily at the cost of seeing it whole. He sees little bits of it with very perfect vision indeed, but his power of *integrating* life by his imagination—we apologise for a pedantic and detestable word—is not large, not nearly so large as that of those who have less of the critical faculty than he and more of the instinctive.[16]

The distinction between the critical faculty and the instinctive can be added to those other distinctions between intellect and faith, between pure thought and moral sympathy, and between reason and imagination.[17] According to Hutton's argument, Arnold's intellectual energies were aimed most creatively not at 'integrating' life, but at integrating his own life or his own character. Hutton does not himself refer to the demands or traditions of the intel-

---

[16] *Spectator*, 20 Feb. 1869, 223.

[17] Hutton sums up Arnold's 'aristocratic creed' as consisting of 'rationality for the few and imagination for the many' (*Spectator*, 27 Dec. 1862, 1439). See also his comment: 'the point where Mr. Arnold's prose style branches off from Dr. Newman's is at the point where a purely intellectual imagination branches off from a moral and spiritual imagination' (*Spectator*, 25 Feb. 1865, 215).

lectual and cultural clerisy.[18] Only in Arnold's poetry does Hutton find him less concerned with self-cultivation: he finds there 'a guarantee of something like passionate belief'.[19]

Arnold, on the other hand, saw Hutton's notion of 'imagination' as dangerously philistine. He argued that criticism had failed to remain in the 'pure intellectual sphere' and had for that very reason achieved little 'spiritual work', since such work is intended to 'lead him towards perfection, by making his mind dwell upon what is excellent in itself, and the absolute beauty and fitness of things'.[20]

The issues at stake here are what is the practical aim of 'criticism' and what are the sources of the power and authority of the critic, do they lie outside his character, and what is his character? Both Arnold and Hutton agreed that the general aim of cultural criticism was 'spiritual perfection', but they gave significantly opposing accounts of the values behind each of those words 'spiritual' and 'perfect'.

Hutton did not believe that spiritual work could be defined by aesthetic aims, and denied the notion of 'absolute beauty' and its identification with moral 'fitness'. He did, however, believe that spiritual ends and practical work were quite consistent with each other:

What is it which, in the passion and fever of life, truly transforms and chastens human purposes? Surely nothing but the *knowledge* of realities,— sensible realities more than spiritual abstractions,—spiritual realities most of all; mere *things* painful or delightful far more than any abstract ideas.[21]

'Spiritual realities' would have been an unintelligible phrase to Arnold. Hutton's 'knowledge of realities' might remind us of Arnold's 'seeing things as they are', but they actually imply quite different versions of the 'real'. Hutton is thinking of the power of religion in the world, and in literature the power of the realistic novel as a sort

---

[18] Ben Knights, *The Idea of the Clerisy in the Nineteenth Century* (London, 1978), Ch. 4.

[19] See *Spectator*, 7 Dec. 1885, 815, and Hutton's feeling that Arnold was 'not bound by conviction, not conquered by it . . . but merely playing with it' (*Spectator*, 27 Dec. 1862, 1439). Arnold's critical pose is discussed by W. A. Madden, *Matthew Arnold: A Study of the Aesthetic Temperament in Victorian England*, Indiana University Humanities Series, 63 (Bloomington, Ind., 1967).

[20] Matthew Arnold, 'The Function of Criticism at the Present Time', *Lectures and Essays in Criticism*, ed. R. H. Super, *Prose Works of Matthew Arnold*, iii (Ann Arbor, 1962), 271.

[21] Hutton, *Theological Essays* (London, 1871), 116.

of secular religious force. To Arnold the real is opposed to the apparent, knowledge is not for him 'knowledge of realities', which was the sort of provincialism he thought was expressed in the novel.

Thus it is instructive to compare the two critics' reactions to real events with moral implications, to see what they made of political 'realities'. The most important of such events during the period under discussion was undoubtedly the American Civil War. For although the war had some practical effects in England, the public reaction to it—and it is specifically the *public* we are concerned with—was couched in terms of a moral debate. Hutton presents his readers with the moral reality of slavery in his attempt to transform their attitudes; Arnold presents *his* readers with the idea of injustice and the middle-class's insensitivity to it.

To be more precise, Hutton took over editorship of the *Spectator* the year the war broke out and immediately threw its support behind the Northern States. This, as an initial position, was shared with only one other London newspaper and put the *Spectator* in some financial danger. General public opinion on the war was complex and unpredictable, and undefined by existing political or social categories. The war was generally discussed in this country as a war of abolition, most newspaper opinion distrusting the abolitionist aims of the North and being credulous of the likelihood of emancipation in an independent South.[22] Several newspapers, most notably *The Times*, the *Saturday Review*, the *Standard*, and the *Morning Herald*, argued for a transformation of slavery into some distinguishable form of perpetual serfdom in an independent South.[23] Hutton's *Spectator* consistently argued the case for the North on abolitionist grounds, though he thought that Mill, for example, gave too much credence to Northern abolitionist aims, and was sceptical of Lincoln's declared war aim of abolition.[24]

[22] D. P. Crook, 'Portent of War: English Opinion on Secession', *Journal of American Studies*, 4 (1970–1), 163–79 (p. 171).

[23] Douglas A. Lorimer, 'The Role of Anti-Slavery Sentiment in English Reaction to the American Civil War', *Historical Journal*, 19 (1976), 405–20 (p. 411). See also Leslie Stephen, *'The Times' on the American Civil War: An Historical Study* (London, 1865).

[24] 'Mr. John Stuart Mill on the Civil War', *Spectator*, 1 Feb. 1862, 126–7; 'The Northern Treatment of the Slaves', *Spectator*, 15 Mar. 1862, 294–5. See also Arnold Whitridge, 'British Liberals and the American Civil War', *History Today*, 12, No. 10 (Oct. 1962), 688–95 (p. 694).

Arnold, on the other hand, was most concerned with the state of English culture as reflected in English public opinion. In his retrospective essay 'My Countrymen' he attacks the English middle class, much as Hutton had done at the time of the war, for shifting their sympathies to the North as that side appeared to be winning.[25] In this respect Hutton and Arnold had the same target, but Hutton was concerned about Arnold's tone, the source of his energies, and the general intention of his argument. Hutton wrote that Arnold judged the middle class from 'his serene station above the clouds of their dull atmosphere', but suggested that 'others have convicted them of the same blunders from a far less elevated and yet far more hopeful position in the very midst of that zone of prejudice and custom-blinded intelligence by the mere force of that genuine sympathy with freedom which overpowers, even without dispelling, the cautious fears of selfish conservatism.'[26] Hutton does not make the contrast with himself any more explicit, but his very modesty risks glamorizing and dramatizing his own profession 'in the very midst of that zone', as if he is not only commenting on a war but also taking part in one. Hutton here seems to be drawing on two sources of strength. The first is his genuine sympathy with freedom, implying that he is as interested in freeing the custom-blinded English middle class as in freeing Southern slaves. The second is his very position as a working journalist. He argues that, conversely, Arnold is as insular as the class he attacks, and prefers 'contemplating blankly the gulf between him and the uncultured people he pities' to the active 'stirring-up of English moral feeling against a gigantic moral iniquity'.[27]

Although the argument concerns different issues, Hutton made the difference between them clearer still in criticizing Arnold's 'Anarchy and Authority' series in *Cornhill Magazine*, the series which became *Culture and Anarchy*—and it is important that in the change of title Arnold's 'Authority' became his 'Culture'. Hutton comments on Arnold's complaint that the disendowment and disestablishment of the Irish Church merely replaced one injustice with another:

Even admitting that the plan of universal endowment is natural and wise,—Mr. Arnold yet seems to concede that it is at present simply impossible in

25 *Cornhill Magazine*, 13 (1866), 153–72.
26 *Spectator*, 3 Feb. 1866, 126.
27 Ibid.

Ireland, and he would therefore have statesmen wait, and set in motion this 'free play of consciousness' till it *becomes* possible . . . We postpone the only pledge of sincerity and desire for equal dealing which we could give because Ireland is not ready for the one we should like to give . . . [It is a] genuine act of justice,—narrow, if you please,—but still justice.[28]

This belongs, of course, to another debate, but it highlights the issues more starkly still: the failure of imagination and concern for the inadequacies of Arnold's writings as for the Civil War. Hutton's moral concern with the contemporary is not restricted to literary production; rather his interest in the contemporaneity of literary production is a product of his interest in the general state of 'things as they are'. To him, Arnold's political postponement is analogous to his want of sympathy, his holding-off: Arnold's critical judgement fails to amount to doing 'justice'. In this particular instance, Arnold uses the abstract noun 'equality', while Hutton turns it into an action, into 'equal dealing'. Hutton sees all these critical writings, political, literary, and theological, as 'acts of justice' or of injustice, and it is on these moral grounds that he judges Arnold.

I have been considering Hutton's question, 'what is it which transforms and chastens human purposes?', and his reference, in answer to it, to 'realities'. As a political commentator Hutton finds Arnold unconcerned with present realities. The explanation of their differences can be found in part in that phrase 'human purposes', which, of course, Hutton is opposing to God's purpose. The notion of individual 'purpose' enters little into Arnold's perception of the spirit of the age and its spiritual work, and his political sensitivity seems dulled by this. The end of cultural improvement for Arnold seems to be a general sense of 'purposefulness', of concentration, though it is not focused on particular objects.

Hutton saw a contradiction between Arnold's aim for the absolute beauty and fitness of things, and his recommendation of a cultivation which is neither absolute nor a reflection of real things. That is to say, Arnold seems to take no account, in his literary or his political criticism, of the individuals who are the readers or the subject-matters of his writing. Hutton writes of Arnold's 'Culture and Its Enemies':

The aesthetic aims which Mr. Arnold insists on holding up before us are, we contend, not moral means of regeneration at all. When he praises Dean

[28] *Spectator*, 4 July 1868, 790. See also J. P. Farrell, *Revolution as Tragedy: The Dilemma of the Moderate from Scott to Arnold* (London, 1980).

Stanley's wisdom and sweetness, and Mr. Jowett's moral unction, and Spinoza's 'beatific vision', as a critic, he does well. But anyone attempting to subdue his own ruggedness from an aesthetic perception of the beauty of Dean Stanley's sweeter wisdom, or to attain unction because he sees that Mr. Jowett's unction is a real beauty of his character, or to reach a 'beatific vision' of his own because it added something to the richness and serenity of the great Pantheist's philosophic calm, would only fall into conscious affectations.[29]

To Hutton, Arnold is recommending as a moralist qualities which he sees only as a critic, that is on purely aesthetic grounds. For Hutton, both as a Christian and as a believer in the importance of individuality, moral authority does not reside in other men's characters. Arnold's spiritual work is really an aim at 'beauty of character', but 'it is better', wrote Hutton, 'to grope your way almost blindly to what seems morally better . . . than to begin aiming at a quality which *really* has no direct moral authority over us—mere harmony or mental grace'.[30] This aim, he argues, would lead to mere sentimentalism and 'aesthetic melodrama'. This is Hutton at his most Newmanite, following the clues of moral sympathy, aiming at authority rather than following it. This poise of Arnold's, or 'mental attitudinizing', is not, Hutton argues, culture at all, but manifests 'a neutral equipoise and incapacity for resolve' which is 'but another phase of anarchy'.[31] This neutrality is at odds with the indecision Hutton actually admires in George Eliot: indecision because there is always more to consider, and which comes of a perception of determinism without religious guidance.

Though I described those words of Hutton's on 'groping your way' as authorized by Newman, Arnold also looked to Newman for authority for what Hutton calls 'mere harmony or mental grace'. It is the secularization of Newman's work that Hutton is really attacking, even though he does not quite see it. Hutton is resisting the paradoxical *religionizing* of culture by Arnold. In a passage of 'Culture and Its Enemies' which Hutton interestingly does not quote, though it lies behind all his remarks, Arnold wrote:

Religion says: *The Kingdom of God is within you*; and culture, in like manner, places human perfection in an *internal* condition, in the growth

29 *Spectator*, 6 July 1867, 747.
30 Ibid., 748.
31 *Spectator*, 11 Nov. 1876, 1402.

and predominance of our humanity proper, as distinguished from our animality.[32]

Arnold's connecting words 'in like manner' are more important than they seem. Arnold is not merely saying that the aims and effects of religion and culture are analogous, but that their *manner* is analogous, and that the aims of a work of art can be discovered from its manner and style. I shall come back to this second point later, but it is important to notice that Hutton's stress on Arnold's manner and style is appropriate even though he misses Arnold's intention. For Arnold, manner *contains* meaning in some very literal sense, and a sense which Hutton did not fully recognize.

Arnold, as Eliot saw, tried to mediate between the spiritual and the material positions. Pater, a generation later, took Arnold's analogy to its next logical step with his reference to 'the poetry of the few, the elect and peculiar people of the kingdom of sentiment' in 'Aucassin and Nicolette'. But Hutton saw Arnold as fulfilling Newman's own prediction in 1841 that on the premises of the liberal Anglican, such as Hutton was to be, Christianity will 'have done no more than introduce a *quality* into our moral life-world, not anything that can be contemplated by itself, obeyed and per-petuated'.[33] It is ironic to find Hutton resisting a tendency which Newman foresaw in Hutton's own principles: Hutton is continually focusing on a matter for which he must have felt some affinity and even responsibility.

We can trace the phrase 'grace of mind' back to Newman's early (1829) essay on 'Poetry in Relation to Aristotle's Poetics'. Newman writes of 'the peculiar grace of mind of the New Testament writers' as evidence of the 'poetical' nature of revealed religion.[34] The point is that Newman argues that religion should be poetical in theory and finds that 'it is so in fact', not merely in like manner. It is the 'factual' status of religion which Arnold's poetics would *replace* to produce a 'surer and surer stay' in a secular future. Nevertheless, Arnold looks back to Newman for his notion of grace of mind. Indeed, when writing to Newman in 1871, Arnold admitted that Newman's influence on him amounted to 'a general disposition of

---

[32] *Culture and Anarchy*, ed. R. H. Super, *Prose Works of Matthew Arnold*, v (Ann Arbor, 1965), 94.

[33] *Essays Critical and Historical*, 2 vols. (London, 1872) ii. 242.

[34] Ibid., i. 23. See also Norman Friedman, 'Newman, Aristotle and the New Criticism: On the Modern Element in Newman's Poetics', *PMLA* 81 (1966), 261–71.

mind rather than a particular set of ideas'.[35] We could extend Arnold's words to suggest that not only did Arnold take from Newman a 'disposition of mind', but also a justification of 'disposition of mind' as itself the end of culture, having replaced religion by culture, and a notion of 'disposition of mind' as a guide in aesthetic matters just as the Illative Sense was Newman's guide in moral matters.

Though Newman's *Grammar of Assent* was published the year before Arnold's letter to Newman, he makes no reference to the book, nor is there any evidence that Arnold read it, though it is impossible to believe that he did not at least read reviews of it. The book is, though, the outcome of Newman's defence of the faculty of Implicit Reason over many years, and as such its argument was well known to Arnold. The book was, of course, read and used by Pater, most evidently in *Marius the Epicurean* and in his *Guardian* essay on Amiel's *Journal*. We might characterize the difference between Hutton and Arnold as different reactions to the *Grammar of Assent* and to one of its precursors, the sermon on 'Unreal Words'.

Arnold would have approved of Newman's attack in the *Grammar of Assent* on liberal knowledge, and his argument that real (i.e. 'imaginative') assent is its own witness and standard. It is a contemplative account of religion as Arnold's is a contemplative account of culture. Newman argues that reason demands absolute certainty which can never be found in 'paper logic', but must be looked for in the mind itself. The sole and final judgement as to the validity of an inference is committed, he argues, to the personal action of the reason, 'the perfection or virtue of which is the Illative Sense—a use of 'sense' parallel to the use of it in "a sense of beauty" '.[36]

Those final words would have been Arnold's authority. Newman suggested that an inner faculty which is associated with conscience acts analogously to the faculty we call taste. Arnold retained the analogy but inverted it: what was once Hebraistic conscience is now acting 'in like manner' as Hellenistic taste. Moral sympathy is converted into pure thought. Both Newman and Arnold have no place for differences of opinion. Arnold, though, is vulnerable because

---

[35] *Unpublished Letters of Matthew Arnold*, ed. Arnold Whitridge (New Haven, 1923), 56–7.
[36] *Grammar of Assent*, p. 345.

his taste depends on inner intuition which in turn is only valid if it produces the right results, not because it *is* inner intuition. Hence Hutton's suspicion that Arnold's final object of cultivation is himself.

Arnold might be said to have taken Newman's aesthetic principles and lopped off the religious roots of beliefs which Hutton, for one, continued to hold. If there were a specific passage in the *Grammar of Assent* which Arnold would have had to secularize it would, I suggest, have been the following:

It does not prove that there is no objective truth, because not all men are in possession of it. But this it does suggest to us, that there is something deeper in our differences than the accident of external circumstances; and that we need the interposition of a Power, greater than human teaching or human argument, to make our beliefs true and our minds one.[37]

Arnold did find a uniting 'not-ourselves' but he found it in a human and secular consensus of like minds. It has to be said, though, that Newman's words do not rule out an Arnoldian reading, indeed that phrase 'make our beliefs true' is just the sort which a man like Kingsley could easily find implicitly sceptical. Yet Hutton objected particularly to Arnold's adaptation and detachment of arguments which he felt should be referred to the beliefs of the originator. Arnold's 'detachment' is not merely the 'disinterestedness' which Pater took to be the most vital 'souvenir' of Christianity, but an argued willingness to appropriate characteristics, arguments and quotations.[38]

The deduction of these characteristics (of Stanley, Jowett, and Spinoza) has 'no real direct moral authority' partly because Arnold does not imagine the purpose which produced those characteristics as, so to speak, side-effects. Hence the nature of Arnold's own attempt to define himself in terms of Wordsworth, Goethe, and Sophocles, to combine Wordsworth's 'sweet calm', Goethe's 'wide and luminous view', and to see life, as Sophocles did, 'steadily and whole'. Hutton argues that Arnold took from Goethe and Wordsworth 'a style of clear heroic egotism' which he could express in poetry, but that this style does not become Arnold's since 'he has not borrowed from either of them the characteristic *motive* and

[37] Ibid., p. 375.
[38] Walter Pater, 'Coleridge's Writings', *Westminster Review*, NS 29 (Jan. 1866), 127.

individuality which in them justifies that style.'[39] Consequently Hutton grants Arnold's poetic personality a certain grandeur and meaning but denies these to Arnold himself.

We can see this self-cultivation at work in one of Arnold's few recorded responses to Hutton. Hutton had written of him with reference to Goethe and Shelley:

Everywhere he loves *measure* in literature. He cannot bear that rampancy of insatiable, unmeasured longing with which the intellect stands on no terms. He worships Goethe for that steady and constant recognition of limitation which was the intellectual rather than the poetical side of his mind . . . [He shows] a deficiency in sympathies lying beyond the intellectual sphere. What Goethe called the 'daemonic' in himself, he prefers to ignore, yet it is often (as in Shelley) the essence of poetry.[40]

The content is by now familiar: Arnold has perfect vision to see what he prefers to ignore; his admiration of limitation is itself limiting. But the point here is Arnold's reaction to this criticism, expressed in a letter to his mother:

The article has Hutton's fault of seeing so very far into a millstone. No one has a stronger and more abiding sense than I have of the 'daemonic' element,—as Goethe called it,—which underlies and encompasses our life; but I think, as Goethe thought, that the right thing is, while conscious of this element, and of all there is inexplicable round one, to keep on pushing one's posts into the darkness, and to establish no post that is not perfectly in light and firm. One gains nothing on the darkness by being, like Shelley, as incoherent as the darkness itself.[41]

This does not contradict Hutton who said, not that Arnold had no sense of the 'daemonic element', but that he preferred to ignore it, and Arnold can be seen articulating that preference to his mother. To Arnold, Shelley is an adversary, and what Hutton posits as the essence of Goethe's poetics Arnold sees as the anarchic undergrowth through which he makes his way. What to Hutton is characteristic of Goethe, Arnold sees as lying all around *him*. It is this self-consciousness of playing a role in literary history, taking on the aspects of some writers and battling against others, which Hutton calls Arnold's 'aesthetic melodrama'.

[39] *Literary Essays* (1896), pp. 314–15 (my italics).
[40] *Spectator*, 25 Feb. 1865, 215.
[41] *Letters of Matthew Arnold, 1848–1888*, ed. G. W. E. Russell, second edn., 2 vols. (London, 1889), i. 249.

Although Hutton may not have seen Arnold's letter, the figure of the Explorer, an important Victorian 'character', to which Arnold likens himself, is for Hutton also *the* image of the individual in a secular society. He wrote in a symposium on 'The Influence upon Morality of a Decline in Religious Belief' in 1877:

Whether the belief in 'Our Father Man' and in a tentative Providence which does not *foresee*, but only accommodates the individual to his 'environment', be wild or sober, this, I think, is clear, that it does not provide the martyr or the reformer with the stimulating power of a *faith* . . . it leaves him a mere *pioneer* amidst dangers and difficulties to which it may turn out that both he and his race are quite unequal.[42]

For Hutton the disbeliever has abandoned the sense that life has a God-given function, that individual lives can be seen as wholes and individual actions as contributions to a known end. The Christian sense that life can be seen as a quest or journey to a goal is replaced by the secular sense that every man is alone in a sort of moral jungle, pushing his posts into the darkness. If Arnold tried to construct a persona from the characteristics of others without their individualities, his literary criticism is also, in Hutton's view, a construction without regard to the individuals whom he studies. To Hutton, Arnold's 'ranking' of authors, typical of the age though it might have been, is typical of Arnold and the secular critic in its privacy bordering on subjectivism. Arnold's subjects are treated like actors in this private melodrama. Yet it is a privacy presented as objective taste with Arnold as Culture personified, the pioneering leader of the vanguard of the clerisy. Hutton comments on the 'dramatis personae' of Arnold's criticism:

He will tell you whether a poet is 'sane and clear', or stormy and fervent; whether he is 'rapid' and 'noble', or loquacious and quaint; whether a descriptive writer has 'distinction' of style, or is admirable only for his vivacity; but he rarely goes to the individual heart of the subjects of his criticism; he describes their style and class, but not their *personality* in that class; he *ranks* his men, but does not portray them; he hardly ever seems to find much interest in the *individual* roots of their character.[43]

'Style' and 'class', both in society and writing, are Arnold's concerns, 'personality' is Hutton's. The word 'character' they both

---

[42] 'A Modern Symposium: The Influence Upon Morality of a Decline in Religious Belief', *Nineteenth Century*, 1 (May 1877), 531–46 (pp. 543–4).
[43] *Literary Essays* (1896), p. 351.

use, and it clearly refers to different things. 'Character' is to Arnold a quality which a person may or may not possess: it is what keeps a man pushing his posts into the darkness. He comments on Haydon's remark that Keats had no 'decision of character': 'we should look for some evidence of the instinct for character, for virtue, passing into the man's life, the man's work'.[44] 'Character' is itself a characteristic of an author. He goes on to say that in Keats's poetry 'there is that stamp of high work which is akin to character, which is character passing into intellectual production.' Character, then, is akin to virtue which is akin to Culture ('high work'). It is an aesthetic distinction disguised as a moral one and retrospective in character.

Hutton, however, *is* concerned with Arnold's moral character, with his lack of sympathy for individuals outside his clerisy and for the individuality of his subjects. The basis of Hutton's criticism of Arnold must therefore be found in his comments on Arnold's religious writing. There is a clear connection between Hutton's belief that Arnold undervalues the personal and the intended, with Arnold's disbelief in a personal God and an immanent Will. For Arnold the only source of objectivity in a secular world, one which has lost its object of devotion and its object in individual lives, is the spirit of Hellenism. For Hutton the source of objectivity was still the personal God, though in literary terms he found it in the novel. So we find them differing both in theology and literature: Hutton Hebraistically defending real belief and the realistic novel, Arnold reviving Hellenism and High Culture and finding the novel 'provincial'.

Religion

Hutton's point in objecting to the exclusivity of the Arnoldian clerisy, its monopoly on the perception of 'things as they are', was made more powerful by his argument that the very word 'life' carried for Arnold the authority of a creed that only a few could afford to believe in. '*Life* is the word which, in Mr. Arnold's teaching, takes the place of *Faith*', Hutton wrote.[45] The word did have at least talismanic power for Arnold: 'we must', he wrote in his essay

---

[44] Matthew Arnold, 'John Keats', *English Literature and Irish Politics*, ed. R. H. Super, *Prose Works of Matthew Arnold*, ix (Ann Arbor, 1973).
[45] *Modern Guides* (1887), p. 111.

on Wordsworth, 'let our minds rest upon that great and inexhaustible word *life*'.[46] In 1863 Arnold cited the words of Maurice de
Guérin:

There is one word which is the God of my imagination, the tyrant, I ought
rather to say, that fascinates it, lures it onward, gives it work to do
without ceasing and will finally carry it I know not where; the word *life*.[47]

Like 'character', life is to Arnold a quality of some lives, and one
which 'faith' can produce: it is this production of 'life' which is to
him 'spiritual work'.

Hutton argued that Arnold's teaching not only devalued faith,
but also misconstrued the realism to which Arnold himself appealed. Hutton asked, in an article on one of Arnold's sermons to
the working people of Whitechapel:

Has Mr. Arnold lately read Dr. Newman's great Oxford sermon on 'Unreal
Words'? If not, we wish he would refer to it again, and remember the warning addressed to those who 'use great words and imitate the sentences of
others' and who 'fancy that those whom they imitate had as little meaning
as themselves' or 'perhaps contrive to think that they themselves have a
meaning adequate to their words'.[48]

This matter of imitating religious language without taking over
its intention is not merely analogous to but actually lies behind
Hutton's criticism of Arnold's imitating the manner and style of
Goethe or Jowett without their motive or intention.

The sermon of Newman's in question was written in the 1840s
and is one to which Hutton makes frequent reference.[49] It was for
Hutton something of a touchstone, a means of discriminating
between 'all the religious and sceptical thinkers in this curious
century of ours'.[50] Hutton's reading of the sermon explains his
criticism of Arnold's language as a critic.

The most important argument Hutton took from Newman's
sermon on 'Unreal Words' is summed up in Newman's notion that
'words have a meaning whether we mean that meaning or not'.

---

[46] 'Wordsworth', *English Literature and Irish Politics*, p. 46.

[47] 'Maurice de Guérin', *Lectures and Essays in Criticism*, p. 31.

[48] *Spectator*, 6 Dec. 1884, 1611. See also D. J. DeLaura, *Hebrew and Hellene in Victorian England* (London, 1969), 157–8.

[49] J. H. Newman, *Parochial and Plain Sermons*, new edition, 8 vols. (London, 1868), v. 29–45.

[50] *Spectator*, 24 July 1886, 982. See above, pp. 48, 62–3.

When, therefore, Hutton criticizes Arnold it is for not 'meaning the meaning' of words. Just as Arnold translated the Will of God into 'that stream of tendency not ourselves which makes for righteousness', so Hutton criticized him generally for seeing the intention of a writer and his language as a 'tendency', though a tendency without historical roots and therefore one which can be categorized and imitated. Arnold's 'tendency' is weak, it takes away volition without substituting materialism: it is determinism without either God, economics, biology, or psychology. A 'tendency' might easily be deflected and channelled elsewhere: it is in this sense a 'manner' and not a 'meaning'. If Arnold translated God into something both secular and unreal, 'not ourselves', he also translated Homer into something both Victorian and unreal, 'too intellectual'.

Arnold's use, Hutton argues, of biblical language in a 'new and washed-out sense of his own' shows 'a hardened indifference to the meaning of words and the principles of true literature'. He accuses Arnold of 'a great literary misdemeanor'. He claims to be attacking Arnold not for his scepticism, but 'as a *literary* man' for 'trying to give currency in a debased form to language of which the whole power depends on its being used honestly in its original sense'. The word 'literary' is, as I suggested in my first chapter, being used with moral overtones.

The particular 'literary misdemeanor' Hutton finds in Arnold's lay sermon is a failure to choose between the literal and the metaphorical in biblical language. He had made the same charge ten years earlier, in 1874, where the tone is much more impatient:

It is not criticism at all, it is playing fast-and-loose with language in the most ridiculous manner, to regard the long series of passionate appeals to God as mere efforts of poetry, while all the words describing the moral conceptions of man are interpreted with scientific strictness . . . He cannot pick and choose, and say that this is poetry, because he does not think its drift can be 'verified'; and that that, on the other hand, is prose because he has persuaded himself that he has 'verified' it.[51]

Prayer, to Hutton, involves the belief in 'one who hears and answers' and he needs 'no more scientific definition of a *person* than this'. Similarly, he distinguishes between the use of the word 'righteousness' as a moral abstraction and its use as an attribute of God. For Arnold there is no such distinction: to him God is

51 *Spectator*, 10 Oct. 1874, 1257.

righteousness, while to Hutton God is righteous. This is the source, and the most important example, of Hutton's argument that Arnold failed to appreciate the attribute of personality in any author.

In his review of the essays which were to form *Literature and Dogma*, Hutton asks why Arnold preserved the personal pronoun for his 'tendency' which makes for righteousness.[52] It was a common question, and one that Arnold answered in the book form of the essays:

It has been urged that if this personifying mode of expression is more proper it must also be more scientifically exact. But surely it must appear on reflection that this is by no means so. Wordsworth calls the earth 'the mighty mother of mankind' . . . Wordsworth's expression is more proper and adequate to convey what men feel about the earth, but it is not therefore more scientifically exact.[53]

Hutton dismisses this reply in his review of the book as an irrelevant 'literary misdemeanor'. Wordsworth, he argues, may have wanted to convey what men feel about the earth, but he did not want to produce the effect of making us *trust* in the earth as if she were a person who could answer our appeals. The word 'mother', that is, is a metaphor which we tacitly agree not to over-interpret, its sense is 'emotional'. The word 'He' when applied to God is not, however, appropriate merely because it 'adequately' describes our feelings about religious experiences or the laws of righteousness.[54] In confusing language which refers to a real God and language which actually describes his own feelings, his own attraction to that which he takes 'God' to stand for, Arnold is in Hutton's terms making the same error as Feuerbach. The point is that this is not to Hutton a purely theological matter but a 'literary' one in its broadest sense: Arnold is accused of misreading or disregarding the language and the intentions of the Author, and, by extension, of any author.

This account of Arnold's attentions to his own emotions may seem paradoxical and contradictory: it seems paradoxical in comparison with Arnold's own wish to remain in the 'intellectual

---

[52] *Spectator*, 22 Feb. 1873, 243–4.

[53] 'Literature and Dogma', *Dissent and Dogma*, ed. R. H. Super, *Prose Works of Matthew Arnold*, vi (Ann Arbor, 1968), 189 n.

[54] *Spectator*, 22 Feb. 1873, 243–4. See also F. H. Bradley's attack on what he calls Arnold's 'piece of literary clap-trap' in defining religion as 'morality touched by emotion' and God as 'the Eternal not ourselves', in the 'Concluding Remarks' to his *Ethical Studies* (London, 1876), 278–305 (especially pp. 280–5).

sphere' and perhaps with our own received impressions of Arnold; it seems to contradict Hutton's other verdict that Arnold was 'too intellectual'. Yet my argument is that Hutton's study of Arnold's theology discovers the emotional exclusivity which Arnold translated into intellectual exclusivity in his more strictly 'literary' criticism. Only in the poetry Arnold wrote does this oscillation—like that of a shuttlecock, says Hutton—show itself. Hutton is himself placed and limited by this theological concern, since he only deals with those texts where Arnold is dealing with the *intrinsically* ethical. Hutton, therefore, chooses to discuss the texts which Arnold attempts to alter to suit his ideology, a rendering into what Hutton calls an 'emotional' form.

Hutton distinguishes between an 'emotional' form of text and a 'mystical' one in discussing Arnold on St Paul.[55] Hutton takes as his text Colossians 3: 1–3:

> If ye then be risen with Christ, seek those things which are above, where Christ sitteth on the right hand of God. Set your affection on things above, not on things on the earth. For ye are dead, and your life is hid with Christ in God.

Now Arnold takes St Paul's words 'being in Christ' to mean 'identifying yourself with Christ by attachment, so that you enter into his feelings and live with his life'. Such a translation implies a secular notion of individuality, a relative self which can lose its own identity. The change brought about in an individual by such a belief as Arnold's would be attributable to the feeling of sympathy with Christ, not to Christ Himself. It would be comparable to changes brought about by feeling 'sympathy' with the characteristics of Stanley or Jowett.

Hutton suggests that the biblical text in question would have to be rewritten in an inverted form to comply with Arnold's reading and belief, to read thus:

> If ye then seek those things which are above, where Christ sitteth on the right hand of God, ye are risen with Christ. Ye are dead, and your life is hid with Christ in God, for ye set your affections on things above, not on things of the earth.

This is a secular version of the first, aiming to retain Christian morality without its prior beliefs. The first version, says Hutton, is

[55] 'Mr. Arnold on St. Paul and his Creed', *Contemporary Review*, 14 (June 1870), 329–41 (pp. 336–7).

a 'mystical' form, the second an 'emotional' form which refers the reader back to himself and his own values. For Arnold, seeking 'things above', whether it be spiritual or literary 'high work', results in feeling like a Christian; for Hutton, Christ is the *cause* of seeking 'things above'.

To put it another way, for Hutton Christ's promise 'I am come that men might have life' is one given by someone who can fulfil that promise. For Arnold, that promise is a *method* of obtaining what he called 'life'. For, as Hutton said, 'life' is the word which in Arnold's doctrine takes the place of 'faith'. Arnold wrote in *Literature and Dogma*:

The breaking the sway of what is commonly called *oneself* is not, Jesus said, being thwarted or crossed, but *living*. And the proof of this is that it has the characters of life in the highest degree—the sense of going right, hitting the mark, succeeding.[56]

Does this, Hutton asks, mean 'Blessed are the pure in heart, for they shall succeed?' This 'misreading of the language of the conscience' provides the grounds, the vocabulary, and the terms for Hutton's general account of Arnold's misreadings. He describes Arnold's religion as founded on a 'very mild and aesthetic emotion': an aesthetic emotion because it is self-regarding, and because it affects Arnold's aesthetic as well as his religious judgements.[57]

The breaking of the sway of self-interest is, says Arnold, 'the secret of Jesus'. In his poetry, Hutton argued, Arnold is most impressive when he is resisting the emotion he is delineating: not being thwarted or crossed but going on living. This is the 'clear heroic egotism' Arnold took for his poetic personality. In other words, 'what Mr Arnold calls "the secret of Jesus" is in reality the secret of his own poetry.'[58] Hutton wrote this in 1886, though he may have remembered what Arnold wrote in 1880, foreseeing the progress of secularization:

The future of poetry is immense, because in poetry, where it is worthy of its high destinies, our race, as time goes on, will find an ever surer and surer stay. There is not a creed which is not shaken, not an accredited dogma which is not shown to be questionable, not a received tradition which does

---

[56] 'Literature and Dogma', *Dissent and Dogma*, p. 293.
[57] See 'Newman and Arnold—II: Matthew Arnold', *Contemporary Review*, 49 (Apr. 1886), 513–34 (p. 524).
[58] Ibid., p. 530.

not threaten to dissolve. Our religion has materialised itself in the fact, in the supposed fact . . . and now the fact is failing it.[59]

In criticizing Arnold, Hutton is defending the Faith, questioning the implicit equation of the real and the 'factual'. His appreciation of Arnold's poetry is such as to refer it back to its author, to demonstrate that it is the poetry where the open 'aesthetic melodrama' is played out, and to suggest that this is no 'sure stay' for the race, given Arnold's own instabilities.

Poetry

In those well-known words on the future stability and reliability of poetry, Arnold has effectively taken Newman's notion of the *analogous* nature of poetry and religion and made the two *identical* by reference to their sheer manner. It must be said that Arnold's view, 'the strongest part of our religion today is its unconscious poetry', had some simple truth in it. Wordsworth, Tennyson, and Browning, in particular, were used as secular bibles, sources of wisdom and consolation. In practice, Arnold's dictum was inverted to be realized: the strongest part of poetry was its unconscious religion. Ironically, Hutton applies this dictum to Arnold himself, finding in his poetry a source of faith in spite of the efforts of the poetry. His implicit distinction between Arnold's poetry and his prose seems to be that the poetry carries him along with a life of its own, while the prose demands that he takes sides.

I suggested earlier that the differences between Hutton and Arnold might be characterized as different reactions to Newman, and especially to the *Grammar of Assent* and the 'Unreal Words' sermon. Arnold, I suggest, would have read differently the line, 'words have a meaning whether we mean that meaning or not'. For Arnold, this would have *freed* words from the tyranny of intention. Just as for Newman 'paper logic' is not convincing, so for Arnold a word is 'real' in being autonomous of its author. Just as Newman, as I have said, attacked Anglican liberalism for replacing real belief with a mere 'quality', 'not anything that can be contemplated by itself', so Arnold found in literature works that could be contemplated by themselves. Arnold's 'real words' are the touchstones

[59] 'The Study of Poetry', *English Literature and Irish Politics*, ed. R. H. Super, *Prose Works of Matthew Arnold*, ix (Ann Arbor, 1973), 161.

cited in the 1880 essay: they are solid, concrete words whose worth lies *within* their style. And just as for Newman spiritual inwardness cannot be communicated, so aesthetic or stylistic inwardness cannot be communicated according to Arnold.

It has been shown elsewhere that the opening passage of 'The Study of Poetry' was anticipated by Newman's 'Prospects of the Anglican Church' (1839) and that Pater's essay 'Style' was anticipated by Newman's essay on 'Literature' appended to *The Idea of a University*.[60] We might also look to the *Grammar of Assent* for a larger justification for Arnold's notion of the inaccessible 'inwardness' of style. Newman argues that the religious power of words lies in their implicit meaning which is real and inaccessible, and that to infer from them would be to strip them of their real meaning. He wrote:

Words, which denote things, have innumerable implications; but in inferential exercises it is the very triumph of that clearness and hardness of head . . . to have stripped them of these connatural senses, to have drained them of that depth and breadth of associations which constitute their poetry, their rhetoric, and their historical life, to have starved each term down . . . so that it may stand for just one unreal aspect of the concrete thing to which it properly belongs, for a relation, a generalisation, or other abstraction, for a notion neatly turned out of the laboratory of the mind.[61]

Newman opposes the reality of language characterized by the poetical to the unreality of 'inferential exercise'. To treat the Bible as poetry would be to treat its language as independent of the reader's limited understanding of it. To Arnold, literary criticism threatens to be such an inferential exercise as Newman is wary of, so he writes after citing his 'touchstones':

Critics give themselves great labour to draw out what in the abstract constitutes the characters of a high quality of poetry. It is much better simply to have recourse to concrete examples;—to take specimens of poetry of the high, the very highest quality, and to say: The characters of a high quality of poetry are what is expressed *there* . . . They are in the matter and substance of the poetry, and they are in its manner and style. . . . But if we are asked to define this mark and accent in the abstract, our answer must be: No.[62]

---

[60] Denis Butts, 'Newman's Influence on Matthew Arnold's Theory of Poetry', *Notes and Queries*, NS 5 (1958), 225–6; J. H. Newman, *The Idea of a University*, ed. Martin Svaglic (New York, 1960), p. xxiv.

[61] *Grammar of Assent*, p. 267.

[62] *English Literature and Irish Politics*, pp. 170–1.

Hutton's own answer to the question was 'yes', and he felt that Arnold would have been a better critic for inferring the individual motive of the lines he cited. They differ in their views of the accessibility of style, and of the 'inwardness' of what both Arnold and Newman call 'the concrete'. When Arnold uses the word 'in' ('in the matter . . . in its manner') it is with a force that Hutton did not or could not recognize, it is the force Pater used when he found 'the intimate impress of an indwelling soul' in fifteenth-century Italian sculpture.

In the case of Arnold's touchstone from Dante, 'In la sua voluntade è nostra pace' ('In His will is our peace'), the difference between Dante's beliefs and Arnold's is not important to the line's status. Arnold did not believe in a God with a will who could carry out intentions: he took 'God' to refer to a tendency, not an intention, which makes for righteousness. Similarly he does not ascribe the line to Dante's 'voluntade'. The highest poetry, says Arnold in his essay on Wordsworth, is 'inevitable'. He wrote of Wordsworth: 'Nature not only gave him the matter for his poem, but wrote his poem for him. He has no style.'[63] To Hutton nothing is 'inevitable' in this sense. His idea of Wordsworth is very different from Arnold's: to him Wordsworth wilfully resists his own nature, and while Arnold produced a selection of Wordsworth's poems (which, significantly, Pater had recommended in his 1874 essay on Wordsworth), Hutton helped to produce a complete edition of Wordsworth which placed each line in a whole context. Furthermore, the process of inferring from the text which Arnold refuses to carry out is ironically applied to Arnold himself by Hutton. This is what Arnold called Hutton's 'seeing too far into a millstone'.

Hutton took the case of Dante's line to argue that Arnold wanted the advantage of two inconsistent positions. He argued that Arnold held that poetry is its own evidence and so approved of Dante's line, yet also held that poetry is fed on ideas that can be verified and so disapproved of Shelley's 'On the brink of the night and the morning / My coursers are wont to respire'.[64] This ambiguity, he suggested, is expressed in Arnold's own poetry, to which he applies his inferential exercise. Arnold's poetry is to Hutton a morality touched by Arnold's emotions: it expresses Arnold's

---

[63] Ibid., p. 52.
[64] 'Matthew Arnold on Poetry and Religion', *Spectator*, 22 May 1880, 649–51 (p. 650).

faith. Moreover, he takes this combination of trust and scepticism to be typical of the age:

When I come to ask what Mr. Arnold's poetry has done for this generation, the answer must be that no-one has expressed more powerfully and poetically its spiritual weaknesses, its craving for a passion that it cannot feel . . . its desire for a creed that it fails to accept, its sympathy with a faith it will not share, its aspiration for a peace that it does not know.[65]

Hutton's answer to his own question—doing what Arnold refused to do—is couched in terms which criticize while ostensibly merely depicting. He suggests that Arnold is *the* poet of a secular morality based on subjectivism: 'craving', 'admiration', 'sympathy', 'desire', and 'aspiration'. His final words, 'its aspiration for a peace it does not know', suggest the extent to which he felt Arnold was untouched by his touchstone from Dante. He sees Arnold as typical of his age in having emotions which are undercut by intellectual doubts: he sees Arnold's aspiration for 'life' in conflict with Arnold's own critical and intellectual perception of what life really is.[66]

Arnold's poetry is to Hutton composed of 'real words' because only in the poetry is there any real indication of Arnold's unresolved contradictions and any sense of disappointment at the difference between his sympathies and his beliefs. He describes Arnold as the great Victorian elegiac poet and his typical mood as one of 'elegiac regret'.[67] What Arnold seems to regret, if we read Hutton's account of his poetry as expressing the regrets of a generation, is a loss of faith and the lack of any complete alternative; it is the lack of *completeness* of emotion which Arnold seems to regret, and to regret with a vigour which yet cannot compensate for the loss. According to Hutton's account, Arnold, in spite of his own criticism of *Empedocles on Etna* for its lack of resistance, cannot depict doubt without showing what its opposite might produce, 'a kind of imperious temperance of nature'. Arnold has neither a Wordsworthian resistance which reverses emotion nor the abandon of Shelley, but an identifiably post-Romantic uneasy combination of the two. Where Wordsworth says 'rejoice', Hutton comments, Arnold says 'endure'.[68] The implication is that the two can somehow start at the same emotional point but reach different conclu-

---

[65] *Literary Essays* (1896), p. 350. See also Madden, *Matthew Arnold*, pp. 43–4.
[66] *Spectator*, 19 June 1869, 734.
[67] *Spectator*, 7 Nov. 1891, 638–9.
[68] *Spectator*, 20 July 1878, 919. See also Hutton on Arnold's stoicism in *Contemporary Review*, 49 (Apr. 1886), 527.

sions. It is this endurance which Arnold claimed was the secret of Jesus but which Hutton saw as the secret of Arnold's own poetry:

Take his description of the solitude in which we human beings live—heart yearning after heart, but recognising the eternal gulf between us—a solitude decreed by the power which

'bade betwixt our shores to be
The unplumb'd, salt, estranging sea!'

How noble the line, and how it sends a shiver through one! And yet not a shiver of mere regret or mere yearning; rather a shiver of awe at the infinitude of the ocean in which we are all enisled . . . What he calls (miscalls, I think) the 'secret of Jesus' is in reality the secret of his own poetry. Like the East, he bows low before the blast, only to seek strength in his own mind, and to delight in the strength he finds there. He enjoys plumbing the depths of another's melancholy.[69]

'Not mere regret or mere yearning' may be taken as a summary of Hutton's view of Arnold's elegiac poetry, and his reading of those two lines is typical of his discussion of Arnold's poetry. Yet why does Hutton not criticize Arnold for ignoring the personal source, as Hutton believed it, of the power which 'bade betwixt our shores to be . . .', and why does he choose to look at these really rather hysterical pieces of poetry? Hutton himself seems to be taking refuge behind the poetical metaphor: his reaction would have been different had the lines read 'betwixt our *souls*', as they certainly suggest. Hutton seems to treat the poem, any poem, as an 'emotional form', and it is Hutton who seems to enjoy plumbing the depths of another's melancholy. These lines were certainly something of a touchstone to Hutton. He returned to them frequently, having written in 1872 of being 'possessed and haunted' by them:

That line is inexhaustible in beauty and force. Without any false emphasis or prolix dwelling on the matter, it shadows out to you the plunging deep-sea lead and the eerie cry of 'no soundings', it recalls that saltness of the sea which takes from water every refreshing association, every quality that helps to slake thirst or supply sap, and then it concentrates all these dividing attributes, which strike a sort of lonely terror into the soul, into the one word 'estranging'. It is a line full of intensity, simplicity and grandeur—a line to possess and haunt the imagination.[70]

[69] Ibid., p. 530. See also Madden, *Matthew Arnold*, pp. 28–30, on Arnold's relation to the East.

[70] *Literary Essays* (1896), pp. 335–6. See also Erik Frykman, *'Bitter knowledge' and 'Unconquerable Hope': A Thematic Study of Attitudes Towards Life in Matthew Arnold's Poetry, 1849–1853*, Göteborg Studies in English, 18 (Göteborg, 1966), 32, 61.

Arnold found the word 'life', as Hutton finds these lines, 'inex-haustible': both critics are unapologetic in feeling that they refine the material which poetry mines for them. So Hutton elaborates the word 'salt', refines the attributes of the word 'estranging'. It is Hutton who, without drawing attention to it, supplies the word 'soul' ('a sort of lonely terror into the soul'), though in fact his explication of the text is surprisingly, even amusingly, realistic and novelistic. One feels that he is really searching, not quite desper-ately, for some explanation of why the line returns to him, and he does not supply a very good one. His refining of Arnold might be said to be the only way of giving the poetry point without merely repeating those moments when Arnold rather embarassingly wants to 'make a point': Hutton's final review of Arnold was, in fact, an attack on the popular penny selections of Arnoldian 'good words', and Bradley similarly felt that many of Arnold's phrases were no more convincing than 'Honesty is the best policy', or such similar edifying maxims.[71] What Hutton admires, however, is Arnold's sustained equipoise, never allowing, as his 'Stanzas from the Grande Chartreuse' demonstrate, his regret to assume the form of hope for a revival of faith or his hope to take the form of regret for the conditions of intellectual progress. Hutton can admire this as aesthetic purity, disregarding its moral implications except in so far as they help him to criticize the critic.

Hutton admires Arnold's equipoise of style, and found, just as George Eliot did, 'real criticism' in Arnold's choice of words in his poetry. But Hutton holds it, as it were, at arm's length to admire it, as if watching the aesthetic melodrama. He cites, on a number of occasions, Arnold's remark that when he wrote 'Geist's Grave' the tears were streaming down his face: 'but they were gentle tears', wrote Hutton, implying 'gentlemanly', 'the tears of sweet elegiac regret, which brings with it a keener and brighter vision, not that stormy anguish which troubles and bedims the whole earthly scene.'[72] The difference, we might say, is between a sentimental melodrama and *King Lear*, it was the difference between Arnold and Thomas Hardy, as Hardy himself saw.[73] Arnold is not, to com-

---

[71] Bradley, *Ethical Studies*, p. 284.

[72] *Spectator*, 7 Nov. 1891, 638–9; *Spectator*, 23 Nov. 1895, 719–20.

[73] See F. E. Hardy, *The Life of Thomas Hardy*, (London, 1962), 146–7, quoting Hardy: 'Arnold is wrong about provincialism, if he means anything more than a provincialism of style and manner in exposition. A certain provincialism of feeling is

pare the more comparable, 'wild with all regret' like Tennyson or 'buoyant' like Clough, though this latter is the adjective repeatedly applied to Arnold. 'Buoyant in rebounding from melancholy reflection', Hutton says.[74]

'Rebounding from reflection' is how Hutton sees Arnold the critic in the poet. He does not exactly separate the two, the poet and the critic, but he does suggest that the poet helps him to contradict the criticism: like the 'emotional' scripture, the poetry may not express faith, but it 'engenders something akin to faith'.[75] He sees the poetry as both confessional and metaphorical. Hutton's reading of Arnold's poetry is, in Hutton's terms, Wordsworthian in reversing the emotion of the poems: 'though it offers no consolation, nay, often expressly refuses it, yet bears you along with the current of a passionate regret, with such a sense of life rather than loss'.[76] There in Hutton's own words, 'life' seems to have taken the place of 'faith'. The difference for him between Arnold's poetry and his prose is that the poetry could carry Hutton along in spite of itself, but the prose demanded agreement or conflict. The poetry is an 'emotional' form and the prose, according to that distinction between a biblical and an Arnoldian text, a 'mystical' form. Yet Hutton is not thinking of mere 'vivacity' when he writes of the 'sense of life' engendered by Arnold's poetry: he felt that the conflicts of Arnold's poetry were more 'real' than the narrow didacticism of the prose. The aspiration for life in Arnold's poetry coincided with Hutton's aspiration for faith, and it is again the difference in their perceptions of what 'life' was that we are brought to.

Conclusion

Hutton concluded that Arnold's writing was the work of a man 'exaggerating rather than attempting to bridge over the chasm between life and thought', a man whose instinct for life was contradicted by his critical perception of what life actually amounted to. To Hutton his poetry expressed this division. Hutton was haunted by two lines of Arnold because the poetry was for him the expression

---

invaluable. It is of the essence of individuality, and is largely made up of that crude enthusiasm without which no great thoughts are thought, no great deeds done.'

[74] *Modern Guides* (1887), p. 141.
[75] *Spectator*, 21 Apr. 1888, 539.
[76] *Spectator*, 25 Mar. 1893, 383.

of an estranged mind attempting 'to find some new image for the pain that results from the division of the soul against itself, for the restlessness which yearns inconsistently for sympathy and solitude, and rebounds like a shuttlecock from the one desire to the other.'[77] All Hutton's writing on Arnold could be taken as an elaboration of that remark. He can admire the poetry for its attempt to find a new image; yet he criticizes the prose for its falling back on old images. While Arnold cultivated his public persona in prose which laid down general cultural dogma and expressed his personal agony in poetry, Hutton felt he achieved the contrary: that Arnold's Culture as advocated in the prose is a private one relying on personal 'manner', while the divisions expressed in the poetry are not personal but symptoms of the age's upheaval.

However, the very words 'life' and 'thought' have such different associations for Arnold and Hutton that we might look for some concluding common ground in what each wrote about the life and thought of a common friend: not Newman, but Arthur Hugh Clough.

Arnold wrote to Clough in 1848:

The good feature in all your poems is the sincerity that is evident in them: which always produces a powerful effect on the reader . . . The spectacle of a writer striving evidently to get breast to breast with reality is always full of instruction and very invigorating—and here I feel you have the advantage of me: 'much may be seen, tho' nothing can be solved'—weighs upon me in writing.[78]

The key words 'reality' and 'sincerity' appear also in one of Hutton's reviews of Clough in 1861, a piece which was later incorporated into his important essay on Clough:

So eager was his craving for reality and perfect sincerity, so morbid his dislike even for the unreal conventional forms of life, that a mind quite unique in simplicity and truthfulness represents itself in his poems as,

> Seeking in vain, in all my store,
> One feeling based on truth.

Indeed, he wanted to reach some guarantee for simplicity deeper than simplicity itself.[79]

---

[77] *Literary Essays* (1896), p. 335.

[78] *Letters of Matthew Arnold to A. H. Clough*, ed. H. F. Lowry (London, 1932), p. 86 (20 July 1848).

[79] *Literary Essays* (1871), pp. 369–70, first published in 'Arthur Hugh Clough—In Memoriam', *Spectator*, 23 Sept. 1861, 1286. See also the review by Henry

A comparison of the two is not, of course, entirely fair since Arnold
is not writing public literary criticism, but we can conclude something of significance from the two views. When Arnold reads
Clough he sees a 'good feature' and a 'spectacle': Arnold is Pater's
impassioned contemplator considering what might be the appropriate emotions with which to witness this spectacle. Arnold, moreover, describes the poems as 'full of instruction', yet the effect on
him is described in physical terms. When Hutton reads Clough's
poetry, however, he finds a mind represented there, but not a
representative mind. Hutton's difficulty is in finding a description
as new as the mind it describes as 'unique': hence the difficult final
sentence of the quotation. Arnold is reminded of his difference
from Clough; Hutton is forced to find terms which he feels will be
'in sympathy' with Clough's intentions. Arnold quotes a touchstone which will communicate his weight; Hutton cites two lines
which he feels represent the mind behind them.

Arnold was a close friend to Clough, Hutton worked with him as
Assistant Principal of University Hall in the 1850s: both, therefore,
knew what Clough's 'reality' was in the quotidian sense. The
Clough represented to us by Hutton was driven by his own character, by his own 'life', however it may have been realized in biographical terms. The Clough Arnold gives us is measured by his
addition to Arnold's own life: the very closeness of Arnold to his
real subject matter renders the necessary retrospective detachment
impossible. To both critics Clough was a failure. To Hutton he remained in the intellectual sphere, failing to put his thoughts into
action.[80] To Arnold he failed to remain in the intellectual sphere,
and was distracted by action from systematizing his thought.

Sidgwick, 'The Poems and Prose Remains of Arthur Hugh Clough', *Westminster
Review*, 92 (Oct. 1869), 363–87.

[80] See also Hutton's 'Amiel and Clough', *Spectator*, 9 Jan. 1886, 42–3.

5
Wordsworth and Tennyson

THE elements isolated by Hutton in his discussion of Clough were his craving for reality and sincerity, or Clough's desire to express his perception of the real world in words which would express his true self. Similarly, Hutton thought Arnold's true self to be expressed in his poetry and believed his choice of words in writing poetry to be 'real criticism'. These problems of realism, character, and expression are the ones which inform Hutton's interest in poetry in general.

As we have seen, Hutton expressed the position of the non-believer in a secular society by the character of the Explorer, the character Arnold unknowingly adopts. Hutton similarly sees the poet, particularly in choosing his language, as such an Explorer. He describes Browning as a poet who 'hews away right and left, like a pioneer in a jungle, instead of shaping anxiously and lovingly as a sculptor shapes his marble.'[1] Hutton is comparing Browning with Tennyson who, he says, 'treats words and all their associations with the utmost sympathy and reverence'. Hutton's striking image of the pioneer does not apply to all poets, but all are seen as struggling with the problems represented by the image: how to express oneself in a language which has been rendered unstable by changes in belief and society, and is therefore a 'resistant medium', and how to know what 'oneself' is in a world where one has no function, no path marked out before one.[2] The novel seems to have been addressed to the second of these questions by its provision of a narrative sense of selfhood. Poetry, on the other hand, provided the materials for argument on the question of self and self-expression.

Discussing the eccentricity of Carlyle's forms of expression, Hutton wrote in 1871: 'special matter often determines its own form by some occult law of the inner faculty, and it is idle to assume that a man can express his thought in any way he chooses'. Here, choice of expression is not, as it might at first seem, determined by the world, but neither is it possible for the writer *con-*

---

[1] 'Browning and Tennyson', *Spectator*, 21 Dec. 1889, 879.
[2] See Hutton on Tennyson's 'resistant medium', below, chapter 5, 'Tennysonian resistance'.

sciously to choose his words. This choice is made by the 'occult law of the inner faculty'.[3] This is clearly the Illative Sense as depicted by Newman in the *Grammar of Assent* only a few months before the article of Hutton's was written. As I said when discussing Newman, the Illative Sense seems to be an inner counterpart to real life, not an alternative to it. So in Hutton's argument the inner faculty determining expression seems to be an internal equivalent to the determining *Zeitgeist*. The expression of poetry, in particular, is seen as determined by what in religious terms we should call the 'spirit', or the true, unselfconscious self.

Twenty-five years later, in 1896, Hutton wrote a vigorous and moving article on 'Life in Poetry', arguing that poetry was not only expressed *by* the true self, but was also an expression *of* the true self. The article is particularly moving when one considers that Hutton was seventy years old and only a year from his death. For poetry, he says, is not 'the criticism of life', as Arnold defined it, but life itself: 'poetry is a real addition to the life of man, or at all events, an emancipation, a manumission of that life.' Every great poem, he says 'has been a great blow for freedom'. He does not mean, however, that reading or writing poetry frees us from the world or from ourselves. That idea of freedom, he says, belongs to 'the old romantic moulds of thought'. It would be a romantic mistake, he writes, 'to attempt to liberate ourselves from the authority of the truest self within us and seek after an unnatural freedom which is really the most galling bondage'.[4]

The 'authority of the truest self' to which Hutton refers is, once more, the sanction of the Illative Sense. It is specifically not this self from which poetry frees us, as Hutton goes on to say:

After all freedom is a relative word. You cannot be free *from* your nature, you can only be free *in* your nature, in your highest nature. And no bondage is more cruel, more intolerable, than the bondage which comes of fighting against the very law of your own nature.[5]

When Hutton refers to 'your nature' he does not mean 'your temperament', but rather 'your character' as part of 'human nature'. He sees this character as God's creation and its expression an expression of God *irrespective of the writer's belief*. Hence Hutton's frequent discovery of the 'implicitly Christian' in secular works of literature.

[3] 'Mr. Carlyle on Verse', *Spectator*, 7 Jan. 1871, 10–12 (p. 11).
[4] 'Life in Poetry', *Spectator*, 20 June 1896, 866–7.   [5] Ibid., p. 867.

Poetry is therefore 'real' to Hutton in two senses. First, poetical language has a meaning whether the poet 'means' it or not. The poet's expression is in advance of his control of it, unless it is conventional or revised.[6] Second, the unself-conscious mind which is expressed by poetry is the 'real' poet, his 'true nature', and the poem provides the occasion for this expression.

For Hutton Wordsworth is the great realist poet, and his poetry the expression of a real nature resisting the poet's temperament. For the Victorians Wordsworth allied his true nature with the natural world. Hardy wrote in 1881:

Consider the Wordsworthian dictum (the more perfectly the natural object is reproduced, the more truly poetic the picture). This reproduction is achieved by seeing into the *heart of a thing* (as rain, wind, for instance), and is realism, in fact, though through being pursued by means of the imagination it is confounded with invention, which is pursued by the same means. It is, in short, reached by what M. Arnold calls 'the imaginative reason'.[7]

Arnold's 'imaginative reason' was a secularized Illative Sense, and Hardy's notion of the poetic as inward and perceptive derives from Newman rather than Wordsworth. For both Hardy and Hutton, perception of the natural world is analogous to perception of the natural self, though their respective views of this self were, of course, importantly different.

Tennyson was to Hutton a significanܼly more selfconscious poet than Wordsworth. Tennyson's 'reverence' for the associations of words is seen as part of an effort to control them and to present an image which is consciously 'of the age'. He does not, to Hutton, always express his true nature but collusively reflects the dominant tendencies of the day.

Hutton, it is hardly necessary to say, wrote on almost all the major poets of the day, and on literally dozens of minor and long-forgotten ones. I have concentrated on these two poets to represent this bulk of work because he valued their poetry the most highly, because his writing on them was the most influential of all he did on poetry, because his comments on them are least occasional, and because he provides us with a new perspective on the two poets

---

[6] See Hutton on Wordsworth's revisions, below, chapter 5, 'Hutton's restoration of Wordsworth'.

[7] F. E. Hardy, *The Life of Thomas Hardy* (London, 1962), 147 (Journal entry for January 1881).

whom we might regard as the most important of the nineteenth century.

Hutton published two substantial and important essays on Wordsworth and over twenty articles in response to the publication of works by or about him. The essays appeared in the *National Review* in 1857 and in the *Modern Review* in 1882; the one in the latter being first delivered as a paper to the Wordsworth Society in 1882 and republished in the Society's *Wordsworthiana* (1889). The shorter articles all came out in the *Spectator* between 1868 and 1895 and were all, unlike the essays, occasioned by a publication: the first was a review of J. C. Shairp's *Studies in Poetry and Philosophy* which was followed in subsequent years by, for example, reviews of Dorothy Wordsworth's Scotch journal (1874), Matthew Arnold's and William Knight's differing selections from Wordsworth (1879 and 1888), Alois Brandl's *Life of Coleridge* (1887), the first publication of *The Recluse* (1888), and the gradual publication of William Knight's scholarly edition of the poems (1882–86).

My own discussion will centre on the 1857 and 1882 essays, though it will draw on the *Spectator* material. The earlier essay provided a vocabulary for discussing Wordsworth's idealism which directly and explicitly affected the reading of Wordsworth for the rest of the century. I discuss two of the most important 'readings', those of Leslie Stephen and Edward Caird, although others, notably Matthew Arnold's and Walter Pater's, are significant reference points.[8] The second of Hutton's essays reflects on Wordsworth's style as well as on his 'teaching', though it is the latter which most interested the Wordsworth Society, for whose audience the essay was intended. I discuss the consolatory 'use' to which the Society, as a representative late Victorian readership of Wordsworth, put his poetry, and how Hutton's view of Wordsworth responded to the needs of and contributed to the growth of this readership.[9]

[8] R. H. Hutton, 'William Wordsworth', *National Review* (4 Jan. 1857), 1–30; Leslie Stephen, 'Wordsworth's Ethics', *Cornhill Magazine*, 34 (August 1876), 206–26; Edward Caird, 'Wordsworth', *Fraser's Magazine*, NS 21 (Feb. 1880), 205–21; Matthew Arnold, 'Wordsworth', *Macmillan's Magazine*, 40 (July 1879), 193–204; Walter Pater, 'On Wordsworth', *Fortnightly Review*, NS 15 (Apr. 1874), 455–65.

[9] An excellent account of Wordsworth's early readership is given by R. E. Lovelace, 'Wordsworth and the Early Victorians: A Study of his Influence and Reputation, 1830–1860' (unpublished Ph.D. dissertation, Cambridge University, 1951). Bibliographical information on Victorian criticism of Wordsworth may be found in N. S. Bauer, *William Wordsworth: A Reference Guide to British Criticism, 1793–1899* (Boston, 1978), and in J. V. Logan, *Wordsworthian Criticism: A Guide and Bibliography* (New York, 1974).

Hutton devoted some forty-two articles and essays to discussion of Tennyson (though twelve of these cannot be positively identified as his) between 1855 and 1896. This does not represent a large proportion of his total output, but it does represent a major part in terms of subject matter: there were not many subjects or writers to whom he could return so often or on whom he could continually update his opinion. Most of what we might regard as Tennyson's major work had been published by 1855 (*The Princess* in 1847, *In Memoriam* in 1850), but it should be remembered that a critic writing in 1855 had no way of knowing this, though it should also be said that Hutton did, in fact, feel that *In Memoriam* was unsurpassable. The years covered by Hutton's writing saw the finalization of the *Idylls of the King*, the first parts of which were published as *Idylls* in 1859 (namely *Enid*, *Vivien*, *Elaine*, and *Guinevere*, though the cycle may be said to have begun with the publication of *The Lady of Shalott* in 1832), and the last part (*Balin and Balan*) in 1885.[10] Hutton himself discussed the progress of the series with Tennyson, advising him in 1873 to add nothing to the poem, apparently unaware that Tennyson was engaged on *Balin and Balan*.[11] In addition to plotting the course of the *Idylls*, Hutton also gave his first impressions of *Maud* (1855), *Enoch Arden* (1864), *Locksley Hall Sixty Years After* (1886), *The Death of Oenone* and *Akbar's Dream* (1892). He also saw the beginning of Tennyson's career as a playwright with the publication of *Queen Mary* in 1875.

I shall concentrate on the readings of Tennyson in the second half of the nineteenth century, in part because the general reception of his work until the publication of *In Memoriam* has been fully documented already by Edgar Shannon (although he does not discriminate between the significance of individual writers).[12] During the period with which I deal, Tennyson was a well-established poet and was regarded as *the* poet of the age. I shall discuss what currents of thought he was taken to represent and to oppose. I shall be particularly concerned with Hutton's belief that Tennyson was,

[10] See the thorough account by Kathleen Tillotson, 'Tennyson's Serial Poem', *Mid-Victorian Studies* by G. and K. Tillotson (London, 1965), 80–109, and J. M. Gray, *Thro' the Vision of the Night* (Edinburgh, 1980).

[11] See *Diary of Alfred Domett*, ed. E. A. Horsman (London, 1953), 79.

[12] Edgar Shannon, *Tennyson and the Reviewers: A Study of his Literary Reputation and of the Influence of the Critics on his Poetry, 1827-1851* (Cambridge, Mass., 1952).

unlike Wordsworth, not strong in opposing either his own temperament or the tendencies of his age. I shall look at Hutton's analysis
of Tennyson's use of language, and especially at his 'reading' of
two of his lyrics: 'Tears, idle tears', and 'Break, break, break'.

Wordsworthian idealism: Edward Caird, Leslie Stephen, R. H. Hutton

Hutton's first substantial essay on Wordsworth, published in 1857,
provided the terms for discussion of the poet by a discernible line of
critics for the rest of the century. This line runs from Hutton,
through Leslie Stephen, to Edward Caird. The needs and premises
of these three are notably different: Hutton sees Wordsworth as a
poet of Christian reserve, Stephen, as an agnostic, sees him as providing a personal philosophy of consolation, and Caird, as an
Hegelian philosopher of religion, sees Wordsworth as a source of
stability and innocence. Each refuses to recognize any distinction
between poetry and philosophy, and the precise terms of the refusal
can be traced back from Caird to Hutton. The 'Wordsworth' of this
movement is opposed to the 'Wordsworth' of Arnold and Pater.
Indeed, the Wordsworthian haunters of Social Science Congresses
mocked by Arnold in his 1879 essay have something in common
with this 'ethical' movement, not in systematizing Wordsworth,
but in treating his poetry as thought.

In 1892 the philosopher Edward Caird published a collection of
essays on literature and philosophy, including in it an essay on
Wordsworth which had its origins in Caird's review article on
Arnold's selections from Wordsworth.[13] Caird begins his essay by
addressing himself to a question frequently posed by late Victorian
criticism, the question of why Wordsworth could never become
'popular'. He emphasizes the differences between Wordsworth's
poetry and 'usual verse', and between Wordsworthian emotions
and 'commonplace experience':

It courts us with none of the usual subsidiary charms and illusions of verse;
and it requires, at first, something like a moral effort ere we can put
ourselves into the temper for enjoying it; 'we must love it, ere to us it will
seem worthy of our love'. It requires us, in a sense, to become as little

---

[13] Edward Caird, *Essays in Literature and Philosophy*, 2 vols. (Glasgow, 1892), i.
147–89; 'Wordsworth', *Fraser's Magazine*, NS 21 (Feb. 1880), 205–21.

children, to divest ourselves of all artificial associations and secondary interests, of all that hides the essentials of humanity, and to enter a region where everything is estimated at the price which it has for the simplest and most universal affections.[14]

Caird's essays are generally remarkable for his powerful sense of being under an obligation to the subject of them, and this feeling seems to be represented by, not merely to derive from, Wordsworth. It is important to recognize the tone and vocabulary which Caird is able to take for granted: he assumes that no explanation is necessary for treating Wordsworth as a moral philosopher and that the moral effect of the poet is achieved without even reading the poetry (the moral effort being expended on putting yourself into the right frame of mind), though the poetry is appealed to implicitly as justification for this effect. Since Caird is consciously writing for an audience who can be taken to know the poetry (the notion of an audience of *real* 'little children' shows that his idea of simplicity is of a hard-won simplicity), he can use the same vocabulary to describe both the poetry and its effect.

The world in which the poet writes is taken to be a region quite separate from the material world but is entered through a concern with the 'essentials' of common life. This idea of the poet's world is also used by Hutton, who wrote that Wordsworth's passion 'introduces us to a sort of fourth dimension in the poetic world, to a previously untravelled region of poetry where Wordsworth lives almost alone'.[15] Here, once more, the poet is depicted as the Explorer, though the jungle has been replaced by the more modish fourth dimension. The Hegelian philosopher took his idea of the poet directly from Hutton, though he cuts off its Christian roots. Caird explicitly appeals to the knowledge and memory of Hutton, the only critic cited by him, as the writer who established his vocabulary and his tone. Caird wrote:

Mr. Hutton, in his criticism upon Wordsworth, has spoken of his 'spiritual frugality' in making the most of every simple occasion, and refraining from any waste of the sources of emotion; but the secret of this frugality is Wordsworth's belief that there is little difference between small and great occasions, and that, if we cannot find the greatest meanings in the most familiar experiences, we shall find them nowhere.[16]

14 Ibid., p. 205.
15 'Mr. Morley on Wordsworth', *Spectator*, 22 Dec. 1888, 1807.
16 *Fraser's Magazine*, NS 21 (Feb. 1880), 219.

The essay to which Caird refers was first published in the *National Review* in 1857, when the reconciliation which Caird takes for granted, the reconciliation of Wordsworth's 'simplicity' with his 'depth', was still a matter for dispute. In the section referred to by Caird, Hutton is addressing himself to these opposing criticisms that Wordsworth is too simple and too transcendental:

The reconciliation of these opposite criticisms is not difficult. He drew uncommon delights from very common things. . . . He could detach his mind from the commonplace series of impressions which are generated by commonplace objects or events, resist and often reverse the current of emotion to which ordinary minds are liable. . . . Two distinct peculiarities, and rare peculiarities of character, chiefly assisted him in this—his keen spiritual courage, and his stern spiritual frugality. . . . He contests the ground inch by inch with all despondent and indolent humours—turning defeat into victory and victory into defeat. He transmutes sorrows into food for lonely rapture, as he dwells upon the evidence they bear of the depth and fortitude of human nature; he transmutes the periodic joy of conventional social occasions into melancholy as he recalls how 'the wiser mind'

> Mourns less for what age takes away
> Than what it leaves behind.

No poet ever contrived by dint of 'plain living and high thinking' to get nearer to the reality of such life as he understood, and to dispel more thoroughly the illusions of superficial impression.[17]

Hutton's quotation is from Wordsworth's 'The Fountain' and I shall come to his discussion of that poem at the end of this section. Here I wish to show how Hutton has established a vocabulary which Caird has reworked and applied to the poetry (for Hutton's 'He contests . . . He transmutes . . .', Caird has 'It courts . . . it requires . . .'). For Hutton, Wordsworth was able to discover the 'deepest secondary springs of joy' in what ordinary men found uninteresting or even full of pain. For Caird the poetry itself requires him to divest himself 'of all artificial and secondary interests'. That is to say, Hutton argues that Wordsworth's gift for discovering and maintaining secondary emotions was a means of approaching 'nearer to the reality of such life as he understood', while Caird seems to take this position as read, never suggesting that Wordsworth's feelings are 'secondary'. Wordsworth's poetry contained,

---

[17] *Literary Essays* (1896), pp. 90–1.

Hutton argues, the two most important sources of literary power, 'resistance' and 'transmutation', but as reflections of equivalent elements in his character ('keen spiritual courage' and 'stern spiritual frugality'). Caird argues that the poetry reflects on the character of the reader and requires a moral effort, a resistance and a transmutation, in him.

Hutton and Caird, however, share an implicit belief that the Wordsworthian imagination is perceptive, able to penetrate the periodic and the conventional to display or provide access to the 'real', to the 'essentials of humanity'. Both generally treat imaginative works as the product of and source of such perception, though while Caird takes the authority for such treatment on trust (hence the need to become as little children), Hutton reminds his reader, explicitly though fleetingly, of the conception of the penetrative imagination embodied in Ruskin's *Modern Painters*. Unfortunately Hutton's comments on *Modern Painters* are oblique and incidental, while the Ruskin he writes about, in the 1870s and 1880s, is one who Hutton feels has lost control of the earlier perceptions and failed to capitalize on them. We have to reconstruct the precise points at which Ruskin can be seen behind Hutton, partly from Hutton's sense of Ruskin's deterioration: he felt, in particular, that Ruskin's view of Wordsworth in 'Fiction—Fair and Foul' was merely 'the criticism of a clever Philistine'.[18]

Ruskin's trust in the perceptions of the penetrative imagination, as discussed in Part II of *Modern Painters* and as illustrated in the comparison of Turner and Stanfield in Part V, rests on the belief that the imaginative mind may claim meanings which are hidden by the flux of experience, such that every word written by such a mind has 'an awful undercurrent of meaning, and evidence and shadow upon it of the deep places out of which it has come'. Ruskin depicted the imaginative mind as providing 'the Open Sesame of a huge, obscure, endless cave, with inexhaustible treasures of pure gold scattered in it'.[19] These deep places are both inner (the depths of experience and the self) and outer, including the origins of words in

---

[18] 'Mr. Ruskin on Wordsworth', *Spectator*, 7 Aug. 1880, 1000. See also 'Mr. Ruskin on Nature and Miracle', *Spectator*, 8 Mar. 1873, 300–2; 'What is a Strong Imagination?', *Spectator*, 13 Apr. 1889, 506–9; and 'Imagination and Faith', *Spectator*, 2 Dec. 1893, 794–5.

[19] *Modern Painters*, new edition, 5 vols. (London, 1873), vol. ii, part 3, section 2, ch. 3 ('Of Imagination Penetrative'), 160.

other people's experience. Wordsworth, according to Caird's and Hutton's account, felt these two to be analogous and continuous.

Hutton took Ruskin's notion of the evidence supplied by the imaginative mind and so found in Wordsworth 'evidence of the depth and fortitude of human nature'. Hutton regards the evidence as grounds for belief in human nature (as opposed to transient temperament) while Ruskin regards the evidence as an incomplete trace or relic of 'depth' within the work itself. Each account is a justification of the epithet 'profound' as applied to a work of art. Hutton is moved by the depths of Wordsworth's feelings and argues that those feelings belong to Wordsworth's nature and not to any occasion, though an occasion may call them forth. Ruskin leaves the reader to decide whether or not to dwell on the evidence he finds in art. Both writers see the 'highest' art as referring to something beyond itself. For Ruskin this 'something' was 'the dim type of all melancholy human labour' implicit in the Turnerian picturesque. Ruskin calls this 'the real nature of the thing . . . the pathos of character hidden beneath'. Hutton, though, is very sceptical of the human, social lesson to be drawn from art, and for him the 'dim type' represented by art is not human, unless it were Adam.

For Hutton the typical or general is buried beneath and is therefore dim; the occasional or particular is superficial. Wordsworth was for him evidence that the everyday can bring out the essentials of human nature and not bury them. Wordsworth represents for Hutton the struggle of ideal human nature, which is divinely created, with the worldly, occasional, and contingent. Literature, and especially the novel, as I shall discuss later, dealt with worldly experiences and emergencies which brought forth the essential human type.[20] Moreover, Hutton as a reviewer is continually trying to bring his Christian nature to bear on the contingent and the ephemeral.[21]

Hutton saw works of literature and the imagination as forces for penetrating and subverting the conventional and the social by

[20] See below, chapter 6, 'The importance of narrative fiction'.

[21] Hence also the general critical obsession in the last two decades with the question of literary survival and the opinions of posterity. This produced articles like Hutton's 'What Endures in Poetry?', *Spectator*, 24 Aug. 1889, 236–7; 'How Long Will Dickens Hold His Place in the Future?', *Spectator*, 31 Dec. 1892, 950–1; and W. H. Mallock's, 'Are Scott, Dickens and Thackeray Obsolete?', *Forum* (New York), 14 (1893), 503–13.

dwelling on the common and the everyday. Many Victorian critics used literature as evidence for moral perceptions, but these are often no more persuasive than the sort of edifying maxims we might find in Victorian samplers: 'Honesty is the best policy' or 'Handsome is as handsome does'. F. H. Bradley thought Arnold's morality had the same status. The critic who sees writing as the vehicle for decorative morality implicitly sees the imagination as the source of images, not of perceptions, and the writer as purveyor of moments of intense and self-contained experience. Though they might not recognize this description, this criticism is represented by Pater on Wordsworth, Arnold on poetry, or Swinburne on Tennyson. Their work might be identified by their widespread use of terminology from visual art in literary criticism, and by the absence of discussion of the novel.[22]

Conversely, the claims made for all literature by Hutton are essentially the claims made for the novel by novelists. Hutton's notion of Wordsworth's finding depth in common things, followed by Caird's requirement to 'find the greatest meanings in the most familiar experiences' are 'novelistic' answers to Arnold's 'Preface' (1853).[23] They are opposing accounts of those actions and those works of art which might be called 'excellent' or 'profound'.[24]

The excellence of 'great' literature seems to rest for Arnold on its being larger than life, resisting any implication that as a work it belongs to a larger context or refers to things beyond itself. So for Arnold, Sophocles 'saw life whole', not in the sense of seeing all of life but in the sense of having and providing a whole, self-contained view of it which is judged by the treatment of the subject matter. The greatness of a work of art to Hutton does not seem to depend upon the subject matter but upon the power of motivation of which it is the evidence, and the greater moral problems and values to which it sends the reader. Hence Hutton's admiration for and concentration on the life of Walter Scott, rather than the novels.

---

[22] These accounts are discussed by D. J. DeLaura, 'The "Wordsworth" of Pater and Arnold: The Supreme, Artistic View of Life', *Studies in English Literature*, 6 (Autumn 1966), 651–7.

[23] See especially the paragraph beginning: 'The poet, then, has in the first place to select an excellent action . . .', Preface to the First Edition of the *Poems* (1853), *Poems of Matthew Arnold*, ed. Kenneth Allott (London, 1965), 593. See also Hardy on provincialism and greatness, above ch. 4, n. 73.

[24] S. Coulling, 'Matthew Arnold's 1853 Preface: Its Origin and Aftermath', *Victorian Studies*, 7 (1964), 233–63.

   Leslie Stephen's essay on Wordsworth's ethics, published twenty years after Hutton's essay, is important here because he attempts to use the same criterion as Hutton for measuring Wordsworth's greatness, but without the belief in the positive moral or religious values which Hutton finds validated in him. This is what Stephen wrote of what Hutton and Caird called Wordsworth's 'transmuting power':

Wordsworth's favourite lesson is the possibility of turning grief and disappointment into account. He teaches in many forms the necessity of 'transmuting' sorrow into strength. One of the great evils is the lack of power,

An agonizing sorrow to transmute.

. . . Other poets mock us by an impossible optimism, or merely reflect the feelings which, however we may play with them in times of cheerfulness, have now become an intolerable burden. Wordsworth suggests the single topic which, so far as the world is concerned, can really be called consolatory . . . All moral teaching, I have sometimes fancied, might be summed up in the one formula, 'Waste not' . . . The waste of sorrow is one of the most lamentable forms of waste . . . The man who has learnt habitually to think of himself as part of a greater whole, whose conduct has been habitually conducted to noble ends, is purified and strengthened by the spiritual convulsion. His disappointment, or his loss of some beloved object, makes him more anxious to fit the bases of his happiness widely and deeply, and to be content with the consciousness of honest work, instead of looking for what is called success.[25]

Hutton, Stephen, and Caird thus share a common vocabulary for describing Wordsworth's ethics: Hutton writes of his transmuting 'sorrows into food for lonely rapture', Stephen of his 'transmuting sorrow into strength'; Stephen talks of the lamentable 'waste of sorrow', and Caird of Wordsworth 'refraining from any waste of the sources of emotion'. Yet Hutton's and Stephen's needs are crucially different. Hutton is not concerned with consolation but with a kind of redemption, a liberation from the common current of feeling and even from common social concerns (that sense of being, in Stephen's words, 'part of a greater whole' which threatens to diminish your own importance).

   It is difficult to see what Stephen meant by the 'success' we should not look for, but it might be a kind of omniscience, such as that

[25] 'Wordsworth's Ethics', *Cornhill Magazine*, 34 (Aug. 1876), 206–26 (pp. 222–4).

provided in the novel's narration, by which depths and consequences would become visible. Stephen seems to recommend that
we be content with the 'evidence' of the imagination, rather than
question what the product is evidence of, and presents us with a late
Victorian, agnostic version of Wordsworth's 'wise passiveness'.

Though one risks demeaning his words, Stephen is concerned
with specific consolation for two 'occasions' in his life: his 'disappointment or loss of some beloved object' might be taken to
refer to the death of his wife, Harriet (who had died only weeks
before the essay was published), or to a more general 'spiritual convulsion' which led to his renouncement of Holy Orders (which also
happened just before the essay was published).[26] It is impossible to
say whether the lost object of devotion is human or divine, but
though Stephen is writing out of solicitude for his own moral life,
he draws upon a concern for the greater moral life of man of which
his is a part, and which had become by this time (the 1870s) a moral
life without a divine object. For Stephen, Wordsworth is an idealist
in refusing to become cynical in a world in which optimism is impossible, while Hutton uses Wordsworth to resist and deflect the
tendency of secularization. We can see this most clearly in his
discussion of Wordsworth's 'The Fountain'.

Hutton compares Wordsworth's poem with Tennyson's 'Tears,
idle tears', suggesting that while they both begin at a similar emotional point, Tennyson continues to 'picture the profound unspeakable sadness with which we survey the irrecoverable past', but
Wordsworth 'checks the current of his emotion', and is not 'rest-
lessly propelled by it'.[27] Tennyson, it is argued, leaves his tears idle,
while Wordsworth, in Stephen's words, puts his to honest work
even if without hope of what is called success. Hutton quotes four
lines as crucial:

> Thus fares it still in our decay:
> And yet the wiser mind
> Mourns less for what age takes away
> Than what it leaves behind.

[26] See Noel Annan, *Leslie Stephen: His Thought and Character in Relation to His Time* (London, 1951), 69 and 83. See also O. Maurer, 'Leslie Stephen and the *Cornhill Magazine*, 1871–1882', *University of Texas Studies in English*, 32 (1953), 67–95.

[27] Hutton takes the phrase from Wordsworth's 'Reply to "Mathetes" ', published in Coleridge's *The Friend* and reprinted in *Prose Works of William Wordsworth*, ed. W. J. B. Owen and J. W. Smyser, 3 vols. (Oxford, 1974), ii. 18.

It is at this point, Hutton argues, that Wordsworth makes an object of his own emotion, not out of lyrical regret, but as a source of intellectual development. Hutton wrote of 'The Fountain':

And thus meditating, he wrings from the temporary sadness fresh con-viction that the ebbing away, both in spirit and in appearance, of the brightest past, sad as it must ever be, is not so sad a thing as the weak yearning which, in departing, it often leaves stranded on the soul, to cling to the appearance when the spirit is irrevocably lost. There is no other great poet who thus redeems new ground for spiritual meditation from beneath the very sweep of the tides of the most engrossing affections, and quietly maintains it in possession of the musing intellect . . . None but Wordsworth has ever so completely transmuted by an imaginative spirit unsatisfied yearnings into eternal truth.[28]

This is implicitly a description of the resistance to secularization, tacitly a statement that such a resistance is itself a source of fresh conviction or a transmutation of secular feeling back into religion. Hutton considered Wordsworth's 'imaginative spirit' to have turned the subject of his emotions into the object of his thoughts, and Hutton finds this reversal spiritual not transcendental. He describes Wordsworth's source of spiritual faith in terms very like those used by Feuerbach and, following him, by George Eliot, to describe the Christian ideal as an objectification of human nature.[29] Hutton's analysis cuts two ways: he tries to define the particular characteristics of Wordsworth, but the terms of his definition draw unwittingly on the general character of post-Romantic secular-ization. He is not only saying that Wordsworth's poems survive the emotions from which they sprang and have a new life apart from them, but is also saying that secularized morality is attempt-ing to cling to the appearance of Christianity when the spirit of religion has been lost. It was this secularized Wordsworth, refus-ing to accept an 'impossible optimism', which appealed to Leslie Stephen.

In order to see how close Hutton's description of Wordsworth is to his description of contemporary writing, we might compare with his paragraph on 'The Fountain' the final paragraph of his study of *Middlemarch*, published in 1873, and observe the recurrence of the

[28] *Literary Essays* (1896), p. 100.
[29] We might, indeed, criticize Feuerbach's work as an attempt to 'redeem new ground for spiritual meditation' and to explain the nature of religious feelings as the impulse to transmute unsatisfied human yearnings into divine eternal truth.

key words, and their synonyms, 'ebbing away', 'stranded', 'cling', 'the sweep of the tides':

George Eliot means to draw noble natures struggling hard against the currents of a poor kind of world, and without any trust in any invisible rock higher than themselves to which they can entreat to be lifted up. That in spite of any absence of this inward vista of spiritual hope, George Eliot should paint the noble characters in which her interest centres as clinging tenaciously to that *caput mortuum* into which Mr. Arnold has so strangely reduced the Christian idea of God—'a stream of tendency, not ourselves, which makes for righteousness'—and as never even inclined to cry out 'let us eat and drink, for tomorrow we die', is a great testimony to the ethical depth and purity of her mind. When at last this great wave of scepticism has swept by us, the critics of the future will be compelled to infer from it [i.e. from *Middlemarch*], that even in that low ebb of trust in the super-natural element of religion, there was no want of ardent belief in the spiritual obligations of purity and self-sacrifice.[30]

Hutton does not so much discuss writers as allow them to meet in his mind, as here George Eliot meets Arnold. Both were implicit in the piece on Wordsworth. Consequently we can reapply Hutton's words on Wordsworth to a critique of Arnold; in Hutton's terms Arnold reversed the Wordsworthian effect to translate eternal truth into an unsatisfied yearning. While Wordsworth is seen as the poet depicting emotions which are independent of and greater than their apparent causes, emotions which are 'left behind', Arnold, both as a thinker and as a poet (the key words in this passage form the vocabulary of 'Dover Beach'), is seen clinging to the appearance of religious language when the spirit has been lost. Hutton's own feelings are clearly on the side of the Wordsworthian resistance, of which his own work is an example: he is resisting the 'great wave of scepticism' while turning it to good account. For Arnold the *language* of religion is left behind, to be used, as Hutton said, in a 'washed-out sense of his own'. This attempt to put Wordsworth to positive use was unique to the *Spectator* among the Anglican establishment press and unique to Hutton among the establishment critics and apologists (though its positive tone had counterparts in criticism of Wordsworth in support of Arnoldian idealism and Stephen's agnosticism).[31] A brief study of the 'Wordsworth Society'

[30] '*Middlemarch*: A Study in Provincial Life', *British Quarterly Review*, 57 (Apr. 1873), 407–29 (p. 429).

[31] T. E. Casson, 'Wordsworth and the *Spectator*', *Review of English Studies*, 3 (1927), 157–61; John Dover Wilson, *Leslie Stephen and Matthew Arnold as Critics of Wordsworth* (Cambridge, 1939).

will place Hutton's writings on Wordsworth in perspective and in a more narrow context.

The 'Wordsworth Society'

(i) Wordsworth and consolation

It was Wordsworth's lot in the second half of the nineteenth century to be regarded as the writer who saw and described, in Ruskin's phrase, 'the real nature of the thing', penetrating the veil of appearance for the agnostic idealists and providing an alternative scripture for the Christian literary critic. Examples of the latter gathered in the 'Wordsworth Society', and propounded a late nineteenth-century poetic and a Wordsworthian morality. The Society was formed in 1880 and lasted for six years, by which time its Executive Council (of which Hutton, along with Edward Caird, and Robert Browning, was a member) felt it had achieved its aims. These were to form 'a bond of union amongst those who are in sympathy with the general teaching and spirit of Wordsworth', and, more specifically, to carry out three scholastic projects: to prepare a definitive text of the poems, to publish Wordsworth's letters, and to compile a 'record of opinion, with reference to Wordsworth, from 1793 to the present time' (i.e. 1880).[32] Most of the writing to be found in the Society's *Transactions* falls into either the general or specific category: it is either a vaguely 'metaphysical' cementing of the 'bond of sympathy', or it is scholarly and pedestrian. Similarly, the Society's membership was, on the whole, High Church, middle class, and low in critical power.

Hutton was a founder member of the Society and one of its leading members. His interest reflects a strong need on his part to institutionalize his concerns, as is evidenced by his founding membership of the Metaphysical Society and its later equivalent, the Synthetic Society. This need to belong to institutions may be a result of the desire to give some stability to views which were otherwise published in an ephemeral form as responses to occasions, and were not necessarily left behind when the occasions faded.

Of the two categories of contributors to the Society Hutton was regarded by fellow Wordsworthians as one of the metaphysicians. The Dean of Salisbury gave a paper to the Society on 'Wordsworth's

---

[32] *Transactions of the Wordsworth Society Nos. 1–8*, reprinted facsimile, 2 vols. (London, 1966), i, No. 1, p. 4.

Position as an Ethical Teacher' in which he referred to 'the refined and subtle teachings of Mr. R. H. Hutton', quoting Hutton's opinion (or 'teaching') that: 'Wordsworth alone, of all the great men of that day, had seen the light of the countenance of God, shining clear into the face of duty.' One can imagine the preaching style of address, a relic of his days as a Unitarian lay preacher, which Hutton must have employed in order to leave this kind of impression. The Dean's subsequent comments are worth quoting:

I am inclined to think that as the world grows older, a still greater value will attach to the ethical qualities of Wordsworth's verse. Whatever science may achieve, there will still be the stern whisper of a voice saying 'thy duty do', and men, sated with the feverish poetry of emotion and sensation, will return to the sterner and more barren heights of 'verse that builds a princely throne on humble truth'. Again and again, as we all know, throughout Wordsworth's poetry the outward picture is nothing to the poet unless it be connected with the freedom of duty, and the hope of immortality . . . I for one am still loathe to believe that the hour of Wordsworth's empire as an ethical teacher and as a great poet is coming to an end.[33]

It is not easy to see how the writer (or speaker—since the difference may be important) progressed from the first sentence here, stating that the reputation of Wordsworth as a teacher is secure, to the last sentence, stating his reluctance to believe that Wordsworth's reputation is not secure. He seems to be writing from a position which is under attack, appealing to an audience whose bond of sympathy ('Again and again, as we all know . . .') could be interpreted as reactionary prejudice. Implicitly, the Society seems to represent a collective resistance to certain tendencies, and especially to that 'great wave of scepticism' which Hutton referred to while writing on George Eliot. As in that piece, the writer appeals to a future time when the world has 'grown older', but the resisted tendencies are implicitly detailed. These are, in the first place, literary—Swinburnian 'feverish poetry'; in the second place, scientific—poetry is opposed to 'whatever science may achieve' and the phrase 'as the world grows older' sounds like a post-Darwinian catch-phrase with which the stability of ethics is contrasted; and in the third place, political—the refusal to believe, in 1883, that 'the hour of Words-

[33] Ibid., i, No. 5, p. 42.

worth's empire . . . is coming to an end' can hardly be divorced from events in the real Empire.[34]

The most important role of the Society, however, was as a counter force to the pressures of secularization, an anti-materialist force whose most intelligent spokesman was Aubrey de Vere. De Vere wrote on the 'true self' of Wordsworth's poetry, which is not a secular or 'occasional' self:

It is not a single faculty of the mind that originates a true poem, though the imagination is specially needed for that end: it is the whole mind, and not the mind only, but the whole moral and emotional being, including those antecedent habits and experiences which fitted that being for its task. In this respect the highest poetry has some analogy to religious faith. . . . It is in his higher poetry that Wordsworth is most eminently himself. Whatever he looks at he looks at in a way special to him. When he contemplates Nature it is as the mystic of old perused the page of Holy Writ—making little of the letter, but passing through it to the 'spiritual interpretation'.[35]

We might take this as a summary of the Society's notion of imagination and poetry, though its importance to this discussion lies in the survival of ideas implicit in Hutton's 1857 essay and in the implicit opposition to arguments put by Arnold and Stephen. Thus Hutton's interest in 'higher' poetry which refers to something other than itself has become a vague mysticism, while De Vere has attempted to invert Arnold's assertion that religious faith has some analogy to poetry, or that religious language *is* 'high' poetry. Sin.ilarly, Stephen's belief that Wordsworth reminds him that he is 'part of a greater whole' is countered by a defensive individualism ('most eminently himself', 'in a way special to him'). De Vere's thinking is marked by a High Anglican religiosity, as many of the contributors' essays are. Newman is frequently invoked, and religion is offered as literary criticism, making little of the letter, but passing

---

[34] The piece in question was written after a period of unprecedented imperialist activity, from the partitions under the European Congress in 1878 to the invasion of Egypt in 1882, with the attacks on imperial policy by Gladstone during his Midlothian campaign undimmed by his own government's adventures in the Transvaal, Afghanistan, and the Sudan. This, though, only establishes a climate for the remarks and the political content is left implicit. I have only come across one occasion in the *Transactions* when political considerations came to the surface. During the final annual meeting in 1886, Lord Selbourne seemed suddenly to realize a potential meaning of the 'bond of sympathy' and assured members: 'I do not say this in any socialist sense, but I say it in the sense of a man sympathizing with his fellow-men.'

[35] *Transactions*, i, No. 5, pp. 13–15.

through it to the 'spiritual interpretation'. This religiosity is then read back into the poetry: if Wordsworth is thought to have read Nature like Holy Writ it is because his poetry is given such status. The weakness of such an argument as De Vere's is that it relies upon analogy and justifies this reliance in literary criticism by implying that literature is itself analogical and hence open to 'spiritual interpretation'.

The nature of this argument allowed most members of the Society to avoid uniting general discussion with detailed elaboration, although we do find some such discussion in a paper given by the poet and critic Roden Noel entitled 'On the Poetic Interpretation of Nature, with Examples Taken Chiefly from Wordsworth'. Noel writes:

The outer world is but symbol and parable, the imperfect self-manifestation to our defective apprehension of eternal Ideas, which are substantial. That is a truth familiar to mystics of all ages, and in recent times has been virtually restated by two notable teachers, one a man of science, James Hinton, the other a theologian, Cardinal Newman. . . . A true poet is ever a loving and faithful observer of the external features and deportment of his mistress [i.e. of Nature]. But because his look is the long look of the lover, no passing glance, he sees more than that. Real feeling, I hold, must put us into some vital relation with the actuality of things, though the expression of it may be but a striving to body forth the truth about them. . . . When Keats, in describing the slow movement of spent shredding foam along the back of a heavy wave, characterises it by the phrase 'wayward indolence', he fixes and determines the idiosyncrasy of this movement in a manner simply impossible to a poet who should either fail to perceive, or else resolve not to allow himself the language of analogy. There is some occult identity between spent foam and our 'wayward indolence'. . . . When Milton calls the boat that wrecked Lycidas:

> That fatal and perfidious bark,
> Built in the eclipse and rigg'd with curses dark,
> That sunk so low that sacred head of thine,

how unliteral, inaccurate, and true to the inmost fact is he! 'Stone him with hardened hearts, harder than stones', says Shakespeare. Stones are hard because hearts are, not hearts hard because stones are, though that is not the common opinion. To arrive at the true spiritual order, you must reverse the order of experience.[36]

[36] Ibid., i, No. 6, pp. 32–5.

The passage is notable not only for what it says but also for the confidence, even dogmatism, with which it is said and with which its terms are assumed to be acceptable. Noel has taken to the extreme the notion, first asserted, as Caird wrote, by Hutton, that Wordsworth is concerned with the reverse side of common opinion and common emotion, in order to argue that all poetry deals with the real nature of things ('the actuality of things') of which the world is merely a sign. The notion seems shared by the majority of writers in the Society's records and the general readership they represent. There is clearly something comforting and consoling in the thought that a changing and secular material world is not the 'real' one, that a body of men bound by a 'bond of sympathy' have a private access to 'the inmost fact'. The position represented by Noel asserts that the unliteral nature of poetic language is a measure of its truth. The vocabulary of Noel's piece is not unlike that of Hutton's much earlier essay on Wordsworthian spiritual strength which reversed the order of his experience, but Noel is attempting to put Wordsworth to some general consolatory use, while Hutton wanted to illustrate his spiritual strength for its own sake. That is to say, Hutton is moved by Wordsworth's power to retain and control his own emotions regardless of the material cause of them. Noel uses Wordsworth, and poetry in general, as evidence for a criticism of the acceptability of material causes. Hutton is interested in the use of experience, Noel in the use of poetry.

Noel's consolatory use of Wordsworth becomes clearer if we look more closely at the other writer to whom he refers in addition to Newman. He suggests that Newman and James Hinton had restated the mystical view of life for his time. Hinton's best book, *The Mystery of Pain: A Book for the Sorrowful*, was first published in 1866 and R. H. Hutton is credited, probably wrongly, with having written the Introduction to the second edition. However, as Hutton felt that Wordsworth had sunk a 'deeper sounding line' than any other writer 'into the fathomless secret of the mystery of suffering', the book's subject was clearly one to demand his attention.[37]

More importantly, the subject of the book is the same as that of Hutton's 1857 essay, the transmutation of one emotion into another. Consolation, says Hinton, can come from any unexpected

37 'Mr. Ruskin on Wordsworth', *Spectator*, 7 Aug. 1880, 1002–3.

quarter 'to transmute our life, and make its dark threads trans-lucent', though this does not 'alter the nature of things, or invert the essential relation of pleasure and pain'. He goes on to say: 'Pain may be removed passively by the removal of its cause. . . . But it may also be removed actively, positively; not by the absence of the cause, nor by diminished feeling, but by a new and added power, which shall turn it into joy—a joy like God's.'[38] Noel has misread Hinton to find in him an inversion of the nature of things, but Hutton goes further than Hinton in not only 'preferring' the active removal of pain, but in further believing that pain cannot be 'removed by the removal of its cause'. Hutton found in Words-worth one who had the 'spiritual courage', as he calls it, to admit that emotions survive the removal of their causes and have a life independent of them. Hutton, in fact, would seem to be closer to Hinton than Noel, and not only in terminology. For if most of the writers contributing to the Wordsworth Society looked to Words-worth for consolation or a distraction, at best, and a numbness at worst, Hutton looks to Wordsworth for the active, positive hand-ling of heightened states of feeling. Hence the 'inmost fact', which is the subject of Hutton's 1882 paper to the Society, is the status of Wordsworth's delineations of feeling and their trustworthiness.

(ii) Hutton's restoration of Wordsworth

The second of Hutton's major studies of Wordsworth, entitled 'Wordsworth's Two Styles', was read to the Wordsworth Society in May 1882, published in the *Modern Review* for July 1882, and republished in the Society's *Wordsworthiana* in 1889. His study is primarily stylistic, drawing on comparative readings of Words-worth's early and later poetry, but is also an answer to Arnold's argument that Wordsworth had no 'assured poetic style of his own'. Hutton argues that Wordsworth had two styles, that of his youth and that of his age, which were used to the same effect (to 'restore the truth to feeling') but by different means and using dif-ferent resources.

The chief differences between the two styles, Hutton argues, are, first, that 'objective fact' plays a larger part in the earlier; second, that the earlier has a 'pure elasticity' which is unique in poetry; and third, that in the best poems of the earlier phase emotion is sug-

---

[38] James Hinton, *The Mystery of Pain* (London, 1886), 6, 9.

gested rather than expressed, that is 'expressed by reticence, by the jealous parsimony of a half-voluntary, half-involuntary reserve'.[39] The third category clearly develops Hutton's notion of Wordsworth's 'spiritual frugality' first expressed twenty-five years earlier. His comparison of Wordsworth's early and later work seems undertaken almost as a comparison of Hutton's own earlier and later opinion, and just as 'The Fountain' was his example in 1857, so it is again in 1882, but this time compared with Wordsworth's revision of it. Hutton quotes the stanzas immediately following the ones he had previously cited, where the Friend reproves Matthew for his 'complaint':

> Now both himself and me he wrongs,
>   The man who thus complains!
> I live and sing my idle songs
>   Upon these happy plains;
>
> 'And, Matthew, for thy children dead
>   I'll be a son to thee!'
> At this, he grasped his hands, and said,
>   'Alas! that cannot be.'

Hutton compares the last two lines with those with which Wordsworth replaced them in later editions, a revision which Arnold included in his popular selection from Wordsworth (1879):

> At this he grasped my hand, and said,
>   'Alas! that cannot be.'

Hutton comments on the significance of the variation from 'grasped his hands' to 'grasped my hand' as follows:

The earlier reading looks like hard fact, and no doubt sounds a little rough and abrupt. But I feel pretty sure, not only that the earlier reading expressed the truth as it was present to Wordsworth's inner eye when he wrote the poem, but that it agreed better with the mood of those earlier years, when the old man's wringing of his own hands, in a sort of passion of protest against the notion that anyone could take the place of his lost child, would have seemed much more natural and dignified to Wordsworth, than the mere kindly expression of grateful feeling for which he subsequently exchanged it.[40]

---

39 'Wordsworth's Two Styles', *Modern Review*, 3 (July 1882), 525–38 (p. 528).
40 Ibid., pp. 529–30.

The barely restrained disgust at the revision derives from a feeling that more than mere words have been changed, as if the grief of the old man in the thought that his lost child cannot be replaced is weakened by the ease with which its expression *is* replaced. The earlier poem refuses consolation, resists the consoling drift of the emotions to which the later version gives in, and having given in, colludes with the forces of influence and convention. It is Hutton's aim in the paper to resist the attempts to translate Wordsworth comfortably into the 1880s, even though his language, as I have already attempted to demonstrate, may betray him into the contemporary. Matthew's wringing of his own hands, though it is 'a hard fact' in many senses, is for Hutton a measure of Wordsworth's independent 'spiritual frugality', an independence which is given up by Matthew's grasping at the Friend's hand, not in that it asks for aid, but in that it gestures toward the lower moral order of gratitude. In 1857 Hutton had called Wordsworth 'a miser in his reluctance to trench upon the spiritual capital at his disposal . . . he hoarded his joys, and lived upon the interest they paid in the form of hope and expectation'.[41] In 1882 he called Wordsworth's revision not a change but an exchange because it seemed to represent for him a wasting of that capital (the sort of wastage Leslie Stephen saw Wordsworth warning against).

Hutton's resentment of poetic wastage must be seen in the general context of his distrust of over-expression or premature expression in society and literature. In 1887 he wrote of 'the very great and increasing facilities for literary expression, which prevent anything like large reserves of feeling and thought from accumulating till they acquire sufficient mass to produce individual effects'.[42] The press, and especially the periodical press, was seen as attenuating and diffusing what should have been a reservoir of literary feeling. It is important that Hutton chose to write about the exchange of an expression of grief for an expression of gratitude. He seems to find particular power in the conscious, almost ascetic refusal to allow too much force to be spent in exchanges with other men: thus 'Simon Lee' would have shown him that to receive gratitude was as painful as bearing ingratitude. Comparing the poem beginning 'I wandered lonely as a cloud' with the much later 'The Primrose of the Rock', Hutton concluded that the poet expresses

[41] *Literary Essays* (1896), p. 92.
[42] 'The Storing of Literary Power', *Spectator*, 12 May 1887, 594.

himself 'in reflective gratitude' in the second poem for perceptions which the earlier poem draws upon but leaves opaque.[43] It is the opacity and suggestiveness which Hutton seems to admire.

Though Hutton argued that 'objective fact' played a larger part in Wordsworth's earlier poems, he criticizes the realism of the later work and Wordsworth's attempt to give a full account of himself. In 'The Fountain' we might say that the words 'he clasped his hands' is an external detail, an objective fact, before it is understood. The expression is in advance of our ability to understand or 'mean' it: these are 'real words'. The words 'he clasped my hand', however, is a result of conscious reflection: it is a cliché of unreal words. This expression is derived from habitual use, and as Hutton wrote: 'the use to which we ought to turn our words is to remind us of the great realities of life, and when they fail to do so it is simply from the narcotic influence of habitual use'.[44] This narcotic use was welcomed by some Wordsworthians, and they are the ones who do not qualitatively discriminate between Wordsworth's poems.

Hutton's discussion of Wordsworth's revisions culminates in his comparison of 'Yarrow Unvisited' with 'Yarrow Revisited'. The earlier poem, he feels, is more powerful because it attempts to express thought without employing the material world as a support, but rather 'depreciates reality' in favour of the imagined. The subject of the poem, he suggests, is the faculty which expresses by reticence:

The poem may be said to have for its very subject the economy of imaginative force, the wantonness of poetic prodigality, the duty of retaining in the heart reserves of potential and meditative joy, on which you refuse to draw all you might draw of actual delight. . . . And the style corresponds to the thought; it is the style of one who exults in holding-over, and in being strong and buoyant enough to hold-over, a promised imaginative joy. A certain ascetic radiance,—if the paradox be permissible,—a manly jubilation in being rich enough to sacrifice an expected delight, makes the style sinewy, rapid and youthful, and yet careful in its youthfulness, as jealous of redundancy as it is firm and elastic.[45]

To hold-over a joy is to save rather than spend it, but also to refuse the replacement of infinite possibility by particular fact. This refusal is seen elsewhere, in Hardy and Proust, for instance, as a

---

[43] *Modern Review*, 3 (July 1882), 531–2.
[44] 'The Use of Paradox', *Spectator*, 30 June 1888, 881.
[45] *Modern Review*, 3 (July 1882), 533.

Romantic vice. Hutton mediates between the position Hardy took and that which Arnold took in 'Stanzas on the Grande Chartreuse', where he expresses his desire for an 'ascetic radiance'.

Hutton's reading of 'Yarrow Revisited' depends almost entirely upon the belief that expression can be identified with intention: 'the expression', says Hutton, 'is richer, freer, more mellow; but the reserve force is spent; all the wealth of the moment—and perhaps something more than the wealth of the moment, something which was not wealth, though mistaken for it—was poured out.'[46] A great deal seems to rest on that 'perhaps something more' which takes Hutton away from mere textual exposition. He seems to find in the later work and its undeniable Keatsian lingering over colour and feeling, a desire on Wordsworth's part to compensate for the simplicity and what Hutton calls the 'buoyancy' of the earlier. We can recall that those qualities of richness and freedom ('the expression is richer, freer, more mellow') were first attributed to Wordsworth in Hutton's own earlier work, but here they are used to indicate aesthetic means and not spiritual ends. The whole point of this series of comparisons is to restore what Hutton sees as the spiritual truth of Wordsworth's first thoughts about subjects he returned to. Hutton is also affirming his continuity with his own earlier work: the belief that Wordsworth got 'nearer to the reality of such life as he understood' than any other poet has to be reaffirmed in the face of attempts to turn him into a mystic whose truths are immaterial and general.

Conclusion

In 1887 John Hogben, who was to write a biographical monograph on Hutton, published an essay on 'The Mystical Side of Wordsworth' in the *National Review*. Hutton took up the essay in an article and argued that what seems like mysticism in Wordsworth could be shown to be analogous to common sense. It should be remembered that Newman had already described the action of the Illative Sense as analogous to common sense. Hutton wrote:

Where Wordsworth is most mystical, good sense itself . . . is almost identical in its assumptions, though instead of setting out in full the path by which these assumptions are reached, good sense is apt to lead to a conclusion

---

[46] Ibid., pp. 534–5.

without much attention to the . . . mystical reasoning. . . . Wordsworth relied on the conclusions to which his own mind came in what may be called a kind of mental somnambulism, a mood in which the senses seemed to be laid asleep, while *some higher faculty* was all the surer and more penetrating in its judgements on account of that partial sleep of the perceptive powers.[47]

This higher faculty is the Illative Sense, Hutton's fusion of Newman's Implicit Reason, which travels without 'setting out in full the path', and Ruskin's Penetrative Imagination. Moreover, he applies this mystical good sense, as Newman does, to everyday life: 'we are apt to catch our truest and most really informing vision of the deeper aspects of the things around us, in the *least* studied of our glances.'

This is what Wordsworth seemed to mean to the readership with which I have been concerned: he consoled them that self-consciousness was not necessary for wisdom, that truth might be attained by intimations, and that life, which was a series of episodic 'occasions', could provide material for a rich inward life.

Significantly, one of the last articles Hutton wrote, a piece on 'Self-Consciousness in Poetry' published in June 1897, assures his readers that Wordsworth is seldom self-conscious. Individual self-consciousness is fatal, he says, while trust in the higher faculty of intuition is capable of 'bringing out the characteristics of human nature at large'.[48] It was precisely 'enlargement' which Hutton saw as the function of literature, and which he saw most fully fulfilled by Wordsworth.

Tennyson as the poet of the age

When Hutton published the first of his two major essays on Wordsworth in the *National Review* in 1857 it might be said to have been written as an alternative to an essay on Tennyson. It was produced without any particular occasion for an essay on Wordsworth; it was published, however, two years after William Roscoe's *National*

---

[47] 'The Mystical Side of Good Sense', *Spectator*, 6 Aug. 1887, 1051.

[48] 'Self-Consciousness in Poetry', *Spectator*, 12 June 1897, 831–2. See also Hutton's comment that Dorothy Wordsworth's *Journal* showed no sign of 'the conscious seeker after aesthetic feelings' ('Dorothy Wordsworth's Scotch Journal', *Spectator*, 1 Aug. 1874, 980). The author implicitly contrasted with Wordsworth is Dickens, whose characters, Hutton thought, were the products of a highly self-conscious mind.

Review study of Tennyson and two years before Walter Bagehot's (so according to the pattern one can observe in the treatment of other subjects, one might expect each of the three writers, the journal's editors, to have written his piece). The comparison between Wordsworth and Tennyson in Hutton's essay on the grounds of each poet's treatment of grief is made at the expense of the very poem, *In Memoriam*, which was popularly turned to for solace, for the transmutation of pain which Hutton finds in Wordsworth.[49] Hutton seemed to find it difficult to write about Tennyson because of the close identification of the poet with a specific time, a particular generation. He seems reluctant to use the terms of moral obligation in which he can describe Wordsworth's poetry since for Hutton much of Tennyson's poetry is written in response to occasions, or to the force of circumstances which are temporary. He felt the opacity of Wordsworth's lyrics was deliberate and purposeful, but that Tennyson's opacity was evidence of an inability to control a language ill-adapted to poetry. He felt that Wordsworth's resistance to his own emotions was the basis for moral lessons, but that the 'tone' of the emotions studied by Tennyson sometimes risked becoming anachronistic.[50] His was not a temperament in advance of the meaning of its expressions, as was Wordsworth's in writing 'he clasped his hands'.

However, in his obituary on Tennyson Hutton explained the special debt he owed the poet:

Those who, in 1842, when Tennyson's first important poems were published, were just old enough to love poetry, and yet young enough to have no prepossessions or prejudices against poetry of a new type, probably owe more to the great poet who is just dead, than either his own contemporaries, whose taste in poetry was formed before his poems were published, or those younger generations which have grown up to find Tennyson's fame well established and taken for granted by the whole world around

---

[49] The essays by Roscoe and Bagehot are: W. C. Roscoe, 'Tennyson's *Maud*', *National Review*, 1 (Oct. 1855), 377–410, and Walter Bagehot, 'Tennyson's *Idylls*', *National Review*, 9 (Oct. 1859), 368–94. On the transmuting effect of *In Memoriam* see, for example, a comment in the *Athenaeum* in 1851: 'In its moral scope the book will endear itself to all by its vivid appreciation of all their grief and by its transmutation of that grief into patience and hope' (cited by Shannon, op. cit., pp. 143–4).

[50] Voicing the concern with 'the lasting' in literature (see above, note 21), Hutton wrote that 'Locksley Hall' would, among others, 'undoubtedly pass away with the generation in whose tone of sentiment they are somewhat minute studies' (*Spectator*, 1 May 1869, 536).

them. . . . Those who were growing up, but not yet grown up, in 1842, can hardly know how much of their ideal of life they owe to Tennyson, and how much to the innate bias of their own character. They only know that they owe him very much of the imaginative scenery of their own minds, much of their insight into the doubts and faith of their own contemporaries, much of their political preference for 'ordered freedom', and much, too, of their fastidious discrimination between the various notes of tender and pathetic song.[51]

Hutton himself was sixteen years old in 1842 during this hiatus in Tennyson's reputation, and the obituary draws uncharacteristically on his autobiographical recollections, though characteristically only implicitly. The influence attributed to Tennyson seems very considerable, though it is limited here to providing adolescent moulds of thought, mental 'scenery'—the kind of scenery the next generation would recall having found in Dickens. Tennyson provided a purchase, Hutton claims, on some of the thought and poetry of his own contemporaries but left vague the precise obligations under which this readership was put. Hutton's generation of readers, he goes on to say, 'will find some difficulty in determining what it is that Tennyson has most effectually taught them to enjoy and dread, where he has enlarged to most purpose the range of their love and reverence, and stimulated most powerfully their recoil from ugliness and evil.' The important terms here are not only the moral absolutes, but 'effect' and 'purpose', because the question is whether Tennyson's provision of an additional influence to the 'innate bias' of the reader was no more than the 'innate bias' of his own character. Thus the question is, whether Tennyson's writing had an importance, an intended and purposeful importance, beyond the expression of the tendencies of his character and the character of the age? For one's 'innate bias' is a circumstance, not one's 'deep self'.

The generation to which Hutton is addressing himself in the obituary tended to deny, with Swinburne, the association of literature and ethical intention, or to answer that a poet so strongly identified with the life of an age will also be identified with its death. J. M. Robertson, for instance, though attacking Swinburne's criticisms of Tennyson's *Idylls*, suggested in his *Essays Towards a Critical Method* (1889), adopting the fashionable terminology of evolutionary change, that the *Idylls* in particular had 'diverged on a

---

[51] 'The Genius of Tennyson', *Spectator*, 15 Oct. 1892, 522.

line of impermanent variation'.[52] Though Robertson, it would seem, is thinking of a dying genre, as one of a generation of writers whose distinctions between poetry and prose were more distinct and considered than those suggested by writers of Hutton's generation, nevertheless this question of the possible redundancy of writers continued to be raised in the last decade of the nineteenth century.[53] From his earliest articles on Tennyson, however, Hutton distrusted the criteria which judged a poet to be of only temporary meaning. 'Have we', he wrote in 1869, 'any artifice by which we can relieve ourselves from the pressure of the present, and judge the greatest products of our literature by a standard wider than that of our immediate sympathies and slowly engendered tastes?'[54]

Hutton's theoretical answer to his own question is negative, though in practice his studies of Tennyson are in marked contrast to other studies for their refusal to appropriate Tennyson to the 'times'. Moreover, by the time the *Spectator* article was published, in the late 1860s and 1870s, it had become something of a cliché to identify Tennyson with the age: indeed Alfred Austin, in the essay which Hutton's article reviews, turns the identification to Tennyson's disadvantage.[55] The first example of Hutton's practice in writing on Tennyson is, however, taken from the decade before this, the 1850s, when the generation influenced as Hutton describes are just coming to the fore.

Tennysonian 'resistance': 'Tears, idle tears'

The terms of Hutton's discussion of Wordsworth in 1857, in which he compares Wordsworth with Tennyson, are, as I argued above,

[52] J. M. Robertson, 'The Art of Tennyson', *Essays Towards a Critical Method* (London, 1889), 233–82 (p. 277). Robertson is discussing Dickens's comment that he read the *Idylls* 'with the blessedness of reading a man who could write'. Robertson comments: 'The whole question between those of us who sum up against the *Idylls* and those who adhere to Dickens's position, is whether the poet's art here . . . has moved on the lines of healthy evolution, or has diverged on a line of impermanent variation; whether, in short, these poems, pleasant as they may have been to the sophisticated palate of the generation now passing away, will be pronounced a success a generation or more hence' (pp. 276–7).

[53] See above, nn. 21 and 50.

[54] 'Weighing Tennyson', *Spectator*, 1 May 1869, 535.

[55] Austin wrote: 'He thinks with us of this particular day, feels with us of this day, and is the exponent of such poetical feelings as in this day we are capable of. But as far as poetry is concerned we and our day are not great but little.' *The Poetry of the Period* (London, 1870), 30–1.

implicitly concerned with contemporary issues, especially with the resistance to and significance of secularization, even if the 'scenery' is provided by Wordsworth and Tennyson. Most writing on Tennyson, though, concerned itself with explicitly appropriating the poetry to the age and its specific causes. Charles Kingsley gushingly described Tennyson in 1850 as 'the champion of an orthodoxy' which 'justifies and consecrates the aesthetics and philosophy of the present age'.[56]

It seems to have been necessary to make such inflated claims for writers in an attempt to lift them out of the class of occasional literature and to relieve them 'from the pressure of the present'. As I have already observed, this pressure was increased by the dramatic growth in the periodical press. This both increased and fragmented literary productions so that Hutton feared it would attenuate powerful and lasting efforts.

After the lifting of the Stamp Duty in 1857, the number of journals catering for specialist causes rose steeply and editors were quick to presume the support of reputable writers such as Tennyson.[57] An unidentified writer in *Meliora* (the journal for meliorists) claimed, in a long and irrational diatribe against Feuerbach and Max Stirner, that Tennyson represented a resistance to 'the race's' progress towards 'scepticism and suicide', and that he taught 'that knowledge and belief coalesce in lucid union'.[58] Not quite part of this esoteric extreme, but still representative of the appropriation of Tennyson in the non-newspaper periodical press, Gerald Massey, an active Chartist (who made his name much later writing imperialist lyrics) claimed in *Hogg's Instructor* that Tennyson represented contemporary poetry as 'a continual protest against the pressure of tendencies adverse to the full and free human development . . . fighting a continual fight with all kinds of scepticism and mammonism, which seeks to encroach on her [i.e. Poetry's] fields, and commons, and woodpaths, and holy consecrated ground.'[59] One might have expected the name of Wordsworth to have been invoked to support this reactionary sentimental pastoralism (indeed the tone

56 'Tennyson', *Fraser's Magazine*, 42 (Sept. 1850), 245–55 (p. 245).
57 In London alone, an astonishing 115 periodicals were *started* in 1859 (see J. W. Saunders, *The Profession of English Letters* (London, 1964), 200).
58 'Tennyson and His Poetry', *Meliora*, 7 (Oct. 1859), 225–48 (pp. 242–3).
59 'The Poetry of Alfred Tennyson', *Hogg's Instructor*, 5 (July 1855), 1–14, (p. 3).

is reminiscent of the aged Wordsworth's protests against railways), but the appeal to Tennyson is more immediate and convenient.

In the light of the use to which Tennyson's poetry was put Hutton's claim that he provided a generation with its mental scenery and political preferences does not seem as absurd as it might at first sight. In invoking Tennyson as the 'new', writers almost invariably looked upon Wordsworth as the representative of the 'old': the fashionable description of Tennyson in the mid-1850s was as 'a drawing-room Wordsworth'.[60] When Edward Caird and the members of the Wordsworth Society write of Wordsworth opening up a new 'domain', they are contributing to a tradition which saw Tennyson as the poet who reflected the more immediate. So William Roscoe, in the *National Review* essay which preceded Hutton's, found in Tennyson 'the free, *insouciant* demeanour characteristic of modern society. . . . His Muse, if she met and liked you, would drop the Mr. from your name after ten minutes' conversation.'[61] The analogy seems to derive not so much from a sense of its appropriateness as from Roscoe's sense of being on familiar terms with the poetry and his knowledge that his audience share that familiarity. The emotions of *In Memoriam*, in particular, are too familiar to Roscoe:

The things we have really suffered are no poetry for us; they are the things from which we seek refuge in poetry. The questionings, the cries of *In Memoriam* touch us too close—they wring us. The spiritual world is too real for us; we fly to the material—

> The floods, the fields, the mountains,
> The shapes of sky and plain.

Nature is our solace; and we fall back on Wordsworth with that sort of quiet confidence with which the entrance of the calm, gentle, self-reliant physician inspires the fevered sufferer.[62]

Roscoe would seem to have laid the basis for Hutton's more sophisticated account of why Wordsworth's poetry might seem more consolatory than Tennyson's, without the naive pastoralism.

---

[60] See Walter Bagehot, 'Tennyson's *Idylls*', *National Review*, 9 (Oct. 1859), 368–94 (p. 391). Bagehot wrote: 'Mr. Tennyson has given some accounts of the more refined and secondary passions in Wordsworth's intense manner which are not inadmissable in a luxurious drawing-room.'

[61] 'Tennyson's *Maud*', *National Review*, 1 (Oct. 1855), 377–410 (p. 378).

[62] Ibid., pp. 388–9.

Hutton compares Wordsworth's 'The Fountain' with Tennyson's lyric beginning 'Tears, idle tears':

> Tears, idle tears, I know not what they mean,
> Tears from the depth of some divine despair
> Rise in the heart, and gather to the eyes,
> In looking on the happy Autumn-fields,
> And thinking of the days that are no more.

Hutton chooses this point of comparison because, as he argues, both poets begin at the same emotional starting point, 'picturing the profound unspeakable sadness with which we survey the irrecoverable past'.[63] The difference, to Hutton, lies in Tennyson's continuing in the same emotion in the lyric, not turning his tears to account in resisting the emotion, but leaving them 'idle'. Hutton seems to have taken 'I know not what they mean' and 'thinking of the days that are no more' literally and weighed them against Wordsworth's meaning and thinking, which Hutton (*pace* Arnold) thought considerable. However, Hutton felt that in his more thoughtful poems, such as *In Memoriam* or 'The Two Voices', Tennyson entered Wordsworth's domain in employing the spiritual imagination to illuminate the moods of human emotion.[64] The implication is that Tennyson attempted the reverse, to illuminate the spiritual imagination ('some divine despair') through a human emotion—what Roscoe meant when he said that Tennyson made the spiritual too real. Yet here Hutton's assumption that the imagination is a means of thinking, and that therefore poetry is embodied thought, leads him to misread Tennyson, to disregard, that is, the 'strangeness' of the sense that the feeling of loss is endlessly recurrent even as the mind recognizes that the cause of the feeling can never return. There seems to be no 'meaning' to that virtual paradox. The lyric's 'meaning' is self-contained and implicit, yet public and familiar. Its language is defined only by the single emotion of grief and its subsidiary, regret, yet at the same time almost self-consciously 'poetical' ('Fresh as the first beam', 'The earliest pipe', 'by hopeless fancy feign'd'). The analogies and images in the lyric take a form which promises to clarify the poet's feelings, but serves only to intensify them, so that natural objects seem to enter into the scope of the lyric for Tennyson only to measure his distance from them.

---

[63] 'William Wordsworth', *National Review*, 4 (Jan. 1857), 1–30 (p. 9).
[64] Ibid., p. 10.

Hutton appreciates the element of measuring in Tennyson, but he continues to look for a Wordsworthian control of experiences which can be recognized. He writes in a later study of Tennyson that 'Tears, idle tears' is an authentic account of grief and regret ('does not the memory of those days both bring and take away? does it not restore to us the vivid joy of the past only to make us feel that it is vanished?') and concludes: 'No poet has ever had a greater mastery than Tennyson over the power of real things to express evanescent emotions that almost defy expression.'[65] This seems to be where Hutton is too Wordsworthian: it would seem more true to say that Tennyson's power is exercised over keeping real things at a distance, that his uses of natural objects are not intended to bring his emotions closer, and that, anyway, grief and regret were for Tennyson 'real things' and not 'evanescent emotions'.

This misreading, as it seems to me, arises from or results in (it is difficult to say which) Hutton's belief, as he continues to write on Tennyson in the 1860s and 1870s, that the principal importance of the poetry was its attempt to express emotions which resisted expression, and his belief that the very medium in which Tennyson worked resisted the expression of emotion. He wrote in a study of Tennyson in 1872:

It is not want of motion, but rather excessive compression, which gives to so many of Tennyson's poems the air of moving through a resisting medium. There is nothing like 'still' life to be found in his poems. When he puts a half-understood emotion or a new natural fact under his poetic object-glass, it may occupy a larger space than it ever did in the poems of other poets, but that is only because the scale of life is really larger. No poet is less justly liable to the charge of making much of a little or of pottering over his poetic discoveries.[66]

The passage seems to be a further thought on Tennyson and Wordsworth: it was not 'want of motion' that produced the continuous emotion of 'Tears, idle tears', and at least Tennyson cannot be accused (as Clough, for instance, accused Wordsworth) of finding thoughts too deep for tears in wholly inappropriate objects. The clutter of scientific terminology in the passage, including the very phrase *resisting medium*, is fashionable but also reflects a recog-

[65] 'Tennyson', *Macmillan's Magazine*, 27 (Dec. 1872), 143–67, reprinted in *Literary Essays* (1896), 361–436 (p. 374).
[66] Ibid., p. 384.

nition of the importance of the sheer measurement of emotions in Tennyson's poetry, yet still Hutton cannot resist making Tennyson the poet of the age whose emotions are as magnified as the age is expansive: 'the scale of life is really much larger' (than in Wordsworth's day, the implication is). The scientific language also gives us one sense of a 'resisting medium', in that a literary society, especially one with a growing respect for literature in prose, could only justify poetry as a kind of science (hence Hutton's phrase 'poetic discoveries' and his insistence that poetry should contain knowledge). Alfred Austin, bringing Tennyson down to size by identifying him with the age, went on to claim: 'The age is scientific or it is nothing . . . now science and all its processes, its aims and methods alike, are antagonistic to poetry and its aims and methods.'[67] An attempt to describe poetry in scientific terms merely seemed to confirm the ascendency of science, just as the use of terms from psychology had the further effect of recalling the 'psychologizing' in prose fiction: readers were particularly sensitive to 'morbid' and 'hysterical', which Hutton frequently applied to Tennyson.[68]

The description of Tennyson's poetry moving through a resisting medium might seem more aptly applied to Hutton's critical vocabulary, but he does seem to have believed that not only was Tennyson's poetry resisted by parts of the educated classes, but that also the poetry is addressed to a society which cannot find an adequate language for its feelings. For Hutton is still using the phrase 'resisting medium' a decade later, in 1881. Tennyson, wrote Hutton, has a genius 'which requires a resisting medium to do it justice; and it is never nobler than where it gives the . . . impression that the poet is stemming the current of the age, and convinced that the age is all astray.'[69] The phrase which had been applied to Wordsworth ('he checks the current of his emotion') is here

[67] *The Poetry of the Period*, p. 31.

[68] George Brimley advised readers in 1855 'not to be frightened' of these two words, 'which may mean one thing or another, according to the sense, discrimination and sympathy of the man who applies them' (see 'Alfred Tennyson's Poems', in *Essays of Charles Brimley*, ed. W. G. Clark, third edition (London, 1882), 75). F. W. Myers complained in 1889 that the words were 'taking in the Positivist camp the place which the words 'dangerous' and 'unsound' have occupied for so long in orthodox polemics' ('Tennyson as Prophet', *Nineteenth Century*, 25 (Mar. 1889), 381–96 (p. 390)). The writings seem to reflect a fear that the critical vocabulary is becoming subjective and specialized.

[69] 'Mr. Tennyson's Poem on Despair', *Spectator*, 5 Nov. 1881, 1397.

virtually recycled ('stemming the current of the age'), though with much less confidence.

Hutton is less confident, perhaps because Tennyson is still writing, and has produced the post-1850 poems whose polish alone resists analysis. Yet he continues to find in Tennyson evidence of a deeper human nature struggling for and failing to find adequate expression. He writes of Tennyson's dramatic monologue *Despair*:

Such a verse as the following is not the outcome of despair, but of a very different thing,—the wish to find an adequate language for despair, in order that the victims of that despair may realise how much there is in their own souls which asserts or prophesies the falsehood of that language,—

> O we poor orphans of nothing—alone on that
>   lonely shore—
> Born of the ·brainless Nature who knew not that
>   which she bore!
> Trusting no longer that earthly flower would
>   be heavenly fruit—
> Come from the brute, poor souls—no souls—and
>   to die with the brute—[70]

Hutton does not pretend to admire this as poetry, but admires the position, the 'poetic attitude', behind it. Tennyson's despair is not the reversal of his own hope, not a Wordsworthian reversal, yet Hutton felt it was characteristic of Tennyson's poetry to attempt to express that which resisted expression, whether because it was not natural to the poet, because it was not socially fitted, or because the language itself seemed inadequate or unreal. This last category ought particularly to include those occasions when words seem self-sufficient, not only those when words seem insufficient, yet it is this self-sufficiency which seems to lead Hutton to distrust the authenticity of Tennyson's emotions when tested against the counter-claims of familiar reality and the experience of the reader. It is this definition of Tennyson's poetry as the outcome of a general wish to find an adequate language for resisting emotions, which I shall discuss next.

Tennysonian 'breakage': 'Break, break, break'

Hutton discusses Tennyson's lyric 'Break, break, break' in his 1872 study of the poet, a discussion we might take as representative of

[70] Ibid., p. 1398.

his concern with the poetry of Tennyson, and particularly with that
poetry as post-Wordsworthian.

> Break, break, break,
>   On thy cold gray stones, O Sea!
> And I would that my tongue could utter
>   The thoughts that arise in me.
>
> O well for the fisherman's boy,
>   That he shouts with his sister at play!
> O well for the sailor lad,
>   That he sings in his boat on the bay!
>
> And the stately ships go on
>   To their haven under the hill;
> But O for the touch of a vanished hand,
>   And the sound of a voice that is still!
>
> Break, break, break,
>   At the foot of thy crags, O Sea!
> But the tender grace of a day that is dead
>   Will never come back to me.

Observe how the wash of the sea on the cold gray stones is used to prepare
the mind for the feeling of helplessness with which the deeper emotions
break against the hard and rigid element of human speech; how the picture
is then widened out till you see the bay with children laughing on its shore,
and the sailor boy singing on its surface, and the stately ships passing on in
the offing to their unseen haven, all with the view of helping us to feel the
contrast between the satisfied and the unsatisfied yearnings of the human
heart . . . But then the song returns again to the helpless breaking of the sea
at the foot of crags it cannot climb, not this time to express the inadequacy
of human speech to express human yearnings, but the defeat of those very
yearnings themselves. Thus does Lord Tennyson turn an ordinary sea-shore
landscape into a means of finding a voice indescribably sweet for the dumb
spirit of human loss . . . No poet ever had a greater mastery than Tennyson
over the power of real things . . . to express evanescent emotions that
almost defy expression.[71]

All of Hutton's comments here seem intended to apply both to the
internal workings of the poem and to its external effect or influence, so that 'used to prepare the mind' refers not only to the
poem's movement from an expression of helplessness to the expression of the *source* of that feeling of helplessness, but also to the
poem's effect of preparing the mind of the reader for the helpless

[71] *Literary Essays* (1896), pp. 372–4.

inexpressibility of his own deeper emotions. This insistence that the reader is the object of the poem is Hutton's, and is part of an attempt to find the 'real' source of the sense of loss in the poem, a source which is not personal or biographical. Hutton attempts to make the loss expressed in the lyric more final, more 'hard and rigid' (as he describes the language) than it really is. If 'the contrast' is 'between the satisfied and the unsatisfied yearnings of the human heart', and if the corresponding contrast in the poem is between 'breaking' and 'returning', then the source of satisfaction, or at least consolation, in the poem would reside in the sense of breakage, in finality. Hutton finds the expression of breakage in the poem 'indescribably sweet', and attributes Tennyson with 'mastery over the power of real things to express evanescent emotions'. This is Hutton's whole interest in 'real things': he is not interested in the literal 'realism' of the poem. He would not point out, for instance, that what 'really' breaks cannot break again repeatedly, and hence he ignores the suppressed analogy with the broken human heart. Hutton in effect treats 'break' as if it were a transitive verb, supplying an object which is syntactically lost in the poem; the object being the 'unsatisfied yearning' which is defeated in Hutton's account.

The loss in the poem is the loss of an object of emotion, but the pain in the poem is the survival of feelings, the desolate sense that the word 'never' in the final line only refers to a sense of finality which the poet does not 'really' feel. Tennyson is expressing a failure to be over-burdened by a loss, while the lost object of emotion is displaced by tokens ('a vanished hand', 'the sound of a voice') and oblique memories ('a day that is dead') which provide a kind of comfort, though not a comfort which might be said to derive from the survival of the feelings for the object of passion.

In order to find this desolation 'indescribably sweet', Hutton has repressed his belief in the reality of the non-material sources of comfort to which he allows himself to refer with Tennysonian obliqueness ('no poet ever made the dumb speak'). He also represses the contrast with the Wordsworth who had taught him that 'the ebbing away of the brightest past is not so sad a thing as the weak yearning which, on departing, it often leaves stranded on the soul'.[72] Tennyson's stranded yearnings are treated as a real

---

[72] Ibid., p. 100.

alternative to the Wordsworthian refusal to displace the true sources of pain and comfort in the face of breakage which is total collapse (as in 'Michael'). Hutton struggles to avoid introducing the matter of the loss of belief, the great loss of the object of passion which Feuerbach tried to comfort by raising subjectivity to the lost status. Hutton restricts his comments to the literary results of Tennyson's surrender of the real object of his feelings, and thus pronounces the poet a literary success while leaving the impression that he was a moral failure. This is the opposite of his view of Scott and, indeed, Hutton's discussion of the lyric form has a restriction which he is freed from in discussing the narrative form.

Conclusion

Hutton's analysis of 'Break, break, break' in 1872 formed part of his defence of Tennyson against criticism by Swinburne. This defence was a contribution to a larger argument over the place of ethics in literature.[73]

Swinburne argued that morality has no place in art, and that Tennyson threw away the opportunity to produce a modern *Oresteia* in writing the *Idylls* because he omitted the incestuous origins of Mordred. Swinburne suggests that Tennyson pandered to conventional morality and thus spoiled the 'moral tone' of the poem. He uses the phrase 'moral tone' as one might use a term in describing a painting: the point is not the moral issue behind the work, but the effect of its design.[74]

Hutton felt that the Aristotelian notion of tragedy implied by this account no longer applied because the emotions of pity and fear were no longer representative of the age.[75] The tone of the lyric 'Break, break, break' seems to his regret more representative of the age than an Aristotelian version of the *Idylls* might have been: the burden of personal regret he finds more typical than tragic guilt or

---

[73] Hutton's essay discusses two works of Swinburne published in 1872: his essay on Hugo's *L'Année terrible* (*Fortnightly Review*, NS 12 (Sept. 1872), 243–67), and his *Under the Microscope*. Hutton's comments come as the culmination of a series of articles on Swinburne over successive years: 'Mr. Swinburne on His Critics', *Spectator*, 3 Nov. 1866, 1228–9; 'Mr. Swinburne As Critic', *Spectator*, 5 Oct. 1867, 1109–11; 'Mr. Swinburne's Essay on Blake', *Spectator*, 14 Mar. 1868, 320–2.

[74] A. C. Swinburne, *Under the Microscope*, reprinted in *Swinburne Replies*, ed. C. K. Hyder (Syracuse, 1966), 57. Swinburne felt that Tennyson achieved tragedy in the later 'Rizpah' (1880).

[75] *Literary Essays* (1896), pp. 396–407.

spiritual contrition, repetition more typical than sequential climax, and the doubt of any outcome more representative than the certainty of judgement. The loss mourned by Tennyson in the lyric is to Hutton not the death of Hallam, but the loss of an adequate response to suffering which might relieve it.

Hutton argued that in Wordsworth's poems his deep nature resisted his temperament and the circumstances of his time. Tennyson's poems, however, disclosed to Hutton a man whose temperament was stronger than his deep nature, whose feelings for the occasional buried his 'true self'. To Hutton, Tennyson's emotions expressed contemporary doubts which his real, Christian nature could not overcome, in spite of Tennyson's avowals of belief.

Hutton's view foreshadows that of T. S. Eliot, who thought Tennyson's feelings more honest than his mind: 'temperamentally', he wrote, 'he was opposed to the doctrine that he was moved to accept and to praise'.[76] It should not be surprising to find Hutton and Eliot, both High Church men of letters, in some agreement. Eliot felt that Tennyson expressed the mood of his age by accident, supplying a message of hope to the fading faith of his contemporaries while expressing a quite different mood of his own. Hutton, one of those contemporaries whose faith, in spite of everything, was not fading, felt that Tennyson would have been a moral success if he had resisted his own mood and had not colluded with the accidental.

Hutton felt that Tennyson's literary success lay in his resistance to cliché, and his sensitivity to language which did not collude with ready understanding. As Eliot said, Tennyson was 'capable of illumination which he was incapable of understanding'.[77] Similarly, it is likely that Tennyson would not have understood Hutton's illumination of his poetry.

Both Hutton and Eliot found Tennyson's best work in his lyrics. 'His delicate songs', wrote Hutton, 'dignify even the dramas in which he so often failed'. Putting it the other way, Eliot commented, 'for narrative, Tennyson had no gift at all'.[78]

The lyric, we might say, allows the poet to express a single, simple emotion in language which will necessarily belong both to

[76] T. S. Eliot, Introduction to *Poems of Tennyson* (1939), reprinted in *Selected Prose*, ed. John Hayward (London, 1953), 182–3.
[77] Ibid., p. 181.
[78] R. H. Hutton, 'What is a Lyric?', *Spectator*, 23 May 1896, 736; T. S. Eliot, *Selected Prose*, p. 178.

him and to the world but which may leave the connection between the world and the poet unexplored. The lyric's literary opposite is the novel.

The first part of *Middlemarch* and one of the final parts of the *Idylls*, 'The Last Tournament', were published in the same week in December 1871. This accident occasioned an article by Hutton on 'The Idealism of George Eliot and Mr. Tennyson', in which he argues that both works deal with the defeat of higher purpose and noble design by earthly circumstance.[79] In spite of the reassurance available in Tennyson, his idealism was to Hutton a mere secular hope—an attempt to find glory in worldly failure—while the idealism of George Eliot was more honest and thorough-going. Thus, despite his own temperament, Hutton admires George Eliot's 'escape from the limits of concrete detail', her other-worldliness. He believes her to be, like Wordsworth and Scott but unlike Tennyson, imposing her real nature on the complex world. He necessarily believes that this real nature is Christian, and so finds her novels Christian in spite of their author. Furthermore, it seems that only in the novel could George Eliot have provided a 'fit stage' for feelings which are higher and more general than those legitimately bred by the facts of the world.[80]

[79] 'The Idealism of George Eliot and Mr. Tennyson', *Spectator*, 2 Dec. 1871, 1458–60.
[80] 'George Eliot', *Spectator*, 1 Jan. 1881, 11.

6
George Eliot and the Novel

Hutton on the novel

HUTTON published what was probably his first article on a novelist in 1850 ('Puseyite Novels', *Prospective Review*, 6 (November 1850), 512–34) and his last in 1897 ('Sir Walter Scott', *Spectator*, 29 May 1897, 762–3), while between those dates he was publishing his views on novels regularly, even weekly. However, the first and last essays cover subjects in which Hutton was consistently interested: the relation of the novel, particularly the realistic novel, to ideas and theology, the function of ethical fiction in an age of secularized morality, and the standing in the hierarchy of major writers (in which Scott was placed very high by Hutton) of the contemporary novelist.

Hutton's articles on novels, which number around 1,500, were published mainly in the *Prospective Review*, the *Economist*, and the *National Review* before 1861, and thereafter mainly in the *Spectator*. Hutton rarely, unlike his publications on all other forms of writing, wrote lengthy essays on the novel for monthly journals or for books. The major exceptions are his book on Scott, contributed to John Morley's 'English Men of Letters' series, and his essays on George Eliot. The latter was an exception for Hutton partly because he thought her the major Victorian novelist, but also because he treats her both as a thinker and as a novelist. Hence his *Essays on Some of the Modern Guides of English Thought in Matters of Faith* contains chapters on Carlyle, Newman, Arnold, Maurice, and two on George Eliot.

In terms both of the number of articles and the number of words devoted by Hutton to the discussion of George Eliot, she is by far the most significant novelist in his criticism. Generally, though, the subjects of his articles are chosen by a combination of Hutton's taste and, since he is writing about books every week, by the dictates of the publishing trade. Thus the subject matter is largely contemporary, that is, mid- and late-Victorian, and is mainly English or American. Richardson, for example, is discussed only once at any length ('*Clarissa*', *Spectator*, 9 September 1865,

1005-7), and Bunyan only once (even this was, rather oddly, 'Bunyan's Use of Verse', *Spectator*, 14 December 1889, 840-2). Similarly, the only French novelist discussed in a whole article was Hugo (again, this is unexpectedly 'Victor Hugo's Philosophy', *Spectator*, 25 October 1862, 1193-5), and the only Russian is Turgenev (and then as if he were French: 'M. Turgenief's *Liza*', *Spectator*, 23 October 1869, 1242-3). However, Henry James is frequently discussed by Hutton, as is Hawthorne.

My own discussion of Hutton's writings on the novel draws on many of these articles, but I shall focus on his studies of George Eliot, both because she was the focus of his attention (and of ours) and because his general concern with less 'lasting' novelists is also represented there. I shall also compare Hutton's work with that of other critics, particularly with the writings of G. H. Lewes, Leslie Stephen, and W. H. Mallock.[1]

The importance of narrative fiction

The distinction I have made between the ephemeral productions of second-rate novelists and the lasting monuments of the 'great' novelists is not one of which Hutton would have approved. He was, as I have already noted, affected by the debate, in the last decades of the nineteenth century, as to which writers would 'last' and what posterity would make of them. Yet he also made a point of discussing works of literature, especially novels, which he knew would be dismissed and ignored by other contemporary critics.

I have already cited, in my first chapter, Hutton's 'manifesto' as editor of the *Spectator* in which he attacks the Arnoldian notion of 'greatness' and defends the study of the 'everyday literature' of 'ordinary Englishmen' and the appreciation of 'the ephemeral productions of a busy generation'.[2] Hutton's target is the leisured (not 'busy') man of letters like Arnold, who writes of and for a special class whose culture is European (not the 'ordinary Englishmen'). Hutton's is a literary equivalent of the interest in the everyday he admired in Wordsworth, and he finds the literary ideal

---

[1] The most reliable survey of the area to date is Kenneth Graham's *English Criticism of the Novel, 1865-1900* (Oxford, 1965). Richard Stang's *The Theory of the Novel in England, 1850-1870* is extremely unreliable, based as it is on many articles he has mis-attributed.

[2] *Spectator*, 29 June 1861, 697.

embodied in the novel. By 'everyday', Hutton does not mean to make a qualitative distinction: he is referring as much to Dinah Muloch as to George Eliot.

Hutton's interest in the novel was unusual in its depth even for the late nineteenth century. Perhaps only G. H. Lewes paid equally serious attention to the form and tried it by new standards.[3] The motives and criteria of even these two critics were, though, quite different. Unlike Hutton (as far as we know), G. H. Lewes tried his hand at writing novels, while as a critic he attempted to bring the novel into his general effort to decipher the laws of 'success' in all European literature. Hutton wrote about the novel because of its success, as he saw it, in mediating between the inflexible objectivity of dogmatic Christianity and the aestheticism of subjective secular ethics. For Hutton the novel provided what I called in my first chapter a 'narrative sense of selfhood' which secularization threatened to render unavailable. The novel was 'realistic', to use a term also discussed by G. H. Lewes, in allowing for the expression of man's 'true nature' by its very form.[4] The novel was therefore important to Hutton, as it was to Newman, as a means of telling the truth.

Hutton reported that the most frequent ordinary response to the realistic novel (he is discussing Trollope's 'brilliant daguerreotypes of superficial life') was: 'It is all so true!' He suggested, however, that the question in reply should have been: 'But to what is it all true?'.[5] Hutton is not asking if the novel is true to life, but whether it takes for granted implicit beliefs and loyalties. He is asking a specific version of the question 'Is it true?' which he felt a sceptical, secular generation would ask of all literature, from scripture to the novel. He gave warning of this sceptical readership, to which he belongs, in an 1855 article on Mrs Gaskell and Elizabeth Sewall:

There is a *special* necessity for the modern novelist to throw his art into the plot as well as into the characters. . . . The more faithfully he delineates the ordinary tone and manners of cultivated society, the less likely will he be to

---

[3] Lewes had to begin an article on 'Criticism in Relation to Novels' in 1866 with a defence which is also an apology that 'the general estimation of prose fiction as a branch of literature has something contemptuous in it' (*Fortnightly Review*, 3 (1866), 352). For a general account of Lewes's work in this area see M. Greenhunt, 'G. H. Lewes as a Critic of the Novel', *Studies in Philology*, 45 (1948), 491–511.

[4] See also L. Pykett, 'The Real Versus the Ideal: Theories of Fiction in Periodicals, 1850–1870', *Victorian Periodicals Review*, 15, No. 2 (Summer 1982), 63–74.

[5] *National Review*, 12 (Jan. 1861), 211.

help us sound these deeper portions of human nature. Nor will the admitted privilege of mentally diving into the recesses of his actors' hearts effectually extricate him from the difficulty, without the help of an artful and spirited conspiracy of events. For there is a limit to the use of this privilege. It is very right and very pleasing to be told of the strong feelings working *beneath* your hero's unruffled brow, or your heroine's liquid laughter. But it will never do to separate half so completely, in a work of fiction, the outward life and the inward, as they often are separated in reality. It is too trying to faith. Art will not bear the strain. . . . Already a sceptical generation is springing up which will question the author's 'omniscience', and take leave to doubt, here of a fact, there of a feeling. The object must be, to harmonize these statements made 'on authority' with the delineations of manners and life . . . An unbelieving generation will probably some day question whether, in fact, Ivanhoe had the unfortunate taste to prefer Rowena, or Rebecca the still more unfortunate taste to prefer Ivanhoe. Where art ceases to be art, faith will not be persuaded to go its way, nothing doubting.[6]

Hutton is arguing that a novelist writing for a secular audience can no longer rely on 'omniscience' or unquestioned authority. He wants a novelist who does not, on the one hand, merely depict the manners of cultivated society (Jane Austen or Thackeray), or, on the other hand, merely portray the eccentric and accidental (Dickens and Wilkie Collins). He wants a fiction which unites 'the outward life and the inward'. His comments are a remarkable application of religious ideas to aesthetic questions. He also anticipates both George Eliot's strengths and her fears, for she is to emerge both as an ironical and self-critical novelist as well as a leading member of the 'sceptical generation'. At the time of Hutton's essay, George Eliot was still Marian Evans, the translator (in 1854) of Feuerbach, but she had already demonstrated, not least as the translator of Strauss in the 1840s, that she was one of the 'sceptical generation' of readers of the Bible who will 'take leave to doubt, here of a fact, there of a feeling'. Similarly, just as Hutton had warned of the dangers of writing about feelings 'working beneath' the characters' exteriors, so she was soon, as George Eliot in her short story *The Lifted Veil* (written in 1859), to question the limits of mentally 'diving' into her actor's hearts.

It seems that for Hutton the novel was likely to fulfil in England the function of sceptical theology in Europe: it gave a voice to

[6] 'A Novel or Two', *National Review*, 1 (Oct. 1855), 336–50 (pp. 340–1).

doubts about authenticity but replaced Christianity with secular idealism and a new sense of selfhood. Hence his particular, indeed according to Rosemary Ashton, his unique sensitivity to George Eliot as the fruit of European idealism.[7] His particular distinction between 'faith' and 'authority' was later to be important in his reading of *Romola*, but here it is important to notice his insistence on the contemporary novel's harmonizing of the 'outer' and the 'inner' life, of the occasional and the deeply natural.

Hutton takes for granted that literature in general, and the novel in particular, can help him 'sound these deeper portions of human nature': this is the real, inner nature which I have already, in discussing Wordsworth and Tennyson, opposed to the outer nature of temperament and circumstance. We should notice that Hutton, as a critic, reads as a novelist writes, looking *beneath* his text. This way of reading, both sanctioned and exemplified by the novel, is significantly different from G. H. Lewes' method. Writing in the same year as Hutton's article on Gaskell and Sewall (1855), Lewes expressed his regret at the analytical influence of German criticism. He wrote in his *Life of Goethe*:

A work is before the critic, and instead of judging this work he endeavours to get *behind* it, beneath it, into the depths of the soul which produced it. He is not satisfied with what the artist has *given*, he wants to know what he *meant*.[8]

The reality of a work of art is to Lewes the world which it presents, rather than what lies behind the appearance of that world. Arnold also refused to read 'inferentially', although for him art *was* an admission into a life behind appearance. For neither critic is art a personal confession of the artist's 'real' feelings. Ironically, however, considering the mutual influence of Lewes and George Eliot, her novels *were* treated as autobiographical by those interested in what she meant.[9]

Hutton's attention to the reality 'behind' a work of art is focused on the author's character and convictions. It depends upon a care-

[7] Rosemary Ashton, *The German Idea: Four English Writers and the Reception of German Thought, 1800–1860* (Cambridge, 1980), 164, 177.

[8] G. H. Lewes, *The Life and Works of Goethe*, 2 vols. (London, 1855), ii. 202.

[9] Hence the popular notion that her novels took a 'philosophical' turn once she had exhausted the factual 'givens' of her early life, as illustrated in the opening words of Leslie Stephen's chapter on *Silas Marner* in his *George Eliot* (London, 1902), 105: 'George Eliot had not yet exhausted the materials of her early recollections.'.

ful and sceptical reading of texts. Trollope tells the story of how Hutton nipped in the bud his scheme to publish three anonymous novels while at the height of his success by recognizing a single phrase in *Nina Balatka* as characteristically Trollope's. The phrase was 'he made his way', meaning, wrote Hutton, 'walking where there is no physical difficulty or embarrassment, but only a certain moral hesitation as to the end and aim of the walking'.[10]

A more extended example of Hutton's desire to know what a single line 'means' is to be found in his book on Scott. In the early part of the book Hutton discusses Scott's poetry and its general lack of striking verbal felicity. One exception to this lack is, he suggests, the line in *Marmion* describing the Scottish tents near Edinburgh and the nearby wood:

> Oft giving way where still there stood
> Some relics of the old oak wood,
> That darkly huge did intervene,
> *And tamed the glaring white with green.*

Hutton comments: 'The conception of the peaceful green oakwood *taming* the glaring white of the tented field, is as fine in idea as it is in relation to the mere effect of the colour on the eye.'[11] The comment shows a sensitivity to singularity of effect and the need to explain it, a desire to demonstrate the 'idea' as well as its mere readability. Its appeal is to a readership which is used to hearing novels discussed in visual terms taken from art criticism. Yet more importantly, when Hutton came to his conclusion in the book, the line seemed to occur to him again, because he writes: 'The finer spiritual element in Scott was relatively deficient, and so the strength of the natural man was almost too equal, complete and glaring. Something that should "tame the glaring white" of that broad sunshine was needed.'[12] It reads as if his own word 'glaring' brought the line back, but that does not mean that his second thought did not inform his first note on the line. This is just the sort of 'getting behind the lines' and into the soul of the author which

[10] Anthony Trollope, *Autobiography* second edition, 2 vols. (Edinburgh, 1883), ii. 12. The review is in the *Spectator*, 23 Mar. 1867, 329–30. See also Judith Knelman, 'Trollope's Experiment with Anonymity', *Victorian Periodicals Review*, 14, No. 1 (Spring 1981), 21–3.

[11] *Sir Walter Scott*, second edition (London, 1902), 58–9.

[12] Ibid., p. 175.

Lewes thought offensive and misleading, no matter how local, as in Hutton's case, the observations might have been.

Hutton described Arnold's poetry as 'like the parable of the man who said "I go not" and then went, without giving any glimpse of the reason for his change of mind.'[13] The fragmentary, unexplained nature of Arnold's poetry was explained for Hutton by Arnold's nature and the nature of poetry in general. The novel, however, is treated by Hutton as if its meaning is both implicit and whole, as if it were a latent form. To him, the novelist rearranged the 'everyday' and the reader rearranged the data, translating the 'given' into the 'meant'. But if reading the novel was for Hutton like deciphering a parable, as De Vere and Roden Noel read Wordsworth, it was not necessarily to get at a moral meaning sanctioned by the author.

One of the most familiar phrases of late Victorian criticism is 'the secret of', or more precisely, 'the secret of the success of'. So Hutton comments on Walter Besant's *The Art of Fiction*: 'It is quite certain that neither Mr. Besant nor any other novelist could impart to anyone, or could even explain to himself, the secret of his success.'[14] It seems to be the responsibility of the critic to discover the secret, to reveal the real nature of the novelist of which the book is the occasion. Lewes's translation of the phrase into the title of his book *The Principles of Success in Literature* shows the extent to which he was trying to turn qualities which critics generally saw as the property of individual writers into universal laws of creation. The phrase was a cliché of literary criticism and was by no means restricted to the novel. Its currency has an obvious explanation in that it was a useful way of summarizing a writer for a journalist with limited time and space, thus betraying in every sense the close association between publication and commerce. The phrase, however, also suggests that the novel contained a code to be deciphered by the attentive reader. Similarly, Hutton argues that the function of the novelist, not relying on the 'givens' of experience, is to 'decipher latent and suppressed realities by *translating* them into other moral situations so as to make them speak for themselves.'[15]

---

[13] *Literary Essays* (1896), p. 319.

[14] *Spectator*, 24 May 1884, 674. See also, for example, G. H. Lewes: 'The real secret of Miss Austen's success lies in her having the rare and exquisite gift of dramatic creation of character' ('The Novels of Jane Austen', *Blackwood's Magazine*, 86 (July 1859), 99–113 (p. 104)).

[15] 'The Author of *Heartsease*, and Modern Schools of Fiction', *Prospective Review*, 10 (1854), 460–82 (pp. 472–3).

Thus it is the special function of the novel to reveal man's 'true nature' by making characters independent of circumstance, and by giving them an autonomy they do not possess in real life. In addition the novel provides special occasions for the expression of the latent and the unconscious: it thus gives free expression to the Illative Sense. Hutton admired, on similar grounds, the poems of Wordsworth for standing independent of their origins and circumstances, while he criticized Dickens for being 'much encumbered by life-choking detail that was not life'.[16] For Hutton the novel was potentially striking a blow for freedom from the conditions of life. Moreover, his emphasis on the *translation* of the subject matter is an answer to Arnold's notion of the 'fit' subject whose aptness is decided prior to the artist's treatment of it.[17]

Hutton's idea of 'translation' is derived from a general idea of character and does not arise from his reading of novels. His account of the possible genesis of *Hamlet*, for example, is essentially one of novelistic 'translation' of a subject from his circumstances in order to bring out his 'real' nature:

Supposing that 'Hamlet' was a book-keeper in a merchant's office when Shakespeare made his acquaintance; he probably struck no-one but the poet, certainly not himself, as affording subject for a great drama. He cannot have been an energetic, orderly clerk; he was certainly not up to business emergencies: if he was tender, imaginative, and weak of purpose—not equal to facing his employer—only on Shakespeare's genius would his mind have so worked as to suggest to him the great tragic elements in such a character, if strained by the demands of wronged affection and burdened with a responsibility which he could not sustain.[18]

Hutton's view of fiction is that of an art form which provides emergencies: occasions for the real nature of a person to emerge. He therefore anticipated the view of George Eliot taken by a recent critic and saw her authorship as an 'emergent self'. The depiction

---

16 'Strauss and German Hellenism', *National Review*, 4 (Jan. 1857), 181–211 (p. 195). see also Lewes's attack on 'detailism which calls itself Realism' in 'Principles of Success in Literature: Of Vision in Art', *Fortnightly Review*, 1 (1865), 572–89 (p. 588).

17 See Arnold's Preface to the first edition of his *Poems*, in *The Poems of Matthew Arnold*, ed. Kenneth Allott (London, 1965), 590–607 (pp. 593–4). For some sense of the later familiarity of the notion, see the tired words of Leslie Stephen: 'novels should, I take it, be transfigured experience.' (*George Eliot*, p. 200).

18 *Prospective Review*, 10 (1854), 471–2.

of realities does not mean to him a reliance on the details of everyday life, but that which provides space for the elaboration of 'character'. The unique interest in fiction, he wrote, lies in 'the simultaneous exhibition of the external and internal history of a human life, in the display to a single glance of the inward forces and the external fate'. He called this the creation of a 'double life'.[19] The depiction of reality in this way is distinct from the work of the 'Realistic School' in fiction (in which Hutton places Jane Austen, Trollope, and Thackeray), which he describes as 'a sort of accidental school of fiction, in which men are delineated by random dots and lines'.[20] Hutton sees real fiction as an opportunity to subvert the acceptability of contingent-based materialism.

The novel was for Hutton a kind of taxonomy, a means of defining the human 'type' or ideal. He wrote:

Just as science finds the true *type* of a class of flowers which actual nature seldom or never does more than *approach*, reaching it in some particulars in one specimen, in other particulars in another specimen, so that in a certain sense science knows what the flower *ought* to be, while nature never quite produces it . . . [so] we may fairly say that if Cleopatra, for instance, were not what Shakespeare has represented her, it was a mistake on her part, not on his. He seized the essence of her character, and all that she was different from this was a deviation from her natural type, an artistic error.[21]

One of the answers to the question 'True to what?' seems to be 'True to type'. Hutton's words also imply a teleology, or rather a lack of one. His idea of the 'essence of character' carries with it the notion that the basis of human nature is unchangeable. This is not because he believes human progress to be impossible, on the contrary, one of the central tenets of his liberalism was a belief in human possibility. Yet the 'essence of character' is, for Hutton, Christianity, and the truths of Christianity are unchangeable. Hutton thought that a progressive teleology, such as George Eliot's, was worldly and materialistic. Hardy's static teleology is in one sense close to Hutton's, since neither put their trust in earthly progress of happiness. For Hutton, however, the atheism of Hardy was itself just a phase which would pass, it was only an occasion, though its passing was not necessarily progress.

[19] 'Puseyite Novels', *Prospective Review*, 6 (1850), 512–34 (pp. 512–13).
[20] *National Review*, 1 (Oct. 1855), 337.
[21] *Prospective Review*, 10 (1854), 476.

For Hutton the novel could provide a teleology and a moral vocabulary against which he could compare the world. His use of the word 'character' supposes an agent who is not merely the aggregate of individual traits nor merely the representation of a function. Hutton uses the novel to create what I have called a 'narrative sense of selfhood', mediating between objectivity and subjectivity. A 'character' to Hutton is one who is seen to be living out a personal history, but one who is also the subject of a story which has a meaning for that character alone: 'the simultaneous exhibition of the external and internal history of a human life . . . a double life'. He supposes that a character, both in life and in fiction, performs actions which are partly imposed from outside (by 'external fate') but which also belong to the character's real, essential nature. When the secular writer speaks of revealing the 'real' person beneath the role, he means the individual, whose inner conflicts are personal and arbitrary. When Hutton speaks of the 'real' person, he means the essence of man as the servant of God. When Hutton looked for a 'double life' in fiction, he was looking with the eyes of a Christian who felt at home in a secular world, and who believed in both the 'inwardness' of Christianity as well as the power of circumstance.

Because of his own 'double' view, Hutton finds most attempts to write explicitly 'ethical' fiction unsatisfactory. George Eliot is the writer whom his criticism anticipates as an ideal in all respects but one, namely that she points to beliefs to which she is not, in fact, prepared to be true.

Ethical fiction: Charlotte Yonge and Elizabeth Sewall

Writing on the moral effect of great art, Hutton wrote:

After reading the *Heart of Mid-Lothian* or *King Lear*, we experience a sense of pain which, though not unmixed with pleasure, does not exercise half the motive power upon us that sympathetic pain *can* exercise for the developing and elevating of character. . . . To see the meshes of fate entrap the innocent, and harden the guilty, and crush out all the loveliness and glory of life, is painfully depressing, if the shadow is not seen to be cast by a light beyond. We want to feel that writers who possess such power to paint both good and evil, have a pervading reliance on the dynamic superiority of good over evil.[22]

22 'Ethical and Dogmatic Fiction: Miss Yonge', *National Review*, 12 (Jan. 1861), 212–29 (pp. 212–13).

Hutton writes about his feelings 'after reading' because he is pained not only by the reading, but also by the lack of any palliative for that primary pain. He does not want to feel that the description of powerful suffering in art is an end in itself. He would like to see evidence of a source of power which was greater than literary power, which was outside the writer and could in that sense be relied upon: a moral theodicy beyond relativism. Hutton's argument might imply that *King Lear* is too painful because the moral vocabulary made available to describe it is too limited. To Hutton, tragic art suggested that the ideal was attainable only in God. For the Romantic, as Hutton sees Shakespeare, Scott, and Hardy, tragic art suggests only that the ideal is unattainable on earth. Thus in Hutton's *King Lear* it would not have been necessary for Cordelia to die: that 'full look at the worst' he considered a Romantic vice.

Hutton always addresses himself both to the effect on the 'eyes' of the reader (using, as was common, the terms of art-criticism to describe writing[23]), and to the latent, suppressed meaning. So he wrote that Hardy, in *The Return of the Native*, 'treats tragedy itself as hardly more than a deeper tinge of the common leaden-colour of the human lot'.[24] Similarly, he wrote in a letter to Hardy, in response to the novelist's complaint that the *Wessex Tales* was not reviewed by the *Spectator*, that Hardy's writing 'was appreciated very highly except on its ethical note, on which it seemed . . . to be open to some objection, not for what it delineated, but for the lax standard of morality *implied* in the picture'.[25] Again, what this suggests is that Hutton finds the moral vocabulary used by Hardy to be insufficiently suggestive. He would, for example, have found Marty South's 'he was a good man who did good things' to lack moral richness and to fail to provide the reader with the means of combating the tendency of the narration.

However, if Hutton found Romantic tragedy 'lax' because of its limited moral vocabulary, he finds the mid-nineteenth century 'ethical novel' to be unacceptable because its moral vocabulary was

---

[23] So, for instance, Charlotte Brontë's distinction lay 'in the Rembrandt-like distinctness with which all that the mind conceived was brought into the full blaze of light' while 'the light flows more evenly over George Eliot's pictures', wrote Hutton (*Modern Guides*, p. 152). See also Stang, op. cit., p. 116.

[24] *Spectator*, 8 Feb. 1879, 181.

[25] *The Collected Letters of Thomas Hardy*, ed. R. L. Purdy and M. Millgate, (London, 1979–), i. 312. Hutton's reply of 18 July 1888 is in the Dorset County Museum. *Wessex Tales* was, as a result of Hardy's letter, reviewed in the *Spectator*.

unlimited: it had no *other* vocabulary. The novels of Charlotte Yonge and Elizabeth Sewall, for example, try to make a 'standard of morality' itself the explicit subject-matter of the novel. Yet writing on them in the 1850s did, at least, enable Hutton to work out what he did and did not expect from the novel.

Writing on *Heartsease* in 1854, Hutton found the novel 'realistic' only in reflecting the *status quo*. Looking back on the novel, in which he thought 'the strict impartiality of the Daguerreotype process has seldom been carried so fully into fiction', was 'less like the review of a story than the memory of a few years of ordinary life'. Charlotte Yonge's notions of moral welfare were, he felt, identified by her with other notions of 'civilisation and order' which did not seem to be sources of character and powerful motive. She 'chains down' her imagination, he wrote, to the exact forms of life to which her experience had accustomed her and to the values of 'a civilisation and order which imply by their very meaning that half the realities of human nature are in a state of chronic suppression'.[26]

Hutton's objection to Charlotte Yonge seems to be the opposite of his objection to Hardy. While Hardy fails to imply any moral order behind his novel, her novels consist entirely of an inflexible moral order which circumstances are never allowed to contradict. Hutton elaborates his views in another essay, where he compares Charlotte Yonge's early novels, *The Heir of Redclyffe* and *Heartsease*, with the later *Hopes and Fears*. He finds her 'mental horizon' to have been 'enlarged', but finds the change unreflected in the novel's essential meaning:

She has a quick eye for the different shades of intellectual power which characterise different minds . . . But whether she does, or does not, endow her heroes with the intellectual and moral capacity which would enable them to transcend the conventions of life, the practical result always comes out the same. They must fit into the hierarchical order of society which Miss Yonge has been taught to accept, and must never alter it in any direction.[27]

What seems to be at stake here is not Charlotte Yonge's failure as a novelist, but the failure of a popular moralist, which she certainly was, to imagine a secular society in which Christian values were *effectually* maintained. Curiously, and among

26 *Prospective Review*, 10 (1854), 461, 471.
27 *National Review*, 12 (1861), 216.

fellow-commentators uniquely, he does not have much to say about her archaic Christian chivalry, but attacks her attachment to social bases which would soon seem archaic. He sees her ethics as therefore one-sided, concerned with moral imperatives but not with social expansiveness. In literary terms he finds lofty attempts to *form* the reader but no attempt by narration to *inform* the reader; in moral terms he finds that claims based on eternal verities are employed merely to sanction the status quo.

Charlotte Yonge seems to want to construct, in her novels, a feudal system peopled by passionate individuals reliant on a 'Higher Will'—hence her most characteristic publication is her *Kings of England*, a version of history intended to 'inculcate faith, loyalty, obedience and reverence'. The central anomaly of Charlotte Yonge's work rests in the fact that her moral idealism is given free play only within the limits of dogmatic values which she feels under no obligation to question. In theological terms, she does not face up to the anomalous appeal which High Anglicanism makes to personal conscience within dogmatic values, as Hutton did in his letters to Newman.

An even more extreme dogmatism, however, is preached by the Puseyite novelist Elizabeth Sewell, who pushed the ethical content of the novel to greater lengths. Hutton wrote of her *Amy Herbert* in 1850, commenting on Puseyite novels in general:

All human feelings and sentiments require, in fiction, to have an outward as well as an inward life, objects for their activity, and times when external events load them with satisfaction or disappointment: inward hopes must be staked on external circumstances. . . . But this does not seem to be so, when spiritual life is in question. To give it also a distinct external career, seems an infringement of its nature . . . here, if anywhere, in the spiritual secrecy of the individual soul, should all the doubt, and risk, and trial of mere outward fate find its explanation, and lose the arbitrary character that it has to spectators from without.[28]

This is tantamount to admitting that the novel is the most active contemporary form *because* it is a necessarily secular one. Hutton's criticism of Puseyite novels is a translation of his criticism of the Puseyite movement itself: of its staking of spiritual life on externals, its embodying of mysteries in institutions, and its giving (in its theory of Apostolic succession) divine power over to a human line

[28] *Prospective Review*, 6 (1850), 531–2.

which has an 'arbitrary character' to 'spectators from without'. The evangelical religious novel is a contradiction in terms to Hutton, since it presents as arbitrary that which should itself explain the arbitrary.[29]

Yet George Eliot's novels *are* 'religious' in giving an account of the complex and the contingent: they give some sense of the spiritual secrecy of the individual soul to the Paterian 'spectator from without'. She would not, however, have accepted Hutton's implied distinction between 'inward hopes' and the spiritual life. For Hutton, while inward hopes 'must be staked on external circumstances', the spiritual life only *attaches* itself to external circumstances, it cannot be altered by them. For George Eliot, the inward hope *is* the spiritual life, and it is staked on the external. Again, the difference is teleological: Hutton's spiritual life is static, while George Eliot's is a worldly idealism. We find the difference represented, as I hope to show later, in George Eliot's depiction of Savonarola's heretical staking of his spiritual life on external circumstance in promising to perform a miracle.

Hutton's criticism of the 'ethical' novel can always be translated into a criticism of the ethics of that particular novelist, while implying that the novelists themselves lack this kind of self-consciousness. Both Charlotte Yonge and Elizabeth Sewall are specifically criticized for lacking any ironical or testing insight into the values they preach. They are ethical without being speculative, that is they make no use of the ironical anomaly of the 'novelistic' character as one making personal judgements within ethical boundaries and within conventional social limits.

As interest in her grew in the 1860s, both Hutton and Lewes thought they had found this self-consciousness in Jane Austen, so that for both she provided a basis from which to criticize the novels of the previous decade and to judge the work of George Eliot.

Jane Austen

After years of critical neglect, a revival of interest in Jane Austen followed the publication in 1870 of Austen-Leigh's *Memoir* of her. G. H. Lewes was exceptional in having produced an important study of her in *Blackwood's Magazine* ten years before this, which

---

[29] Elizabeth Jay, *The Religion of the Heart: Anglican Evangelicalism and the Nineteenth Century Novel* (Oxford, 1979), 207–43.

study was itself the culmination of enthusiastic appraisals dating
back to a review by him in *Fraser's Magazine* in 1847. Hutton had
written about Jane Austen throughout the 1860s but did not devote
an essay exclusively to discussion of her until the publication of the
Memoir. However, this book did little to alter his views on her, and
he wrote: 'It is always a pleasure to know that any popular writer
was what he or she "must have been" '.[30]

Thus it does seem that the inferred character of a writer can be
more important to Hutton than the biographical 'facts', and it is to
him merely pleasing when the two coincide. There were, indeed,
two 'versions' of Jane Austen for virtually the whole of the nineteenth century and each found confirmation in Austen-Leigh's
Memoir that she *was* what she 'must have been'. The first view is
represented, though in notably different ways, by Hutton and
Lewes, the second is represented by Richard Simpson, who discusses
her in the *North British Review* in 1870, and by Julia Kavanagh in
her earlier *English Women of Letters* (1862).

However, the seminal text is Archbishop Whateley's 1821 essay
on Jane Austen, and later critics might be classed by the extent to
which they agree or disagree with it. He wrote of Jane Austen's
characters as follows:

In Miss Austen's hands we see into their hearts and hopes, their motives,
their struggles within themselves, and a sympathy is induced which, if
extended to daily life and the world at large, would make the reader a more
amiable person; and we must think it that reader's own fault who does not
close her pages with more charity in his heart towards unpretending, if
prosing worth; with a higher estimation of simple kindness and sincere
goodwill.[31]

Whateley was, in fact, trying to 'novelize' and Christianize Wordsworth. Yet after his essay all criticism of Jane Austen is largely
concerned with 'character' in the novel, and with the function of
the novel in affecting the character of the reader.

Hutton, in effect, contradicts Whateley's view of Jane Austen's
characters with their internal struggles, and in classing her with
Mrs Gaskell and Trollope as 'society novelists' he expressed the
view that their characters' minds are never 'exhibited in any direct
contact with the ultimate realities of life; none of them are [sic] seen

[30] *Spectator*, 25 Dec. 1869, 1534.
[31] Cited by G. H. Lewes, 'The Novels of Jane Austen', *Blackwood's Magazine*,
86 (July 1859), 103.

grasping at the truth by which they seek to live, struggling with a single deadly temptation,—or, in short, dealing with any of the deeper-elements of human life.'[32]

His idea of 'the ultimate realities of life' is based on a faith in the value of inner struggles, emergencies rather than mere daily occasions, which reveal one's real nature and draw out the whole person. Hutton sees the novel as providing expression for inward states in outward forms, and giving a forum for doubt, temptation, contradiction, and self-consciousness, rather than for singleness of mind or firm belief in external authority. He wrote: 'only the doubtful portions of life, where fates are changing, and risks are great, are fit for the subjects of fiction'.[33] Arnold would have thought this a very debased notion of the fit subject, suggesting as it does a taste for melodrama. Indeed the idea of Shakespeare which seems to lie behind the contrast with the 'society novelist' is of a decidedly sensationalized Shakespeare.

The complacency of his taxonomical classification of Jane Austen, that she 'was' what she 'must have been', is a reflection of Hutton's sense of her own complacency as a writer and as a woman. To Hutton, Jane Austen's mind was the opposite of 'doubtful', rather her mind and life were 'settled'. In 1869 he wrote:

Miss Austen's novels and her life were one of perfect calm, and it was to this calm that we owe that fine, sedate humour and gentle irony which imply a settled standard of life, and an estimate of human follies quite unmixed with bitterness of motive or scepticism of inference. . . . She did not at any time *arraign* either human nature or human society for their shortcomings and positive sins, as our modern novelists, George Eliot, or Thackeray, or even Mrs Gaskell either do, or try to do.[34]

Hutton's sentence is barely grammatically correct in its assumption that Jane Austen's 'novels and life were one of perfect calm'. Yet his reference to the absence of 'scepticism of inference' is very telling, and contrasts with that 'lax standard of morality implied in the picture' which Hardy delineated. Jane Austen seems to exist for Hutton in a presecularized idyll where, as Bagehot said of Scott, beliefs are merely 'data' whose meaning is not expected to be

[32] *Modern Guides*, p. 150.
[33] *Prospective Review*, 6 (1850), 512.
[34] *Spectator*, 25 Dec. 1869, 1533–4.

questioned.[35] Hutton therefore found, as he explains in an article entitled 'From Miss Austen to Mr. Trollope', that the characters in Jane Austen's novels were 'exactly themselves', while those in Trollope's novels were affected by 'the irritation of external pressure'. He sees the change in characters as a reflection of a move in social and political power 'from social home rule to social centralisation' which led to an improvement in the power of fiction.[36]

Unlike Hutton, Lewes approvingly quotes Whateley's view but admits citing it 'for the sake of introducing a striking passage from one of the works of Mr. George Eliot'.[37] If Jane Austen 'was' for Hutton what she 'must have been', then for G. H. Lewes, George Eliot is what Jane Austen 'might have been'. The 'real secret' of Jane Austen, Lewes goes on, 'lies in her having the rare and exquisite gift of dramatic creation of character'. The word 'exquisite' is a revealing one; Hutton also uses it of Jane Austen: 'the secret of her great charm is in the reduced scale of her exquisite pictures'.[38] The word seems to retain its original meaning in applying to the critics' attempt to 'seek out' her secret. It does not suggest keenness or intensity, since that would imply the kind of 'looking beneath' the art which Lewes thinks inappropriate to aesthetic judgement and which Hutton thinks unachieved in Jane Austen's time.

This vocabulary and these methods are, however, in stark contrast to those of Julia Kavanagh, writing in 1863:

If we look under the shrewdness and quiet satire of her stories, we shall find a much keener sense of disappointment than of joy fulfilled. Sometimes we find more than disappointment.[39]

'Quiet satire' is quite different from 'gentle irony', and keen disappointment from 'sedate humour'. The bitterness which Kavanagh finds in the novel is still only tactfully suggested, as if it remained a secret. Hutton, as late as 1894, finds no depth in the novels and no depth in Jane Austen: 'Nothing in the world, not even its sins and

---

[35] See Walter Bagehot's *Literary Studies*, ed. Hutton, ii. 115. He is comparing the novel in 1858, in which a character typically 'desires to attain a belief', with Scott's novels, in which 'creeds are data'.

[36] *Spectator*, 16 Dec. 1882, 1609–11.

[37] 'The Novels of Jane Austen', *Blackwood's Magazine*, 86 (July 1859), 103–4. See also Lewes's 'Criticism in Relation to Novels', *Fortnightly Review*, 3 (Nov. 1865–Feb. 1866), 321–61 (pp. 356–7).

[38] *Spectator*, 22 Mar. 1890, 403.

[39] Julia Kavanagh, *English Women of Letters*, 2 vols. (London, 1863), ii. 230.

vices, move her to the depths'.[40] Lewes, writing thirty-five years before, had rather similarly found no 'profound agitation' in Jane Austen.[41] Yet Julia Kavanagh wrote of her: 'what her extraordinary power wanted in extent, it made up for in depth'.[42] More specifically and, more dramatically, Richard Simpson wrote, echoing Whateley's notion of the internal struggle of Jane Austen's characters, 'the individual mind can only be represented by her as a battlefield where contending hosts are marshalled'.[43]

We are faced, in considering these differences, with conflicting ideas of 'depth'—what it consists of and how it is recognized. To Julia Kavanagh and Richard Simpson, 'poise' is the great sign of depth. Jane Austen's faculties, says Simpson, were 'poised' in that 'their action and reaction were equal'.[44] To Kavanagh she is 'poised' between tragedy and comedy. To Hutton, however, this literary and social tone, given the blanket term 'irony', is a 'neutral equipoise' which does not have 'the nerves to become tragedy'.[45] She cannot, he wrote, 'rise above a tame kind of sweet and refined tenderness. She cannot descend into anything like those depths of self-abasement of which the soul is capable.'[46] Simpson thought her capable of both and poised between each, believing that self-control implies the possibility of its loss.

All this is to say that Hutton takes, or mistakes, irony to stem from a morally and politically neutral mind. He describes irony rather contemptuously as 'educated reticence' which only serves negatively to indicate ideas and individualities its author cannot portray. Irony to him is 'light' in Jane Austen in contradistinction to 'depth' in George Eliot:

What we chiefly care to know of men and women is not so much their special tastes, bias, gifts, humours, or even the exact proportions in which these characteristics are combined, as the general depth and mass of the human nature that is in them,—the breadth and the power of their life, its

40 *Spectator*, 10 Nov. 1894, 645.

41 'Criticism in Relation to Novels', p. 102.

42 Kavanagh, *English Women of Letters*, ii, p. 235. Bagehot seems to question the very use of 'depth' when he writes, of Scott's apparent omission of any full treatment of man's religious nature: 'A reader of a more simple mind, apt to indulge in such criticism, feels "a want of depth", as he would speak' (*Literary Studies*, ii. 120).

43 'Jane Austen', *North British Review*, 52 (Apr. 1870), 129–52 (p. 137).

44 Ibid., p. 136.

45 *Spectator*, 2 Sept. 1865, 979.

46 *Spectator*, 10 Nov. 1894, 645.

comprehensiveness of grasp, its tenacity of instinct, its capacity for love, its need of trust. A thousand skilful outlines of character, based on mere individualities of taste and talent and temper, are not near as moving to us as one vivid picture of a massive nature stirred to the very depths of its commonplace instinct and commonplace faith.[47]

This argument is crucial to an understanding of the importance of George Eliot to Hutton. It is also the basis for his view that Arnold failed to appreciate the literature of the everyday—to preserve the connection between the everyday and the general (the particular flower and the ideal type)—while Jane Austen, by direct contrast, remained merely preoccupied by the everyday in local application; neither won through to the 'double life' of both, to power and conviction combined. Those four qualities by which the breadth and quality of life might, according to Hutton, be measured ('comprehensiveness of grasp, tenacity of instinct, capacity for love, need of trust') are qualities which he would feel the machinery of life was suppressing: narrowing a man's grasp to the detail of the quotidian, loosening the grip of instinct, channelling love through acceptable institutions, and defining human needs in those material terms by which it hopes to satisfy and nurture them. The social equivalents of these qualities are tastes, bias, gifts, humours: all occasional, and defined in terms of other people's possession of them. It is Jane Austen who, it seemed to Hutton, took these social equivalents as her subject matter.

Hutton admired George Eliot for avoiding the portrayal of 'mere individualities of taste and temper', and he judges her novels by examining her own beliefs, the 'high ideal of life', he found lacking in Jane Austen.[48] The latter, says Hutton, only 'indicates a personality', which he takes to be her own pliable personality. Hutton said that Browning, in his indifference as to the outcome of the battles he describes between characters, had no 'narrative force' (see above, chapter 2, 'Utilitarianism and literature'). We might say that Hutton felt George Eliot's narrative power derived from her ability to take every side, while Jane Austen's weakness derived from her poised refusal to be partisan.

Hutton's remark on 'narrative force' is echoed in his argument that dialogue in what he calls the 'society novel' is marked by a character's willingness or even obligation to alter his or her tone in

---

[47] *Modern Guides*, pp. 157–8.
[48] *Spectator*, 22 July 1871, 892.

response to the collective tone, a characteristic which is the fruit of 'social elasticity'. He reprints William Roscoe's comment that Thackeray 'treats a subject like a shuttlecock, raps it to and fro between his disputants, and lets it fall in the middle for those to pick up who list'.[49] Though Hutton does not make the direct comparison, be believes that George Eliot's dialogue is not open to this social modification. In other words, according to Hutton's reading, the play of feeling articulated in an exchange between Emma and Jane Fairfax is built on social community, while the exchange between Dinah and Hetty in *Adam Bede* is based on a fundamental community of nature. Dinah and Hetty might almost be said to be, respectively, the incarnation of the capacity for love and the need of trust, regardless of self. Hutton found this latter exchange the finest achievement of *Adam Bede*, not as an illustration of the conventional conflict of good and evil, but as an attempt to find a meeting-point where there seemed no hope of one. Hutton is moved, that is, by 'the infantine cry for divine mercy which poor little Hetty puts forth to Dinah rather than to God'.[50] Yet at the same time it is this mistaking the human for the divine which Hutton feels he has to correct: 'how strange', he comments, 'and painful it is to realise that the great author who painted this for us did not herself believe in the divine mercy which she makes Dinah proclaim!'. This is one of those points in George Eliot which, tested by the standards of Hutton's realism, he finds 'so true', especially when placed beside Jane Austen's mere indications of realism. Yet it is just this sense of realistic truth, comprising truth to life, truth to type, and truth to self, which leaves Hutton shocked when he reflects that it is a sense contained in a form in which George Eliot did not believe.

George Eliot and 'spiritual irony'

By 1889, after years of 'studying' George Eliot's novels, Hutton contrasts the irony of her novels and that of Jane Austen's as differing in kind, but not in intensity. Directly George Eliot attempts irony, says Hutton, 'you hear the falsetto note'. The heaviness of her style, he says, 'will not admit of the light touch in which there is just a laughing echo, and no more'.[51] He complains, for instance,

[49] *Poems and Essays by the Late William Caldwell Roscoe*, ed. R. H. Hutton, 2 vols. (London, 1860), ii. 284.

[50] *Modern Guides*, p. 185.   [51] *Spectator*, 20 July 1889, 81.

of the 'what a vulgar world we live in' tone of the beginning of chapter 17 of *Adam Bede* as if George Eliot were trying to reproduce *Vanity Fair*.[52] Yet when he explains this tone of 'bantering depreciation' as the result of her having 'indulged in the pleasure of being her own critic', he is not only echoing Trollope's well-known remarks on George Eliot's analysis of her own characters, but also anticipating Herbert Spencer's view that her current of self-criticism was 'an habitual accompaniment of anything she was saying or doing'.[53] Hutton saw criticism of herself, and the selves she created, as the impetus behind the novels while recognizing that she would have her reader believe that her impetus was sympathy, or the reverse of criticism. Furthermore, however, Hutton takes the criticism, the heavy-handed irony of her novels, to be closely related to her scepticism with regard to religious belief, and he understands this scepticism to have specific aesthetic consequences in George Eliot's 'spiritual irony'.

Hutton was the only contemporary critic, even according to George Eliot's own account, to appreciate fully the connection between her novels and the *specific* origins of her views of God and human self-hood, namely her translation of Feuerbach's *Das Wesen des Christentums*. As a critic who, in the 1850s, had praised the novel as a form of translation, Hutton has great admiration in theory for her use of the translated form. However, in practice he deplored the content and, especially in the case of the novels set in an identified past (particularly *Romola*), he criticized her failure to translate anachronistic secularism and scepticism. He wrote to George Eliot complaining that *Romola* had failed as a transposition of religious sentiments into secular conditions, much as he had felt Elizabeth Sewall to have failed to do the reverse. He wrote of Romola herself:

She struck me throughout as rather modern and separating the doubtful from the ethical germs of Savonarola's faith with too much of our modern habit of discriminating between the righteous principles which prove themselves and the divine authority on which they were proclaimed. . . . Romola seems to me not so much to *take* as almost to *imply* a knowledge of such distinctions as she might have picked up by a study of Feuerbach. I do not mean, of course, that any such questions came up, but that her mind seems

    52 *Modern Guides*, p. 162.
    53 Ibid.; Trollope, *Autobiography*, ii. 66–7; Herbert Spencer, *An Autobiography*, 2 vols. (London, 1904), i. 396.

to have had that habit of hanging back, suspending belief before any mere accidental adjunct of what compels her faith which the study of the subtlest negative analysis of religious belief would give.[54]

Hutton's distinction between 'take' and 'imply' suggests that the reader is expected to be sensitive to sceptical inferences, while his phrase 'suspending belief' may be a reversal of the state of the Coleridgean reader. Hutton feels, that is, as if the reader must suspend not disbelief but belief in everything but George Eliot's authority. Nevertheless, his precise suggestion that Romola seemed to have read Feuerbach was, as George Eliot conceded in her reply, a unique perception. His reading makes *Romola* 'modern' in spite of its historical setting, and might imply that *Loss and Gain*, for example, belonged to an old phase of thought in spite of its modern setting.

It is, of course, George Eliot whom Hutton sees separating righteous principles from the divine authority on which he bases them—distinguishing righteousness from a God who is personally righteous. Hutton, though, took this fading of personality to have aesthetic consequences in the fading of character in the novel. He found Daniel Deronda 'little more than a moral mist, a mere tentative in character-conceiving', one whom George Eliot found 'difficult to crystallize into distinct form'. He kept on: 'Is not this to some extent the result indeed of George Eliot's philosophy, which has parted with all the old lines of principle, except the keen sympathy with every noble sentiment which she always betrays, and imported nothing new and definite in their places, except the vaguest hopes and aspirations?'.[55] George Eliot would certainly have bridled at that parenthetic 'except . . . betrays', relegating her prime aim to a source of secondary consolation. It is as if her early collusion with the rationalist attempt to remove personality from the idea of God (her translation of Strauss's *Das Leben Jesu* was published eight years before her translation of Feuerbach, in 1846) had undermined Hutton's ability to believe in the authorship of *Daniel Deronda*. 'We admire, but we do not believe in, the states of mind which are attributed to him', Hutton says of Daniel Deronda. We might, to put it crudely, say that George Eliot thought the same about God.

54 Yale University Library Eliot MS (6 Aug. 1863).
55 *Spectator*, 10 June 1876, 734.

We are reminded, in those comments on Daniel Deronda, of Hutton's warning in 1855 (see above p. 155) of the coming of a sceptical generation of readers who will 'question the author's "omniscience" '; George Eliot seems to fulfil all Hutton's worst fears while being, in another sense, the novelist he had been waiting for. In *Daniel Deronda*, Hutton felt, George Eliot had failed to present what he called the 'double life' of staking inner beliefs on external circumstances, but had instead produced the impression of 'double consciousness', of habitually seeing things as they appeared to others. It was this 'double consciousness' which Feuerbach saw as both evidence of the non-existence of a personal God and as the product of a secularized self-conscious morality.[56]

What Hutton describes as George Eliot's difficulty in crystallizing characters into distinct forms is related to her sceptical idealism which refused to ally itself with the distinct forms of materialism. In strictly literary terms, Hutton seems to suggest that George Eliot's characters can have *too much* in common, and all employ the same idiom because she is directly concerned with inner human nature. Hutton found the opposite in Scott and quoted, in 1877, a thought from Scott's *Journal* which anticipates the fears expressed by George Eliot in *The Lifted Veil*:

Once he says: 'What a strange scene if the surge of conversation could suddenly ebb like the tide, and show us the state of people's real minds! . . . Life could not be endured were it seen in reality.' But this is not irony, only the sort of meditation which, in a mind inclined to thrust deep into the secrets of life's paradoxes, is apt to lead to irony. Scott, however, does not thrust deep in this direction. He met the cold steel which inflicts the deepest interior wounds like a soldier, and never seems to have meditated on the higher paradoxes of life till reason reeled. The irony of Hamlet is far from Scott. His imagination was essentially one of *distinct embodiment*. He never seemed so much as to contemplate that sundering of substance and form, that rending away of outward garments, that unclothing of the soul, in order that it might be more effectually clothed upon, which is at the heart of anything that might be called *spiritual irony*. The constant abiding of his mind within the well-defined forms of some one or other of the conditions of outward life and manners among the scores of different

---

[56] Ludwig Feuerbach, *The Essence of Christianity*, trans. Marian Evans (i.e. George Eliot) (London, 1854), 12–13: 'What was formerly contemplated and worshipped as God is now perceived to be something human . . . Man has given objectivity to himself, but has not recognised the object as his own nature . . . Consciousness of God is self-consciousness.'

spheres of human habit, was, no doubt, one of the secrets of his genius; but·
it was also its greatest limitation.[57]

The quotation from Scott's *Journal* is not, Hutton implies, the
kind of comment which one would expect to find in his novels,
though it is the kind of reflection we find in George Eliot's. Her
'spiritual irony', to adopt and apply Hutton's phrase, is a development of Scott's tentative and private reflection on the power of
showing 'the state of people's real minds'. Yet to Hutton, even
Scott's 'distinct embodiments' are preferable to George Eliot's
'moral mists' because the sundering of substance and form which
he wrote of is paralleled and exceeded in Romola's separating
righteous principles from divine authority. Consequently, he most
admires George Eliot when he feels she combines the expression of
inward needs with the realization of distinct character—as in the
case of Hetty and Dinah in *Adam Bede*.

· If Scott's greatest limitation is his abiding within well-defined
forms, then we might say that George Eliot's fear, though Hutton
did not see it, was of the consequences of the breakdown of the
limitations not of form but of perception—which is properly Scott's
point. Her elaboration of Scott's remark that 'life could not be
endured were it seen in reality' might be said to have been her well-
known reflection in *Middlemarch*: 'That element of tragedy which
lies in the fact of frequency has not yet wrought itself into the
coarse emotion of mankind; and perhaps our frames could hardly
bear much of it'.[58] Yet George Eliot's thrust into the 'state of
people's real minds' until, as Hutton puts it, 'reason reels', produced
the strange short story, *The Lifted Veil*. Hutton does not discuss
the text anywhere, though it might be said to be central to his idea
of George Eliot while contradicting his feeling that to George Eliot
self-criticism was 'a pleasure'.

The short story, as Ruby Redinger has suggested, represents
George Eliot's 'second thoughts about her right to invade other
people's psyches'.[59] The story expresses the fear that there is
nothing but occasions and pettiness underneath life, as well·as on
the surface.

[57] *Sir Walter Scott*, pp. 120–1. See also J. H. Raleigh, 'What Scott Meant to the
Victorians', *Victorian Studies*, 7, No. 1 (1963–4), 7–34, and David Brown, *Walter
Scott and the Historical Imagination* (London, 1979), 108–9 and 197–9 on Scott's
materialism.
[58] *Middlemarch*, 4 vols. (London, 1871–2), i. 351.
[59] Ruby Redinger, *George Eliot: The Emergent Self* (London, 1975), 404.

It illustrates, that is, the painful and destructive side of George Eliot's 'translation' of herself, her lifting of the veil. She tries to get behind intentions as Hutton tried to get behind books, but unlike him she sacrifices her own position in doing it. To George Eliot, her 'double consciousness' is a consciousness, like Feuerbach's explanation of God, that she is at once the subject and object of her thoughts. The 'double life' which Hutton looked for in the novel involved a further knowledge of people and also of their 'otherness'.

What George Eliot takes to be a painful necessity and a means of perception and understanding, Hutton takes to be a measure of aloofness. He does not believe that she always includes herself in her criticism, whereas she would argue that she writes *principally* about herself. Thus for him she is as often scornful as she is sympathetic. Although he reviewed *The Impressions of Theophrastus Such*, very unfavourably, Hutton does not mention the following passage which might help to define the difference between them:

Thus if I laugh at you, O fellow-men! if I trace with curious interest your labyrinthine self-delusions, note the inconsistencies in your zealous adhesions . . . it is not that I feel aloof from you: the more intimately I seem to discern your weaknesses, the stronger to me is the proof that I share them. How otherwise could I get the discernment?[60]

Hutton could not justly have said of George Eliot what he had said of Arnold, that 'of these blunders he convicts them from his serene station above the clouds of their dull atmosphere'.[61] Yet Hutton would not have accepted George Eliot's position because he felt that the source of his discernment was an essentially spiritual one; she argues that her discernment comes entirely from herself, to the extent that she is the object of it. What is essentially external for Hutton, translated into the outside world, is utterly internalized by George Eliot, retranslated into herself. In this sense George Eliot is Hutton's true opposite. In her view weakness, for instance, is translated into strength by the very thought that it *is* weakness: it is not merely closely allied to self-knowledge, it is the necessary precondition for self-knowledge. Cognition of others, according to Feuerbach, is a recognition of yourself, 'consciousness of the objective is the self-consciousness of man'.[62] This attempt by

---

[60] *Impressions of Theophrastus Such* (Edinburgh, 1879), 6.
[61] *Spectator*, 3 Feb. 1866, 126.
[62] Feuerbach, *Essence of Christianity*, p. 5.

Feuerbach to unite the inner and the outer life of man is the key to Hutton's refusal to believe that George Eliot's scorn is really sympathy or that her criticism is self-criticism and not spiritual irony.

Mark Wartofsky has remarked in a recent study of Feuerbach that the 'split consciousness' or 'double consciousness' as Hegel calls it is in fact the real subject of *The Essence of Christianity*.[63] The thesis of the book, however, is that the divine is the objectification of human nature ('in the being of God it is only thy *own* being which is an object to thee, and what presents itself *before* thy consciousness is what lies *behind* it'), which George Eliot takes to imply an almost divine capacity for sympathy in the cultured, self-conscious spectator.[64] When Hutton came to defend George Eliot after an attack on her in the *Church Quarterly* in 1877, he referred with some contempt to the fact that the writer in that journal had made no reference to 'one of her first literary efforts . . . the translation of Ludwig Feuerbach's attempt to explain away both Theism and Christianity as the mere idle echo of human hopes', because, he adds, to the careful student of her books that translation informs all her subsequent work.[65] Thus for Hutton the translation informs all his criticism of George Eliot, and he makes a crucial comment in his essay on Cross's *Life and Letters of George Eliot*, suggesting that George Eliot came to use irony so freely because 'Feuerbach's is an *ironic* explanation of the religions of the world . . . which makes the most momentous factor in the history of the world to consist in a grand procession of pure illusions.' Consequently, he goes on, her belief is 'that every attempt to represent ideals as actually existing in any world has led to the blunders and follies which

---

63 Mark Wartofsky, *Feuerbach* (London, 1977), 207. The most recent factual account of George Eliot's knowledge of Feuerbach is that given by Ashton, *The German Idea*. But see also U. C. Knoepflmacher, 'George Eliot, Feuerbach and the Question of Criticism', *Victorian Studies*, 7, No. 3 (1963–4), 306–9; T. R. Wright, 'George Eliot and Positivism: A Reassessment', *Modern Language Review*, 76 (1981), 257–72; M. Vogeler, 'George Eliot and the Positivists', *Nineteenth-Century Fiction*, 35 (1980), 406–31; K. M. Newton, *George Eliot, Romantic Humanist: A Study of the Philosophical Structure of her Novels* (Totowa, N.J., 1981).

64 Feuerbach, *Essence of Christianity*, p. 228. In her essay 'Evangelical Teaching: Dr Cumming', George Eliot goes as far as to suggest that 'the idea of a God who not only sympathises with all we feel and endure for our fellow-men, but who will pour new life into our too languid love, is an extension and multiplication of the effects produced by human sympathy'. The essay was first published in the *Westminster Review*, 64 (Oct. 1855), 436–62 (p. 461), and is reprinted in *Essays of George Eliot*, ed. T. Pinney (London, 1967).

65 *Spectator*, 3 Nov. 1877, 1363.

make men rely solely on another world for help which they ought to find, and would otherwise find, for themselves.'[66]

George Eliot is to Hutton her own God, her own judge, 'her own critic'. That 'being her own critic' is, in fact, the process of Feuerbach's argument: his was, says Wartofsky, 'a self-critical method'.[67] *Daniel Deronda* seems to illustrate the possible dangers of this mental effort, dangers to which Hutton is particularly sensitive. He wrote that 'fiction alone enables us to look at once on both sides of that barrier which usually divides men's visible and invisible life. . . . there is a double life, inward and outward'. George Eliot wrote, translating Feuerbach, 'man has a two-fold life, an inner and an outer life' but that 'it is not until a man has reached an advanced stage of culture that he can double himself so as to play the part of another within himself.'[68] This is where the difference seems to lie, both ethically and aesthetically, between Hutton and George Eliot. For him it is the novelist's duty to translate experience into distinct embodiments external to himself which constitute this double life. For George Eliot, the distinct embodiment of a character is not properly external at all, but is the result of and not the cause of this double life. By 'culture' she means not only 'self-culture' but also *the* culture—the climate of thought and feeling of the age. Hutton recognized that the implication of George Eliot's work was that the whole culture had advanced beyond the objectivist ethics of Christianity; he can see that her connection with the stage of culture to which his beliefs belong, as in Arnold's connection with Newman, was through the 'inwardness' of Christianity. Hence the importance of his defence of her ethics against the attack by the established Church in the *Church Quarterly*.[69]

The writer of the anonymous article, said Hutton, 'is too unconscious of what Christian morality really means, to criticise George Eliot's ethics with a shadow of success.' 'Not', he goes on, 'that we regard George Eliot's ethics as Christian, but that we hold them to have all the *inwardness* of Christian ethics, all the sincere desire to judge not by outward acts and conventional appearances, but by

---

[66] *Modern Guides*, pp. 275–6.

[67] Wartofsky, *Feuerbach*, p. 11.

[68] R. H. Hutton, 'Puseyite Novels', *Prospective Review*, pp. 512–13; Feuerbach, *Essence of Christianity*, pp. 2, 82.

[69] *Spectator*, 3 Nov. 1877, pp. 1363–4; 'The Romance of Modern Scepticism', *Church Quarterly Review*, 5 (Oct. 1877–Jan. 1878), 91–119.

the quality of the interior motive and purpose.'[70] Her novels, we might say, are to Hutton an illustration of the inside of Christian ethics even if they are not crystallized into a distinctly Christian form. This is the reverse of his view of Elizabeth Sewall's emphasis on the formal conventions of Christianity and Church dogma.

Nevertheless, it must be said that Hutton is trying, in effect, to make George Eliot into the Christian moralist she certainly is not. Perhaps this is why, in the article in question, he aims his idea of the inwardness of Christian ethics at the *Church Quarterly* writer. This critic suggests that her novels undermine the institution of marriage, and in spite of Hutton's repeated criticism of George Eliot's association with G. H. Lewes, he comments on the anonymous writer: 'What the writer is really thinking of is not spiritual Christianity, but *propriety*. "Is this proper?" is the real question besetting the writer's mind, not "Is this conceived in the right spirit?" . . . his morality stands on too conventional a plane to enter into George Eliot's ethics'. Hutton takes the writer to be concerned only with 'outward acts and conventional appearances' and to have, therefore, only the 'outwardness' of Christian ethics. Hutton, that is to say, seems to be using what he has learnt from George Eliot in order to defend her, and is not arguing from a position he might have taken up thirty years before. Though his criticism of Charlotte Yonge and Elizabeth Sewall was on the grounds of their allegiance to the conventional, it was through studying George Eliot that Hutton seems to have learnt the secular answer to conventional Christianity.

Moreover, Hutton's defence of George Eliot is that of a literary critic of the novel and has an aesthetic equivalent. His interest in the novel is fired by his interest in human character, in motive and purpose, and it reflects his anti-utilitarian ethic that the adjective 'good' attaches to people and not to acts. His critical search for 'meaning', the kind of search criticized by Lewes, reflects the 'inwardness' of Hutton's Christianity and his letters to Newman chart the painful effort to hang on to *real* belief in the face of the acceptable alternative offered by George Eliot. There is also, however, an aesthetic equivalent of the ethics of the *Church Quarterly*. Such literary criticism as that of W. H. Mallock, Leslie Stephen, and even G. H. Lewes appeals to the authority of convention, and to formal artistry, propriety, and legitimacy.

[70] *Spectator*, 3 Nov. 1877, 1363.

The aesthetic and the moral laws

The identification of the moral and the aesthetic law among critics of George Eliot is most clearly illustrated by the work of the political and literary critic, W. H. Mallock. He discusses her philosophy in his *Is Life Worth Living?* (1879), but puts his aesthetic criticism more dogmatically in his *Edinburgh Review* essay on *The Impressions of Theophrastus Such*.[71] The novel, he insists, is a work of art and therefore 'must conform to certain artistic laws' which require, for example, that incidents be presented in 'due proportion' and be 'properly subordinate to some central interest'. Using analogies from painting, Mallock requires 'moral perspective and moral chiaroscuro', a picture in whose composition 'everything must not be made an unrelieved darkness by vice or sorrow'.[72] Hutton rather similarly describes George Eliot as 'painting the world a shade darker', but Mallock lends the analogy authority, deriving from it ¬ sense of compulsion and the sanction of propriety. Hutton's reaction to George Eliot is to question the truth of what she implies—she evokes in him 'a combative disposition to challenge the fidelity of the pictures'—while Mallock's reaction is to question their propriety.

Mallock's criticism is itself, as he insists the incidents of a novel should be, part of an organic whole. It refers to the larger context of his belief just as he suggests that George Eliot's novels are a 'gradual setting forth of a philosophy and religion of life, illustrated by a continuous succession of diagrams'.[73] The fundamental tenet of George Eliot's thought, and the fundamental difference between her philosophy and Christianity, he argues, 'lies in this, that it asserts the part to be more complete and greater than the whole; that it asserts those human hopes, loves and enthusiasms which Christianity has developed for us, and bequeathed to us, to be in reality *complete in themselves*.'[74]

This summary is reapplied directly to the novels, which are therefore 'not so much so many pictures, as so many separate canvases . . . neither in conception nor in execution fused together into con-

---

[71] 'Impressions of Theophrastus Such', *Edinburgh Review*, 150 (Oct. 1879), 557–86.
[72] Ibid., pp. 557–8.
[73] Ibid., p. 565.
[74] Ibid., p. 564.

sistent artistic wholes'.[75] He does, though, argue that the novels are part of a consistent philosophy, an 'atheistic pietism', and he attacks George Eliot, in essence, for failing to separate fiction and philosophy. Though Mallock does not distinguish much between novels, *Romola* comes in for particular and representative criticism, especially for Savonarola's words of advice to Romola, 'make your marriage sorrows an offering, too, my daughter: an offering to the great work by which sin and sorrow are made to cease.' Mallock finds these words especially distasteful since they imply the notion that a sacrifice could be made to 'some force of human progress' and not to 'the God who has made us, loved us, and suffered for us'.[76]

Mallock is objecting, it seems, to a change from a belief in the claims of a personal God to a belief in the claims of every person, from an appeal to Divine right to an appeal *avant la lettre* to 'human rights', as the jargon of secular morality has it today. Hutton expresses a commitment to individuality which places his sympathy, even as a Christian, with George Eliot. He therefore separates his notion of the total effect of the novels, that which induces a 'combative disposition', from what he calls their 'unit of effect'; he also distinguishes more rigorously, as a reviewer would, between novels, and concentrates on character rather than 'incident'.

So, to return to *Romola* and Savonarola, Hutton writes:

George Eliot's drawings all require a certain space, like Raffael's cartoons, and are not of that kind which produce their effect by the reiteration of scenes each *complete in itself*. You have to unroll a large surface of the picture before even the smallest *unit* of its effect is attained. And this is far more true of *Romola* than of her English tales.[77]

The painting analogy is much more active here, contradicting Mallock's translation from a system of ethics which sees human emotions as 'complete in themselves'. The very metaphor from painting is generous and itself a virtual retranslation of George Eliot's ethics, not Hutton's own, since her avowed aim was the production of a certain greater inner space in her reader, a magnanimity.[78] Indeed, it is significant that this statement on *Romola*

[75] Ibid., p. 561.
[76] Ibid., p. 564.
[77] *Modern Guides*, p. 189.
[78] See her letter to Charles Bray (5 July 1869): 'If Art does not enlarge men's sympathies, it does nothing morally' (*Letters of George Eliot*, ed. G. S. Haight, 9 vols. (London, 1954–78), iii. 111).

was not part of his original review of the book (which appeared in July 1863) but from his *Essays Theological and Literary* which appeared in 1871, after the correspondence on *Romola* cited above. His words might be seen as a version of the remarks in her letter to him describing it as the habit of her imagination 'to strive after as full a vision of the medium in which a character moves as of the character itself'.[79] She also, quite unwittingly, contradicts Mallock's assertion that her incidents are not 'properly subordinate to some central interest'. She wrote to Hutton: 'There is scarcely a phrase, an incident, an allusion, that did not gather its value to me from its supposed subservience to my main artistic objects'. That word 'artistic' distinguishes Mallock from George Eliot—he takes her main object to be philosophical and outside the novel. Hutton appreciates more specifically the doctrine to which *Romola* is subservient but, as in the case of the exchange with Hardy, he restricts mention of it to the letter.

Though George Eliot's remarks on the representative status of single phrases and single allusions might be said to serve as a sanction for his method of inferring from partial readings what a novel is being 'true to', Hutton does not take up the meeting of Savonarola and Romola seized upon by Mallock. In fact he expressly dismisses the scene as uncharacteristic. He refers instead to Savonarola's inner debate on the trial by fire:

George Eliot was too sceptical at heart to desire to paint a finer picture of the believer than of the half-believer. And she threw her whole mind into the profoundly pathetic scene in which Savonarola, having in the fervour of his eloquence committed God to working him a miracle at the right moment, is brought to book both by his enemies and friends on the question of the trial by fire, and kneels in prayer that in fact refuses to be prayer, but rises into a political debate within himself as to the policy of seeming to take a step which he knows he must somehow evade . . . The scene is too long to snatch from the context and is, indeed, closely bound up with the picture of the encounter of Tito which follows.[80]

Hutton begins with George Eliot's scepticism, and sees the scene as an expression of that, of what Arnold called, in 1853, 'the dialogue of the mind with itself'. Mallock follows the reverse process and takes an excerpt as an accidental revelation of scepticism. Con-

---

[79] *Letters of George Eliot*, iv. 97 (8 Aug. 1863).
[80] *Modern Guides*, pp. 199–200.

sequently, Hutton does not choose the scene in which Savonarola's faith overcomes Romola, but the scene in which Savonarola is at odds with his own faith. Hutton praises George Eliot on just those grounds where Mallock criticized her, for putting her whole mind into half belief. Moreover, in an early article on fiction Hutton had observed that the writer 'must not only catch and paint the distinct natures' of his characters, but also 'the uniting purpose which broods over them'. The writer, he went on, 'must imbue his tale with the feeling of that secret relation between the characters which suggests the reason why their destinies are interwoven, and determines the limits of their mutual influences on each other's career.'[81] Hutton's final comment on Savonarola ('the scene . . . is closely bound up with the encounter with Tito') illustrates Hutton's feeling for what he calls the 'retarding nature' of a scene which both holds up the action and suggests the connecting 'context'. His comment also illustrates his feeling that the reader has to have knowledge of a large part of George Eliot's 'canvas' in order to understand any part of it. The scene he chooses leads on to the encounter with Tito, and Hutton hints at what lies 'behind' the text to see the 'secret relation' (the phrase is closely associated with the critical search for 'the secret of George Eliot'), never more than implicit in the novel, between Savonarola, whose prayer becomes political debate, and Tito, whose internal life might be said to consist *entirely* of such debates.

We do not know Mallock's reaction to Hutton's analysis of *Romola*, but we should compare Hutton's reaction to George Eliot with that of the agnostic critic Leslie Stephen. The 'excellent R. H. Hutton' is the only critic repeatedly cited as a contrast to his own point of view by Leslie Stephen in his book on George Eliot. Yet Stephen dismisses the whole question of the place of the scene in the larger context of belief in the organization of the novel. He writes:

Hutton considers the portrait of the reformer to be one of George Eliot's great triumphs, and appeals especially to one scene. I am the more glad to be able to point to an appreciative and genial criticism, as I have to confess my inability to accept it. I should have taken the same scene for the clearest illustration of failure . . . What we really have is not the concrete man at all, but a long and very able psychological analysis of his mental state . . .

[81] 'A Novel or Two', *National Review*, 1 (Oct. 1855), 336–50 (p. 336).

Savonarola's mind was surely, in this respect, constituted like most people's: we all think we can bear the dentist's forceps till we get into his armchair.[82]

Stephen first exaggerates Hutton's claims for the portrait of Savonarola in the attempt to make the contrast with his view more stark. He would have preferred something 'short and pithy' for the scene which then made way for the action. 'We want to see the crowd and bustle and the play of popular fun and passion', says Stephen.[83] Even the phrase 'psychological analysis' is used with a rather scornful irony, making use of the critical jargon which Stephen rarely uses without drawing attention to its distasteful vulgarity and his reluctance to employ it.[84] He does not tell us why the 'portrait' of Savonarola is a failure, and any faith in his assurance that it is an 'able psychological analysis' is undermined by the inadequacy of his bathetic summary: we all think we can bear the dentist's forceps till we get into his armchair. In fact, bathos is the most characteristic feature of Stephen's book on George Eliot.[85] In effect, Stephen shares with Arnold an inability to accept and discuss the novel as the translation of thought and belief in the way they both discussed Wordsworth.

It might be added, however, that just as I suggested Leslie Stephen had some autobiographical occasion for finding Wordsworth consolatory, so there may have been some 'secret relation' between Hutton and Savonarola. The debate which Savonarola has with himself has certain affinities with the debate Hutton had with Newman in private. Hutton may have seen in Savonarola an expression of his feeling committed to a certainty in public which did not guarantee his certainty in private.

[82] Leslie Stephen, *George Eliot*, pp. 133–4.

[83] Ibid., p. 135.

[84] So Stephen writes, for instance: 'It is proper, I believe, to speak of such writing as "subjective" ' (Ibid., p. 87). That 'I believe' is frequently used by Stephen to suggest its opposite, his scepticism of such proprieties.

[85] Commenting on George Eliot's suggestion that she 'had no soul for music', Stephen writes: 'Perhaps the want of "soul" meant only a specific aptitude for the musician's calling; or possibly the singing at Coventry was out of tune' (Ibid., p. 13). Again, he quotes her explanation of why she could not use the Moors or Jews for what became *The Spanish Gypsy*, 'the facts of their history were too conspicuously opposed to the working out of my catastrophe'. Stephen comments: 'Facts have that awkward habit' (p. 160).

7
Conclusion

HUTTON asked of any part of a novel the question 'To what is it true?'. He tries to answer the question by referring to the novel's and the reader's rough familiarity with life as it appears everyday ('truth to life'), to the psychological consistency of the recognizable character ('truth to type'), to the internal aesthetic consistency of the novel (its truth to itself), and to the novel's fidelity to its author's complete beliefs (the author's truth to himself or herself). Yet this last category raises a further question, especially to the practising reviewer, namely 'to what end is it being written?'— meaning by 'end' both its artistic conclusion and its moral intention of effect.

That the weekly reviewer was in every sense a partial critic was a fact faced by Hutton, who opens his review of the complete *Middlemarch* with a contemptuous reference to those who, in his words, 'say, with a kind of virtuous assumption of artistic feeling' that they will not read novels published in parts. Hutton welcomes publishing and reviewing in parts because 'that is the only way in which human life itself can be studied'.[1] Hutton seems to have removed absolute derogatory comment from criticism just as George Eliot removed it from morals, and to have translated into criticism George Eliot's obsessive question of which part of a man's life might be taken to represent the whole. For her, however, this represented whole was the whole race, 'man'; for Hutton this whole was the whole nature of a man. To George Eliot the terms are sociological, while to Hutton they are essentially biographical and religious.

Practically, Hutton was prepared to risk making literary judgements which might prove wrong and, indeed, did prove wrong. As he had warned in 1855, he belongs to that generation of readers who are prepared to doubt whether incidents 'actually happened', to suspect George Eliot of adding unreal traits to characters which 'bear out her own *criticism* rather than her own imaginative conception.'[2] So Hutton finds George Eliot prejudiced in the apparently

---

[1] *Spectator*, 7 Dec. 1872, 1554.   [2] *Spectator*, 5 Oct. 1872, 1263.

heartless way in which Celia explains Casaubon's codicil to Dorothea.[3] Similarly, he refuses to believe that Lydgate's 'rare nature' would have failed to turn his mistakes into 'the conditions of purer strength and less accidental happiness'. He concludes of Lydgate that 'in pursuing that course from the high and right motive from which, on the whole, he pursued it, he should have gained no new power over either her [i.e. Rosamond] or himself, but should have become bitter on his side, and left her as vain and shallow as he found her is, I think, not *true to nature*, but a picture due to that set theory of semi-pessimism which George Eliot evidently regarded as the best substitute for faith.'[4] Hutton would have preferred to think that Lydgate 'was' what he 'should have been', but his reaction to Rosamond is the most remarkable. In the first reviews his reaction to her is rather like Lydgate's own reaction to her: his impression is one of 'grace, gentleness, propriety, conventional sense, soft tenacity of purpose' and that hers is 'really a sweet and lovable nature at bottom'.[5] Hutton finds, at first, George Eliot's portrayal of Rosamond as 'stagey' to be a product of her spiritual irony; he believes her feelings, though feeble, to be genuine. He later reverses the judgement precisely, to find Rosamond's emotions, though genuine, to be feeble.

Hutton's sensitivity to his own reversals of feeling and opinion mark his sensitivity to George Eliot's own reversals. This brings us to the conclusion of *Middlemarch*, and to Hutton's remarks on the *'Finale'*:

One sees, on looking back over the tale, that it was an essential of George Eliot's purpose to make this high-minded and enthusiastic girl marry twice, and in *neither* case make an 'ideal' marriage . . . The author, indeed, attempted at the close to ascribe the first mistake partly to causes which she had never before indicated, and in doing so made, as I think, a faulty criticism on her own creation. She attenuated Dorothea's responsibility for her first marriage after a fashion hardly consistent either with the type of the character itself, or with the story as it had been told . . . The remark as to the world's 'smiling on a proposition of marriage from a sickly man to a girl less than half his age' really has no foundation in the tale itself. . . . I find in this passage a trace that George Eliot was, on reviewing her own work, dissatisfied with her own picture of the 'prosaic conditions' to which she ascribed Dorothea's misadventures.[6]

---

[3] Ibid.   [4] *Modern Guides*, p. 207.
[5] Ibid., pp. 220–1; *Spectator*, 30 Mar. 1872, 405.
[6] *Modern Guides*, pp. 208–11.

Hutton is comparing his reviewing with George Eliot's reviewing. Both feel that Dorothea's motivation is insufficiently realized but while Hutton looks for an explanation in the text, George Eliot looks for an explanation in the world. For George Eliot a character is to the plot of a novel what an individual is to society, and Hutton resists that equation. He feels that George Eliot, in this Finale and in the novel as a whole, empties the world of the force of God in man's real nature, or at least narrows the moral world to issues which are within human reach. This, he wrote in 1880 in an essay on 'The Atheistic View of Life', is the very narrowing effect of atheism itself: 'Our moral life becomes, on this philosophy, a series of careful adjustments to the great object of rendering that part of the world within our influence, beginning with ourselves, capable of as much healthy and happy life as may be in our power'.[7]

Hutton's criticism of the presentation of small effects as part of a large object could, if he had formulated it differently, have become an analysis of the failure of the secular provincial novel. But he sees *Middlemarch* as unusual in its coincidence of artistic and philosophical aim. The novel's moral and aesthetic tendencies, he wrote in 1872, 'convey the same sort of shock with which, during the early days of eclipses, men must have seen the rays of light converging towards a centre of darkness . . . one feels a positive sense of vacancy'.[8] This is what Hutton cannot quite accept, that he and George Eliot share so many beliefs except the authority for them. Hence the aptness of the phrase 'positive vacancy', since it is said in reaction to vacant positivism. George Eliot is her own authority, as Hutton tacitly recognizes in his phrase 'a criticism on her own creation'. He had, however, foreseen this authorial status and his reaction to it while writing on Elizabeth Sewall and Mrs Gaskell in 1855. He wrote then:

The Germans teach of the 'retarding nature' essential to a romance. They do not mean that which retards the reader, but that the absence of which is apt to retard the reader,—the retarding elements of the action,—the holding back from the coming issue,—a sense throughout the tale of an end, but a constantly increasing anxiety as to *what* end: a feeling of convergence of moral destinies to an unseen focus. . . . A great artist must, in a certain sense, be the providence to the conceptions he has created . . . From the beginning there should be a foreshadowing of the coming knot of destiny,

---

[7] *Fraser's Magazine*, NS 21 (May 1880), 652–67 (p. 665).
[8] *Spectator*, 7 Dec. 1872, 1556.

though not of its solution, so as to give a unity of meaning to the whole as
well as individual life to the parts . . . We doubt if any really great writer of
fiction ever thought *up* from his individual characters, to his scenes and
events. The action is conceived first as an organic whole.[9]

Here Hutton anticipates his reaction to the 'converging rays' of
Middlemarch and foreshadows, in his remarks on the artist's need
to be 'the providence to the conceptions he has created', his study
of George Eliot and Feuerbach. He could not have foreseen how
literally he was to see in George Eliot 'the spectacle of a woman
who was her own God', a woman who could write 'I have sinned
against my own laws'.[10] Ironically, George Eliot perfectly fulfils
the requirements of Hutton for a great artist to 'think down' to her
characters from an organic whole. Hutton had, in this sense,
always been waiting for George Eliot—hence his combative shock
when he discovered that, unlike Jane Austen, she 'was' not what
she 'should have been'.

Although George Eliot may not have realized Hutton's ideals
fully, it is important that she *was* his ideal writer and significant,
also, that he should have appreciated her intentions in art while not
necessarily always approving her realization of them, since this
distinction between intention and action is one of which she would
have heartily approved. We might, indeed, most fittingly conclude
by surveying the common ground between Hutton and George
Eliot, especially as this can be inferred from late Victorian verdicts
on Hutton's work.

Julia Wedgwood wrote a moving obituary of Hutton for the
Contemporary Review in which she confesses to be 'chary of re-
opening a review of George Eliot' because 'so much was written
about her at the time recording . . . the spell of a great genius dealing with the problems of the hour'.[11] Hutton is regarded in the same

---

[9] *National Review*, 1 (Oct. 1855), 336–8. See also D. A. Miller, *Narrative and Its
Discontents: Problems of Closure in the Traditional Novel* (Princeton, 1981),
107–10. The notion of a 'retarding' element entered the language of literary criticism
without further comments. It surfaces in Henry James's review of *Felix Holt*: 'It is
as a broad picture of midland county life in England thirty years ago that *Felix Holt*
is, to our taste, most interesting. On this subject the author writes from a full mind,
with a wealth of fancy, of suggestion, of illustration, at the command of no other
English writer, bearing you along the broad and placid rise of her speech, with a
kind of retarding persuasiveness which allows her conjured images to sink slowly
into your very brain' (*Nation*, 16 Aug. 1866, 128).

[10] *Modern Guides*, p. 264; *Letters*, v. 459.

[11] 'Richard Holt Hutton', *Contemporary Review*, 72 (1897), 457–69 (p. 460).

light—as one who dealt with the problems of the hour and their relation to 'eternal verities'. Similarly, Julia Wedgwood defends Hutton against charges that were, and still are, also made against George Eliot. Hutton's *Spectator*, she records, was said by some to be dull reading and over-written because it was 'so just':

I remember well the laugh . . . of a Saturday Reviewer, who confessed he found it a difficulty in the way of reading the *Spectator*, that it was 'so just'. He was the spokesman of the larger half of the newspaper-reading world. Nothing, indeed, is really less dull than justice.[12]

Readers made the same accusation of George Eliot and received the same moral lesson from her admirers.

Both Hutton and George Eliot wrote a 'just' prose which tried to be all-inclusive. So Julia Wedgwood went on to confess that Hutton wrote in 'an involved style', and other commentators were less polite in making the same observation. Thus a writer in the *Dial* described Hutton as 'entangled in the network of his own verbiage', while the *Athenaeum* commented: 'his sentences are frequently of an exasperating length and of the most ungainly character; he gives the impression that his thoughts are running away with his pen and that he is ignorant of the virtues of revision'.[13] All these writers are in context contrasting their *fin de siècle* 'modern taste' with Hutton's 'lack of excursions into brilliant paradox or exaggerated epigram'.[14] Yet if we were to try to put forward Hutton's case we might say that his prose reflects a mind which, like that of his hero Newman, was 'wide and delicately sympathetic' and yet attached to 'a dogmatic and theological view of the universe' (see above, chapter 3, 'Apologia Pro Vita Sua'). His prose has sympathy with, and even expresses, the sort of doubts he expressed in private to Newman, yet it also contains assurance and faith. Similarly, when writing on Arnold's comments on the American Civil War, he opposes Arnold's view to a 'sympathy . . . which overpowers, even without dispelling, the cautious fears of selfish conservatism' (see above, p. 89). So we might say that Hutton's prose aimed to overpower problems without dispelling them: he held difficulties in solution.

With a similar regard to the prose of the sympathetic imagination, a recent critic could have been writing of Hutton when she

12 Ibid., p. 458.
13 *Dial*, 1 July 1894, 18; *Athenaeum*, 2 July 1894, 704.
14 *Athenaeum*, 18 July 1897, 389–90.

commented on George Eliot's prose: 'the long and usually well-balanced sentence served her well, protectively enveloping the pith of the content . . . even if at times rendered almost incomprehensible by an excessive burden of meaning. . . . she paid a price for the style which emerged as her own, for as it was being shaped, it was also determining she would never be a true wit or a genuine poet'.[15]

We might say that both Hutton and George Eliot wrote with a prose which, like their minds, tried to do justice to every side of an issue, and both express and conceal their prejudices and aggressions. Far from being ignorant of the virtue of revision, each writes in a style which is full of second thoughts—not in the sense of being self-contradictory, but in the sense of anticipating the contradictory and trying to appropriate it.

To some late Victorian critics the style, content, and even imagery of Hutton and George Eliot seem dated.[16] However, the retrospective accounts by writers less anxious to dissociate themselves from the century suggest very important similarities between Hutton and George Eliot, even on religious grounds. Wilfred Ward, writing in 1888, described Hutton's religion as 'of his own manufacture', went on to write of his 'individual and self-evolved creed', and suggested that 'a more individual and independent journey forward in religious truth has rarely been accomplished'.[17] A comparison with Newman immediately comes to mind, but perhaps the other great self-evolved creed of the age belonged to George Eliot. Although it may seem paradoxical to describe as close the religious positions of Hutton and George Eliot, their views of the moral aims of Christianity are almost identical, and these views are translated into their style and their literary judgements.

Thus the tone of Hutton's work is described in the same terms as that of George Eliot's. He is said to have written 'with never a shade of doubt in his own infallibility', while some readers of his *Spectator* articles found themselves 'resenting their omniscience

---

[15] Ruby Redinger, *George Eliot: The Emergent Self* (London, 1975), 78–9.

[16] A comment in the *Athenaeum* on Hutton's imagery, for instance, is strikingly applicable to George Eliot: the writer condemns Hutton's 'free use of examples derived from esoteric science in a manner that was commoner twenty years ago than today' ('*Aspects of Religious and Scientific Thought*', *Athenaeum*, 22 Apr. 1899, 489).

[17] 'Mr. R. H. Hutton as a Religious Thinker', *Dublin Review*, third series 20 (1888), 1–21 (pp. 18, 19, 5).

and their casual introduction of recondite information'.[18] Similarly, the omniscient narrator of George Eliot's novels is given particular authority by her moral position as 'a woman who was her own God'. Yet we know that in private both writers had doubts: they both belonged to a sceptical generation which only found certainty in introspection. The difference between Hutton and the novelist is that he believed that his nature was the creation of God, while she believed that her nature was her own and could be made to play the part of every man.

When Henry Sidgwick reviewed Hutton's essays in 1871 he might have been speaking of George Eliot when he describes Hutton's 'general statements about human nature' as 'derived from introspection'.[19] As I suggested when discussing *The Impressions of Theophrastus Such*, George Eliot's moral strength derived, she felt, from a discernment of her own shared weakness. Each writer had a 'religious' attachment to the provincial and the everyday in the belief that they were like all other men but only unlike them in knowing it. Thus the novelist and the critic occupy a position diametrically opposed to that occupied by Arnold and Pater, the spokesmen for exclusivity and subjectivism.

Henry Sidgwick also suggested, in the same review, that Hutton's literary essays do not examine writers' 'methods and technical performance', but instead study their nature and genius: 'what they aimed at rather than what they effected'. This judgement, as I hope to have demonstrated, is not quite true, since Hutton often (as in the case of Arnold and Tennyson) judges on the basis of technical performance. If we take Sidgwick's words in their implicitly ethical meaning, however, such a judging by intention and not by action certainly is a crude summary of the anti-utilitarian creed of both George Eliot and Hutton.

It is true that Hutton judged writers on the basis of their intentions, although he was also more sensitive than most of his contemporaries to the extent to which a writer's language is outside of his control: Hutton was most interested in the conflict between a writer's intention and his age's 'tendency'. This is the 'resistance' he found in Newman, Wordsworth, Tennyson, and in the poetry of Arnold, but he found it dramatized most adequately in the novel, and pre-eminently in George Eliot. Yet one of the consequences of

---

[18] *Bookman*, 6 (June 1884), 85–6; *Academy*, 22 Apr. 1899, 451.
[19] *Academy*, 1 July 1871, 325.

judging writers by their intention is a certain relativism of judgement. Thus Julia Wedgwood had to confess that Hutton had 'hardly
any sense of *rank* in literature', and while this is not quite accurate
(the writers in this thesis comprise the major part of Hutton's
canon), he is clearly setting himself against Arnold when he complains that the latter *merely* ranks the subjects of his criticism
without portraying them (see above, p. 96).[20]

On first consideration, Arnold seems the 'modern' critic and
Hutton the reactionary. On further examination, however, Arnold
can be seen to be holding on to a dying past and Hutton to be
accommodating himself and his readers to new needs and new
forms of expression. I have suggested that Arnold places himself in
the role of moral Explorer and that Hutton sees this role as
representative of the non-believer. Yet in 1871 S. D. Collet percep-
tively described Hutton as belonging to 'an advanced guard of
religious pioneers' who are maintaining spiritual values in a secular
world.[21] We might say that George Eliot belonged to the same
advanced guard, and that both she and Hutton saw the realistic
novel as the form which cleared the way forward.

In concluding as I have on Hutton's affinities with George Eliot,
I might be accused of using, or abusing, Hutton's own technique of
looking for common ground in divergent writers and thinkers.
Several contemporary accounts of his work speak of 'Hutton's
method of showing that the views of other people, although they
knew it not, were fundamentally in harmony with the views held by
himself and his readers'.[22] This comment, however, only demonstrates further the affinity with the novelist: in both art and morals
each is committed to discovering and enlarging a fundamental community of human nature. It is true, however, that Hutton repeatedly
finds writers 'implicitly Christian' in spite of those writers' own expressions of disbelief, because he takes their words and actions to
be the occasions for the emergence of a nature which must, given
his beliefs, be God-given. On this point, the question of the *reality*
of spiritual causes, he and George Eliot differ sharply and finally.
We might say, however, that their *aims* are essentially close, even if
their ideas of cause and effect are vitally different.

---

[20] Wedgwood, *Contemporary Review*, 72 (1897), 459.
[21] 'Mr. Hutton as Critic and Theologian', *Contemporary Review*, 16 (1871), 635.
[22] *Academy*, 22 Apr. 1899, 452.

Hutton's criticism, like George Eliot's writing, is both flexible and personal, introspective and absolute. He provides, therefore, a view of Victorian literature and thought which is, I would say, unique in its combination of consistency of purpose and standpoint with a flexible sensitivity to divergence and diversity. Indeed, I can do no better than conclude with the verdict of Marcus Dodds in the *Bookman* for 1894, reviewing *Criticisms on Contemporary Thought and Thinkers*:

Among his contemporaries have been Carlyle, Emerson, Newman, Darwin, Ruskin, Martineau, Dickens, Arnold, J. Stuart Mill, and for a judicious estimate of these and the other writers who have illustrated the Victorian era there is nothing to compare with Mr. Hutton's criticism. These volumes are not merely a present delight to all lovers of literature, but they will afford the most valuable assistance to the future historian of the nineteenth century.[23]

[23] *Bookman*, 6 (June 1894), 85–6.

Appendix: Hutton's Contributions to the Periodical Press

With regard to attribution and identification, Hutton's contributions to the quarterly press were often signed or noted on file, so that their identification is probably complete. In particular, many articles in the *Prospective Review* are identifiable from the letters, biographies, and works of its chief contributors (especially the unpublished *Diary* of Crabb Robinson), while many pieces in the *National Review* are known from marked files kept by James and Russell Martineau and now held by the Reading University Library, and the Dr Williams Library. Both these journals are dealt with in the third volume of the *Wellesley Index to Victorian Periodicals.*

Hutton's contributions to weeklies, except for those in the *Spectator*, can on the whole only be identified on the basis of internal evidence and from correspondence with friends and colleagues—especially his correspondence with Martineau, Maurice, Bagehot, J. H. Thom, Crabb Robinson, and Clough. Any records kept by Hutton himself would have been lost with the rest of his papers in the 1927 fire which destroyed the home of his nephew, who had inherited them.

The problem of identifying Hutton's *Spectator* contributions dogged earlier attempts to study his work. The author of a 1949 Ph.D. thesis suggested that 'most of the four thousand articles and reviews Hutton must have written for the *Spectator* will probably never be identified' (A. K. Stevens, 'R. H. Hutton, theologian and critic', unpublished dissertation, University of Michigan, 1949, p. 20). Another confessed that 'an authoritative exposition of Hutton's views in full detail is impossible without full access to the marked files of the *Spectator*' (G. N. Thomas, 'R. H. Hutton, a biographical and critical study', unpublished Ph.D. dissertation, University of Illinois, 1949, p. 182).

These records have since come to light, identifying some 20,000 articles from the periods 1874–7 and 1880–99, and attributing about 3,500 of these to Hutton.[1] There are, in addition, marked copies of the *Spectator*, kept originally by the editors and now privately owned or held by the Brixton Central Reference Library. Further articles from Hutton's period as editor can be identified from the four volumes of *Spectator* essays published in collections. A few articles can be identified from Hutton's reference to himself, as editor, or as the author, and a number attributed from internal evidence and from correspondence.

[1] R. H. Tener, 'The *Spectator* Records', *Victorian Periodicals Newsletter*, 17 (Spring 1960), 33–6.

Since Hutton wrote some 6,000 articles and reviews for the *Spectator* it is difficult to give some representative cross-section of his material. If, however, we look at the four decades of Hutton's period as editor we can get some indication of the scope of his work.

In what was probably the first issue he edited, that of 1 June 1861, he probably wrote three articles: 'Intellectual Crazes' (pp. 584–5), a review of two eccentric mathematical books, *The Quadrature of the Circle*, by James Smith, and *Philosophy or the Science of Truth*, by James Haig; 'Tracts for Priests and People' (p. 588), a review of two of these tracts, 'Religio Laici' by Thomas Hughes and 'The Mote and the Beam' by F. D. Maurice, concentrating on the discussion by Maurice of *Essays and Reviews*; 'Archbishop Whateley's *Miscellaneous Essays*' (pp. 590–1), a largely favourable review of material with which Hutton was already familiar.

If we compare these contributions with those of the first week of June ten years later (3 June 1871), we find the same interest in current intellectual events, partly governed by the sheer chance of current publication. Hutton contributed an article on 'Satiric Utopias' (pp. 665–7), reviewing two accounts of the year 2071, and a second on 'Aphasia' (pp. 667–8), a review of a book of the same title by a Dr Bateman. This second article represents an increasing interest on Hutton's part in the progress of research into the operation of the brain and particularly its implications for notions of mind and language.

Ten years later (4 June 1881), this interest is reflected in an article on the limits of intelligence and animal society ('The Ants and their Policy', pp. 729–30). His other two articles for the week are, however, on politics: 'Lord Salisbury in Middlesex' (pp. 725–6), about Conservative attacks on the Liberal's Irish Land Bill, and 'Sir Stafford Northcote's Personal Bias' (p. 727), a comparative study of the temperaments of the leaders of the Conservative party.

The *Spectator* for the first week of June 1891 shows the same kind of scope. Hutton is attributed with having contributed four articles: two are political, 'Mr. Goschen and the Conservative View of Education' (pp. 782–3) and 'The Queen as Statesman' (pp. 783–4), about Victoria's correspondence with Archbishop Tait on the Disestablishment of the Irish Church; the third is an article on research into the relationship between mind and language using early recording techniques ('Apes and Men', pp. 787–8); the fourth is a review of Mrs Sutherland Orr's *Life of Browning* (pp. 793–5).

This is a reasonable cross-section of Hutton's *Spectator* work, writing usually between two and six articles per week on politics, current events and current publications. Although, as Hutton himself announced, he wrote about the most ephemeral publications, he returned most often to those writers which posterity has also remembered, though this is partly because they were the most frequently published and republished and therefore provided most occasions for review.

A brief survey of Hutton's contributions to other, mainly quarterly periodicals during this period is easier to give. The evidence suggests that Hutton wrote three more essays, all in 1863, for the *National Review* before it folded in 1864: these were on Shelley, Browning, and the poetry of Owen Meredith.[2] He also wrote three more articles for the *Economist*, in 1862, 1872, and 1877, the last being an obituary of Bagehot. In May and September 1863 he wrote essays for the first issue of *Victoria Magazine*, the only contributions he made and which were signed, on the spiritual world and on Renan's *Vie de Jésus* and its intellectual background.[3] Between February and December 1865 he seems to have written twenty-seven articles for the *Pall Mall Gazette*, and never contributed again. Seventeen of these articles, on the political characters of individual Members of Parliament, were reprinted in book form as *Studies in Parliament* (London, 1866), including sketches of Gladstone, Stanley, Palmerston, Disraeli, Cobden, Bright, Forster, and Lord Derby. Hutton had written two essays for the *North British Review* in 1858 and in 1866 he wrote his third and last, an essay on '*Ecce Homo* and Modern Scepticism'.[4] Between 1869 and 1873 Hutton wrote three essays each for *Macmillan's Magazine* and the *British Quarterly Review*, on Herbert Spencer, St Paul, and Tennyson, and on Utilitarianism, Matthew Arnold, and George Eliot.[5] One of these was read as a paper to the Metaphysical Society and four others reprinted in book form. Also in the 1870s Hutton wrote for the *Contemporary Review* and for the *Nineteenth Century*: for the former, in fact, he wrote five essays in the 1870s, six in the 1880s, and a final essay in 1894; for the latter he wrote three articles in the 1870s, two in the 1880s, and two in the 1890s. The subjects of these essays include Matthew Arnold, Cardinal Newman, George Eliot, Gladstone, the anti-vivisectionist lobby, and the consequences of a decline in religious belief.[6]

    [2] 'Shelley's Poetical Mysticism', *National Review*, 16 (Jan. 1863), 62–87; 'The Poetry of Owen Meredith', ibid., 17 (July 1863), 174–203; 'Mr. Browning's Poems', ibid., 17 (Oct. 1863), 417–46.

    [3] 'The Unspiritual World of Spirits', *Victoria Magazine*, 1 (May 1863), 42–60; 'M. Renan's *Vie de Jésus*', ibid., 1 (Sept. 1863), 385–96.

    [4] *North British Review*, 44 (Mar. 1866), 124–53.

    [5] 'A Questionable Parentage for Morals', *Macmillan's Magazine*, 20 (July 1869), 266–73; 'St. Paul', ibid., 20 (Oct. 1869), 508–18; 'Tennyson', ibid., 27 (Dec. 1872), 143–67; 'The Latest Phase of the Utilitarian Controversy', *British Quarterly Review*, 50 (July 1869), 68–91; 'The Poetry of Matthew Arnold', ibid., 55 (Apr. 1872), 313–47; '*Middlemarch*: A Study in Provincial Life', ibid., 57 (Apr. 1873), 407–29.

    [6] 'Mr. Arnold on St. Paul and his Creed', *Contemporary Review*, 14 (June 1870), 329–41; 'Cardinal Newman', ibid., 45 (May 1884), 642–65; 'Newman and Arnold—I. Newman', ibid., 49 (Mar. 1886), 327–54; 'Newman and Arnold—II. Arnold', ibid., 49 (Apr. 1886), 513–34; 'George Eliot', ibid., 47 (Mar. 1885), 372–91; 'The Anti-Vivisectionist Agitation', ibid., 43 (Apr. 1883), 510–16; 'Mr. Gladstone', ibid., 65 (May 1894), 616–34; 'A Modern *Symposium*: The Influence Upon Morality of a Decline in Religious Belief', *Nineteenth Century*, 1 (May 1877), 539–45; 'The Biologists on Vivisection', ibid., 11 (Jan. 1882), 29–39.

Hutton wrote for only one other journal in the 1870s, contributing an essay on Walter Bagehot to John Morley's *Fortnightly Review* in 1877. The evidence indicates that Hutton wrote a further eleven essays for some seven journals in the 1880s and 1890s: an essay for *Fraser's Magazine* in 1880, on 'The Atheistic View of Life', two essays in 1881 for the *Expositor*, on 'Secularism' and on Christ's prophecies, an essay on Carlyle for *Good Words* in 1881, which was followed by essays for the same journal on F. D. Maurice (1884), Browning (1890), and Newman (1890), an essay on Wordsworth for the 1882 *Modern Review*, a second essay for the *Fortnightly Review*, this time on Clough (1883), an essay for the revived *National Review* in 1892, on Renan, and finally an essay on Huxley for *Forum* in 1895.[7] All these essays were signed at the time of publication, and several republished in book form by Hutton.

The most obvious reason for Hutton's writing for these quarterly journals was the space it gave him to elaborate an argument: the subject matter is the same as that he was dealing with every week, indeed some of these essays incorporated material already published in the *Spectator*, and the readership was, on the whole, much the same as that addressed by the *Spectator*. Writing for journals like these freed Hutton from the occasional nature of weekly reviewing. Exactly which journal he wrote for seems to have depended on the general tone and content of the journal and Hutton's personal connection with it. So his 1880 essay for *Fraser's Magazine* can be seen as a contribution to John Tulloch's attempt, as editor from July 1879 to January 1881, to revive the flagging fortunes of that journal after its great days under J. A. Froude, under whose editorship, from 1860 to 1874, *Fraser's* became anti-clerical and Conservative. His essay for David Douglas's *North British Review* in 1866 was a contribution to Liberalism in religion before the journal was taken over by a group of Liberal Catholics led by Lord Acton to replace the defunct *Home and Foreign Review*, while the Liberalism of the *Fortnightly Review*, then edited by the Liberal politician John Morley, would have attracted Hutton in 1877. In general, Hutton wrote for journals whose leanings were liberal in religion and politics, and whose interest in politics was from an ethical point of view (this would have been the special attraction of *Macmillan's*). For these

---

[7] 'The Atheistic View of Life', *Fraser's Magazine*, NS 21 (May 1880), 652–67; 'Secularism', *Expositor*, NS 1 (Jan. 1881), 1–12; 'Christ's Prophecies of His Own Death', *Expositor*, NS 1 (June 1881), 457–72; 'Thomas Carlyle', *Good Words*, 22 (Apr. 1881), 282–8; 'Frederick Denison Maurice', *Good Words*, 25 (May 1884), 380–7; 'Browning as a Religious Teacher', *Good Words*, 31 (Feb. 1890), 87–93; 'Cardinal Newman', *Good Words*, 31 (Oct. 1890), 662–9; 'Wordsworth's Two Styles', *Modern Review* (July 1882), 525–38: 'The Poetry of Arthur Hugh Clough', *Fortnightly Review*, NS 33 (June 1883), 790–807; 'M. Renan and Christianity', *National Review*, 20 (Nov. 1892), 301–9; 'Professor Huxley', *Forum*, 20 (Sept. 1895), 23–32.

reasons Hutton did *not* write for, say, the *Quarterly Review* or for G. H. Lewes's and Leslie Stephen's *Cornhill Magazine*.

By far the largest number of Hutton's quarterly writings, some twenty-three essays, were written for the three journals: the *Contemporary Review*, *Nineteenth Century*, and *Good Words*. The last of these was owned by the publisher Alexander Strahan as one of a number of religious journals, and it was Strahan who began the *Contemporary* in 1866, inspired by the example of the *Fortnightly Review* begun the year before, to 'provide a bridge between the secular and the sacred' in literature and thought.[8] Until March 1870 the journal was edited by Henry Alford, the Dean of Canterbury, who edited it 'holding loyally to belief in the articles of the Christian faith' and 'not afraid of collisions with modern thought'.[9] In April 1870, however, Alford was replaced by James Knowles who with Hutton had been a founder member of the Metaphysical Society in 1869.[10] Knowles opened the pages of the *Contemporary Review* to many members of the Society, including Hutton, until he left it in January 1877 to found *Nineteenth Century*, taking with him the Metaphysical Society writers, again including Hutton. Strahan assumed personal control of the journal from 1877 to 1882, when the journal's editorship was taken over by P. W. Bunting, a 'semi-Socialist Liberal', at which point Hutton's contributions were resumed.

[8] F. A. Munby, *Publishing and Bookselling* (London, 1930), 322.

[9] *Contemporary Review*, 13 (1870), 486.

[10] A. W. Brown, *The Metaphysical Society: Victorian Minds in Crisis, 1869–1880* (New York, 1947); R. H. Hutton, 'The Metaphysical Society: A Reminiscence', *Nineteenth Century* 18 (Aug. 1885) 177–96.

BIBLIOGRAPHY

1. R. H. Hutton: manuscripts and published writings

The following bibliography is intended to facilitate reference to works cited in the text and to make available a list of Hutton's writings with special regard to the authors and subjects covered by the present study. Any abbreviations used for purposes of reference are given with the relevant book.

A virtually complete checklist of Hutton's writing will be found in two special numbers of the *Victorian Periodicals Newsletter*: No. 17 (September 1972), 1–183; No. 20 (June 1973), pp. 14–40.

This bibliography lists manuscripts, books, lectures, etc., and periodical articles by Hutton relating to this study.

(*a*) CORRESPONDENCE

There are no known surviving papers of R. H. Hutton, with the exception of letters in the following collections:

Acton Correspondence: letter to Acton written 5 December 1896, Cambridge University Library, Add. MS 6443, f. 186.

Allon (Henry) Papers: 20 letters to Allon written 1868–84, Dr Williams Library, London.

Bagehot: at least 34 letters to Walter Bagehot, Porch Collection, the *Economist*.

Blackwood Papers: letters to Blackwood and to Meredith White written 1864–92, National Library of Scotland, Add. MSS 4209; 4262; 4276; 4291; 4588; 4194.

Gladstone (W. E.) Papers: 44 letters to W. E. Gladstone written 1876–96 (though Hutton did not write at all in the years 1877, 1879, 1881, 1889, and 1893); 5 letters to Herbert Gladstone written 1881–6, British Library, Add. MSS 44215, ff. 283–368; 44785, f. 218.

Hardy Papers: letter to Thomas Hardy written 18 July 1881, Dorset County Museum.

Huxley Papers: 3 letters to T. H. Huxley, Imperial College, London.

Kingsley: letter to Mrs F. E. Kingsley, British Library, Add. MS 41299, f. 270.

Ludlow Papers: 7 letters to J. M. Ludlow written 1861–8, Cambridge University Library, Add. MSS 7348/10 ff. 174–80.

MacColl: letter to Revd M. MacColl written 1880, British Library, Add. MS 44243, f. 316.

Martineau Papers: letters to James Martineau; letters to George Eliot, Yale University Eliot Papers.

Mundella Papers: 33 letters to Maria Theresa Mundella written 1879–84, Sheffield University Library.

Newman: letters to J. H. Newman written 1864–73, 1886–9, The Oratory, Birmingham. Mainly republished in C. S. Dessain and T. Gornald (eds.), *Letters and Diaries of J. H. Newman.*

Robertson (G. C.) Papers: 12 letters to various correspondents, University College, London.

Stephen (J. F.) Papers: letter to J. F. Stephen written 27 November 1868, Cambridge University Library, Add. MS 7349/15/99.

Sully Papers: 5 letters to James Sully, University College, London.

White: letters to R. G. White written 1862–7, New York Historical Society Collection, New York Public Library, Add. MS 71, ff. 1193–1224.

In addition there are 12 letters (1858–95) in the Huntingdon Library.

(*b*) BOOKS

Hutton published twelve books: four were editions of works by W. C. Roscoe and Walter Bagehot, two were critical biographies, and the rest were collections of essays. Several were reprinted, some with important changes which I have detailed below. Two posthumous collections of his articles were published in 1899 and 1900.

Poems and Essays by the Late William Caldwell Roscoe, ed. R. H. Hutton, 2 vols. (London, 1860)

Studies in Parliament (London, 1866). Contains 17 articles reprinted from the *Pall Mall Gazette*, 1865

Essays, Theological and Literary, 2 vols. (London, 1871, revised edition 1877). Reprinted as *Theological Essays* and *Literary Essays*, 1880, 1888, 1896. Contains the following essays:

Vol. i:
'The Moral Significance of Atheism', 3–29
'The Atheistic Explanation of Religion', 30–44
'Science and Theism', 45–67
'Popular Pantheism', 68–94
'What is Revelation?', 95–143
'The Historical Problems of the Fourth Gospel', 144–223
'The Incarnation and Principles of Evidence', 227–84

Vol. ii:
'Goethe and his Influence', 3–100
'Wordsworth and his Genius', 101–46
'Shelley's Poetical Mysticism', 147–89
'Mr. Browning', 190–247
'The Poetry of the Old Testament', 248–93
'George Eliot', 294–367
'Arthur Hugh Clough', 368–91
'Nathaniel Hawthorne', 392–449

1877 edition omits 'George Eliot', and adds 'Christian Evidences Popular and Critical', i. 116–49, and 'Tennyson', ii. 303–69. 1888 edition updates the essays on Shelley, Browning, and Tennyson

Essays in Literary Criticism, Philadelphia, 1876. Reprints 5 essays from *Essays, Theological and Literary*, ii, and adds 'The Poetry of Matthew Arnold', 301–55

Holiday Rambles in Ordinary Places, London, 1877. Contains 6 essays which are collections of articles from the *Spectator*, 1867–76

Sir Walter Scott, London, 1878, reprinted several times

Literary Studies by Walter Bagehot, ed. R. H. Hutton, 2 vols., London, 1879, second edition same year, third edition 1884, fourth edition 1891, fifth edition 1895

Economic Studies by Walter Bagehot, ed. R. H. Hutton, 2 vols., London, 1880, second edition 1888

Biographical Studies by Walter Bagehot, ed. R. H. Hutton, London, 1881, reprinted 1895

Essays on Some of the Modern Guides of English Thought in Matters of Faith, London, 1887. Referred to in text as *Modern Guides*. Contains:
'Thomas Carlyle', 1–44
'Cardinal Newman', 47–94
'Matthew Arnold', 101–44
'George Eliot as Author', 147–258
'George Eliot's Life and Letters', 261–99
'Frederick Denison Maurice', 303–33

Cardinal Newman (London, 1891, second edition same year, reprinted with additions 1892)

Criticisms on Contemporary Thought and Thinkers, 2 vols. (London, 1894). Reprints 77 articles from the *Spectator*

Aspects of Religious and Scientific Thought, ed. E. M. Roscoe (London, 1899). Reprints 54 *Spectator* articles

Brief Literary Criticisms, ed. E. M. Roscoe (London, 1906). Reprints 51 *Spectator* articles

(c) LECTURES, MONOGRAPHS, ETC.

The Incarnation and Principles of Evidence, Tracts for Priests and People, 14 (London, 1862)

The Relative Value of Studies and Accomplishments in the Education of Women: A Lecture (London, 1862)

'The Political Character of the Working Class', *Essays in Reform* (London, 1867), 27–44

'On Mr. Herbert Spencer's Theory of the Gradual Transformation of Utilitarian into Intuitive Morality by Hereditary Descent'. Read to the Metaphysical Society, 2 June 1869

'Reciprocity', *Lectures on Economic Science* (London, 1870), 87–105

'Mr. Herbert Spencer on Moral Intuitions and Moral Sentiments'. Read to the Metaphysical Society, 13 June 1871

'Latent Thought'. Read to the Metaphysical Society, 14 April 1874

'On Wordsworth's Two Styles'. Read to the Wordsworth Society, 3 May 1882

'Walter Bagehot', *Dictionary of National Biography*, ed. Leslie Stephen (London, 1885), ii. 393–6

'George Eliot', *Chambers's Encyclopaedia*, new edition (London, 1889), iv. 294–7

'Robert Browning', *In the Footsteps of the Poets*, ed. David Masson (London, 1893), 299–329

Six addresses to Church Congress are published in the Congress *Reports*, 1869, 1875, 1888, 1891, 1892, 1894

Hutton's addresses to the Synthetic Society are published in *Papers Read Before the Synthetic Society, 1896–1908* (London, 1909), 28–33, 39–40, 54–5

(*d*) ARTICLES, ESSAYS, REVIEWS, ETC.

Hutton probably wrote about 7,000 articles and essays: of these, 3,600 can be positively identified as his, while some 1,500 pieces can be attributed to him with virtual certainty (see the checklist in *Victorian Periodicals Newsletter*, op. cit., and above, 'Appendix', on his journal writing). I have not distinguished, neither in the text nor in the bibliography, between identifications and attributions: I have not used or referred to pieces whose attribution is purely speculative.

About half of Hutton's articles were contributed to the weekly *Spectator* between 1861 and 1897, and several hundred were contributed to the weeklies, the *Inquirer* and the *Economist*, in the 1850s and 1860s. He also wrote for the *Pall Mall Gazette* (about 27 articles), the *National Review* (about 27 essays), the *Prospective Review* (about 14 essays), the *Contemporary Review* (12 signed essays), the *Nineteenth Century* (7 signed essays), *Good Words* (4 signed essays), the *North British Review* (probably 3 essays), the *British Quarterly Review* (3 essays), the *Expositor* (2 signed essays), the *Fortnightly Review* (2 signed essays), *Victoria Magazine* (2 signed essays), *Forum* (1 signed essay), *Fraser's Magazine* (1 signed essay), the *Modern Review* (1 signed essay), the *National Review*, 1883–1960 (1 signed essay), and the *Saturday Review* (1 review). I have given details of these essays in Appendix (nn. 2–7).

I give below details of Hutton's writings which have direct relevance to the subject matter of the present work. The writings are listed in chronological order in each section, regardless of the length of the piece cited.

1. *Newman*

'Newman's *Discourses Addressed to Mixed Congregations*', *Inquirer*, 16 February 1850, 102–4

'Romanism, Protestantism and Anglicanism', *National Review*, 1 (July 1855), 162–96

'Father Newman's Sarcasm', *Spectator*, 20 February 1864, 206–8

'Roman Catholic Casuistry and Protestant Prejudice', *Spectator*, 26 March 1864, 256–8

'Dr. Newman's Apology', *Spectator*, 4 June 1864, 654–6

'Dr. Newman's Apology', *Spectator*, 11 June 1864, 681–3

'Dr. Newman's Catholicism', *Spectator*, 3 March 1866, 243–5

'Dr. Newman's Poems', *Spectator*, 25 January 1868, 102–4

Dr. Newman's Oxford Sermons', *Spectator*, 5 December 1868, 1436–8

'Dr. Newman's *Grammar of Assent*', *Spectator*, 2 April 1870, 436–9

'Dr. Newman's Anglican Essays', *Spectator*, 11 November 1871, 1369–71

'Dr. Newman and Rome', *Spectator*, 16 January 1875, 70–1

'Dr. Newman and the Church of Rome', *Spectator*, 22 February 1879, 237–8

'Cardinal Newman on Liberalism in Religion', *Spectator*, 17 May 1879, 619

'Cardinal Newman on England and the Roman Catholics', *Spectator*, 31 January 1880, 138–9

'Cardinal Newman's Address', *Spectator*, 15 May 1880, 617–18

'Cardinal Newman on Inspiration', *Spectator*, 2 February 1884, 149–50

'Cardinal Newman', *Contemporary Review*, 45 (May 1884), 642–65

'Newman and Arnold—I. Newman', *Contemporary Review*, 49 (March 1886), 327–54

'Cardinal Newman', *Spectator*, 16 August 1890, 205–7

'Authority in Religion', *Spectator*, 23 August 1890, 239–40

'Cardinal Newman's Two Stages', *Spectator*, 30 August 1890, 270–1

'Cardinal Newman', *Good Words*, 31 (October 1890), 662–9

'Simplicity and Complexity of Character', *Spectator*, 11 October 1890, 470–1

'Cardinal Newman's View of Letters', *Spectator*, 24 January 1891, 114–15

'Mr. Leslie Stephen on Scepticism', *Spectator*, 7 February 1891, 199–200

'Cardinal Newman's Anglican Letters', *Spectator*, 7 February 1891, 207–8

'Cardinal Newman's Anglican Letters', *Spectator*, 14 February 1891, 244–6

'Professor Newman on his Brother', *Spectator*, 21 February 1891, 278–80

'Dr. Abbott's Attack on Cardinal Newman', *Spectator*, 18 April 1891, 538–9

'Dr. Abbott and Cardinal Newman', *Spectator*, 25 April 1891, 587–8

'The Defence of Newman', *Spectator*, 8 August 1891, 198–200

'Isaac Williams on Cardinal Newman', *Spectator*, 27 February 1892, 296–7

'The Anglican Career of Cardinal Newman', *Spectator*, 21 May 1892, 712–14

'The *Edinburgh Review* on Newman', *Spectator*, 5 August 1893, 172–3

'Newman and Tennyson', *Spectator*, 18 July 1896, 74–5

2. *Arnold*

'Arnold's *Poems* and Dallas's *Poetics*', *Inquirer*, 3 December 1853, 771–2

'Arnold's *Poems*, Second Series', *Inquirer*, 6 January 1855, 2–3

'Matthew Arnold's *On Translating Homer*', *Economist*, 23 February 1861, 206

'Mr. Grote on the Abuses of Newspaper Criticism', *Spectator*, 29 June 1861, 696–7

'Mr. Arnold's Last Words on Translating Homer', *Spectator*, 22 March 1862, 328–9

'Mr. Arnold on the Aristocratic Creed', *Spectator*, 27 December 1862, 1438–9

'Matthew Arnold's Essays', *Spectator*, 25 February 1865, 214–15

'An Intellectual Angel', *Spectator*, 3 February 1866, 125–6

' "Get Geist" ', *Spectator*, 28 July 1866, 828–9

'Mr. Arnold on the Celtic Genius', *Spectator*, 22 June 1867, 596–8

'Mr. Arnold on the Enemies of Culture', *Spectator*, 6 July 1867, 746–8

'Mr. Arnold's New Poems', *Spectator*, 7 September 1867, 1003–5

'Mr. Arnold on the State', *Spectator*, 4 January 1868, 5–7

'Matthew Arnold *vs* Thomas Carlyle', *Spectator*, 4 July 1868, 788–90

'Mr. Matthew Arnold on the Modern Element in Literature', *Spectator*, 20 February 1869, 222–3

'Mr. Arnold's Poems', *Spectator*, 19 June 1869, 733–5

'The Modern Poetry of Doubt', *Spectator*, 5 February 1870, 166–7

'Mr. Arnold on St. Paul', *Spectator*, 21 May 1870, 642–4

'Mr. Arnold on St. Paul and his Creed', *Contemporary Review*, 14 (June 1870), 329–41

'Mr. Arnold on God', *Spectator*, 8 July 1871, 825–7

'Leading Papers in the Magazines for October', *Spectator*, 7 October 1871, 1213–15

'The Poetry of Matthew Arnold', *British Quarterly Review*, 55 (April 1872), 313–47

'Isaiah for Schools', *Spectator*, 22 June 1872, 782–3

'Mr. Arnold's Gospel', *Spectator*, 22 February 1873, 242–4

'Mr. Arnold on Christianity', *Spectator*, 1 March 1873, 278–9

'Mr. Arnold's Sublimated Bible', *Spectator*, 10 October 1874, 1256–8

'The Magazines', *Spectator*, 5 February 1876, 186

'Mr. Arnold as a Moral and Religious Teacher', *Spectator*, 11 November 1876, 1402–3

'The *Quarterly Review* on Milton', *Spectator*, 27 January 1877, 112–13

'Matthew Arnold's Poems', *Spectator*, 14 July 1877, 889–91

'Mr. Matthew Arnold on Equality', *Spectator*, 2 March 1878, 276–7

'Roman Catholic Education and Mr. Arnold', *Spectator*, 6 July 1878, 850

'The Poetic Place of Matthew Arnold', *Spectator*, 20 July 1878, 918–19

'How to Popularize Wordsworth', *Spectator*, 12 July 1879, 879–81

'Mr. Arnold's Selections from Wordsworth', *Spectator*, 20 December 1879, 1603–4

'The Revivification of Stoicism', *Spectator*, 24 April 1880, 521–3

'Mr. Matthew Arnold on Poetry and Religion', *Spectator*, 22 May 1880, 649–51

'Matthew Arnold's Prose Passages', *Spectator*, 31 July 1880, 969–70

'Living English Poets', *Spectator*, 6 January 1883, 15–16

'The Conditions of the "Grand Style" ', *Spectator*, 10 March 1883, 319–20

'Matthew Arnold in the United States', *Spectator*, 20 October 1883, 1342–3

'Eviscerated Prophecy', *Spectator*, 5 April 1884, 438–9

'Mr. Arnold's Lay Sermon', *Spectator*, 6 December 1884, 1610–11

'Matthew Arnold's New Christian Catechism', *Spectator*, 4 April 1885, 447–8

'The Poet of Elegy', *Spectator*, 18 July 1885, 937–8

'Newman and Arnold—II. Matthew Arnold', *Contemporary Review*, 49 (April 1886), 513–34

'Mr. Matthew Arnold's Retirement', *Spectator*, 13 November 1886, 1519–20

'Matthew Arnold', *Spectator*, 21 April 1888, 538–40

'Poetic Charm', *Spectator*, 14 July 1888, 962–3

'Matthew Arnold as Critic', *Spectator*, 1 December 1888, 1670–1

'The Poetry of Melancholy', *Spectator*, 26 January 1889, 114–15

'What Endures in Poetry?', *Spectator*, 24 August 1889, 236–7

'Our Great Elegiac Poet', *Spectator*, 7 November 1891, 638–9

'Matthew Arnold's Popularity', *Spectator*, 25 March 1893, 382–3

'Matthew Arnold's Letters', *Spectator*, 23 November 1895, 719–20

'Matthew Arnold's Charm', *Spectator*, 7 December 1895, 814–15

'The Popularity of Matthew Arnold', *Spectator*, 6 June 1896, 800–1

3. *Related essays: culture and criticism*

'The Widening Gap Between the Clergy and the Laity', *Spectator*, 16 January 1864, 61–2

'Spirituality Without God', *Spectator*, 13 January 1866, 37–9 [on Walter Pater]

'Greek Tragedy and Modern Literature', *Spectator*, 31 December 1870, 1523–5

'Mr. Ruskin on Nature and Miracle', *Spectator*, 8 March 1873, 300–2

'The Cultus of Impressionability', *Spectator*, 10 August 1878, 1010–11 [on Walter Pater]

'Mr. Ruskin on Wordsworth', *Spectator*, 7 August 1880, 1001–3

'Culture and the Democracy', *Spectator*, 3 June 1882, 714–15

'The Poetry of Arthur Hugh Clough', *Fortnightly Review*, NS 33 (June 1883), 790–807

'The Liberal Movement in English Literature', *Spectator*, 21 November 1885, 1550–1

'Amiel and Clough', *Spectator*, 9 January 1886, 42–3

' "Unreal Words" in Religious Belief', *Spectator*, 24 July 1886, 982–4

'Will Culture Outgrow Christianity?', *Spectator*, 20 November 1886, 1554

'The Conditions of Sound Criticism', *Spectator*, 11 December 1886, 1657

'Literature and Action', *Spectator*, 14 May 1887, 651–2

'Why Mr. Ruskin Failed as a Poet', *Spectator*, 31 October 1891, 590–1

'The Greek Spirit and Modern Life', *Spectator*, 18 March 1893, 351–2

'Plato and Platonism', *Spectator*, 1 April 1893, 422–3 [on Walter Pater]

'Journalism and Public Opinion', *Spectator*, 1 September 1894, 261–3

'The Literary Aspects of the Bible', *Spectator*, 29 June 1895, 894–5

4. *Wordsworth*

'William Wordsworth', *National Review*, 4 (January 1857), 1–30

'Dorothy Wordsworth's Scotch Journal', *Spectator*, 1 August 1874, 980–1

'How to Popularize Wordsworth', *Spectator*, 12 July 1879, 879–81

'Mr. Arnold's Selections from Wordsworth', *Spectator*, 20 December 1879, 1609–10

'Mr. Ruskin on Wordsworth', *Spectator*, 7 August 1880, 1001–3

'Wordsworth the Man', *Spectator*, 11 December 1880, 1581–2

'The Wordsworth Society's Publications', *Spectator*, 18 February 1882, 238–9

'The Weak Side of Wordsworth', *Spectator*, 27 May 1882, 687–8

'Wordsworth's Two Styles', *Modern Review*, 3 (July 1882), 525–38

'The Critical Edition of Wordsworth', *Spectator*, 2 September 1882, 1141–2

'Professor Knight's Wordsworth. Volume III', *Spectator*, 12 May 1883, 614–15

'Wordsworth and Professor Huxley on the Narrowness of Specialists', *Spectator*, 5 December 1885, 1611–12

'Professor Knight's Wordsworth', *Spectator*, 13 March 1886, 355–7

'The Mystical Side of Good Sense', *Spectator*, 6 August 1887, 1051–2

'Mr. Morley on Wordsworth', *Spectator*, 22 December 1888, 1807–8

'Wordsworth', *Spectator*, 29 December 1888, 1852–3

'*Wordsworthiana*', *Spectator*, 16 March 1889, 369–70
'*Lyrical Ballads*', *Spectator*, 5 April 1890, 479–80
'Wordsworth and Mr. Watson', *Spectator*, 27 July 1895, 107–8

5. *Tennyson*

'Tennyson's *Maud*', *Inquirer*, 1 September 1855, 546–7
'*Enoch Arden*', *Spectator*, 20 August 1864, 964–6
'Tennyson's "Northern Farmer" ', *Spectator*, 27 August 1864, 991–2
'Mr. Bagehot on Tennyson', *Spectator*, 26 November 1864, 1355–7
'Dramatic Calamities', *Spectator*, 19 January 1867, 65–6
'Mr. Tennyson's *Death of Lucretius*', *Spectator*, 2 May 1868, 523–4
'Weighing Tennyson', *Spectator*, 1 May 1869, 535–6
'Tennyson's Two Northern Farmers', *Spectator*, 18 December 1869, 1488–90
'Mr. Tennyson's New Poems', *Spectator*, 25 December 1869, 1530–3
'The Modern Poetry of Doubt', *Spectator*, 5 February 1870, 166–7
'The Relative Magnitude of Poets', *Spectator*, 26 March 1870, 397–9
'The Idealism of George Eliot and Mr. Tennyson', *Spectator*, 2 December 1871, 1458–60
' "Gareth and Lynette" ', *Spectator*, 26 October 1872, 1363–5
'Tennyson', *Macmillan's Magazine*, 27 (December 1872), 143–67
'A New Edition of the *Idylls of the King*', *Spectator*, 8 February 1873, 177–8
'Mrs. Cameron's Illustrations of Tennyson', *Spectator*, 29 May 1875, 693–4
'Mr. Tennyson's Drama', *Spectator*, 26 June 1875, 820–2
'Mr. Tennyson's Drama on the Stage', *Spectator*, 22 April 1876, 526–7
'Mr. Tennyson's "Harold" ', *Spectator*, 23 December 1876, 1610–12
' "The Lover's Tale" ', *Spectator*, 21 June 1879, 790–1
'Mr. Peter Bayne on Carlyle and Tennyson', *Spectator*, 16 August 1879, 1044–6
'The Poet-Laureate's New Ballads', *Spectator*, 18 December 1880, 1624–6
'Mr. Tennyson's Poem on Despair', *Spectator*, 5 November 1881, 1397–8
'Tennyson as Dramatist', *Spectator*, 18 November 1882, 1474–5
'Living English Poets', *Spectator*, 6 January 1883, 15–16
'The Parchment Tennyson', *Spectator*, 17 March 1883, 355–7
'The Tennyson Peerage', *Spectator*, 8 December 1883, 1577–8
'*Becket*', *Spectator*, 20 December 1884, 1699–1700
'The Poet-Laureate's New Poem', *Spectator*, 7 November 1885, 1466–7
'The Poet Laureate's New Poems', *Spectator*, 12 December 1885, 1649–51
' "Locksley Hall" in Youth and Age', *Spectator*, 18 December 1886, 1706–7

'Tennyson's New Poems', *Spectator*, 25 December 1886, 1706–7

'Browning and Tennyson', *Spectator*, 21 December 1889, 879–80

'Tennyson's New Poems', *Spectator*, 21 December 1889, 883–4

'The Laureate's Country', *Spectator*, 27 December 1890, 949

'Lord Tennyson's Fancy', *Spectator*, 2 April 1892, 458–60

'The Genius of Tennyson', *Spectator*, 15 October 1892, 522–4

'Tennyson's Theology', *Spectator*, 5 November 1892, 642–3

'Mrs. Ritchie's *Reminiscences of Tennyson, Ruskin and Browning*', *Spectator*, 12 November 1892, 686–8

'Was Tennyson Either Gnostic or Agnostic?', *Spectator*, 7 January 1893, 10–11

'The Late Lord Tennyson on the Future Life', *Spectator*, 4 March 1893, 283–4

'Newman and Tennyson', *Spectator*, 18 July 1896, 74–5

6. *Related essays: poetry*

'Charlatan Poetry: Martin Farquhar Tupper', *National Review*, 7 (July 1858), 160–83

'Shelley's Poetical Mysticism', *National Review*, 16 (January 1863), 62–87

'Mr. Browning's Poems', *National Review*, 17 (October 1863), 417–46

'William Blake', *Spectator*, 21 October 1863, 2771–3

'A Luckless Poet', *Spectator*, 28 May 1864, 615–17 [on John Clare]

'John Clare', *Spectator*, 17 June 1865, 668–70

'Science and the New School of Poetry', *Spectator*, 2 November 1867, 1225–6

'The Public Prepossession for Byron', *Spectator*, 11 September 1869, 1066–7

'Keats', *Spectator*, 18 June 1887, 826–8

'The Victorian Age in Literature', *Spectator*, 2 July 1887, 889–90

'Mr. Gosse on Great English Poets', *Spectator*, 20 April 1889, 539–41

'Browning as a Religious Teacher', *Good Words*, 31 (February 1890), 87–93

'What is a Lyric?', *Spectator*, 23 May 1896, 735–6

'Life in Poetry', *Spectator*, 20 June 1896, 866–7

'Poetry and Landscape', *Spectator*, 6 March 1897, 331–2

'Self-Consciousness in Poetry', *Spectator*, 12 June 1897, 866–7

7. *George Eliot*

'Feuerbach's *Essence of Christianity*', *Inquirer*, 16 and 23 September 1854, 578–9, 595–6

'The Novels of George Eliot', *National Review*, 11 (July 1860), 191–219

'*Silas Marner*', *Economist*, 27 April 1861, 455–7

'*Romola*', *Spectator*, 18 July 1863, 2265–7

'George Eliot's New Novel', *Spectator*, 23 June 1866, 692–3

'*The Spanish Gypsy*', *Spectator*, 6 June 1868, 676–8

'George Eliot's Praise of Death', *Spectator*, 21 May 1870, 638–40

'*Armgart*', *Spectator*, 1 July 1871, 794–6

'The Idealism of George Eliot and Mr. Tennyson', *Spectator*, 2 December 1871, 1458–60

'George Eliot's *Middlemarch*', *Spectator*, 16 December 1871, 1528–9

'*Middlemarch*—Part II', *Spectator*, 3 February 1872, 147–8

'*Middlemarch*—Part III', *Spectator*, 30 March 1872, 404–6

'The Melancholy of *Middlemarch*', *Spectator*, 1 June 1872, 685–7

'George Eliot's Moral Anatomy', *Spectator*, 5 October 1872, 1262–4

'*Middlemarch*', *Spectator*, 7 December 1872, 1554–6

'The Humour of *Middlemarch*', *Spectator*, 14 December 1872, 1582–3

'*Middlemarch*: A Study in Provincial Life', *British Quarterly Review*, 57 (April 1873), 407–29

'George Eliot's Poems', *Spectator*, 23 May 1874, 660–1

'Gwendolen Harleth', *Spectator*, 29 January 1876, 138–9

'George Eliot's Heroines', *Spectator*, 12 February 1876, 207–8

'*Daniel Deronda*', *Spectator*, 8 April 1876, 463–4

'The Hero of *Daniel Deronda*', *Spectator*, 10 June 1876, 733–4

'The Strong Side of *Daniel Deronda*', *Spectator*, 29 June 1876, 948–9

'*Daniel Deronda*', *Spectator*, 9 September 1876, 1131–3

'The *Church Quarterly* on George Eliot', *Spectator*, 3 November 1877, 1363–4

'George Eliot's "Breakfast Party" ', *Spectator*, 29 June 1878, 821–3

'George Eliot's New Book', *Spectator*, 7 June 1879, 727–8

'George Eliot's Ideal Ethics', *Spectator*, 14 June 1879, 751–3

'George Eliot', *Spectator*, 1 January 1881, 10–11

'George Eliot', *Spectator*, 28 April, 1883, 547–8

'George Eliot's *Essays*', *Spectator*, 1 March 1884, 282–3

'Mr. Bray on George Eliot', *Spectator*, 10 January 1885, 43–4

'George Eliot's Humour', *Spectator*, 31 January 1885, 146–7

'George Eliot', *Spectator*, 31 January 1885, 151–3

'George Eliot', *Contemporary Review*, 47 (March 1885), 372–91

'Mr. Oscar Browning's *George Eliot*', *Spectator*, 8 February 1890, 204–5

8. *Related essays: the novel*

'Puseyite Novels', *Prospective Review*, 6 (1850), 512–34 [includes review of Elizabeth Sewall]

'The Author of *Heartsease* and Modern Schools of Fiction', *Prospective Review*, 10 (1854), 460–82

'A Novel or Two', *National Review*, 1 (October 1855), 336–50 [includes reviews of *North and South* and Elizabeth Sewall's *Clare Hall*]

'The Hard Church Novel', *National Review*, 3 (July 1856), 127–45

'Novels by the Authoress of *John Halifax*', *North British Review*, 29 (1858), 466–81 [reviews seven novels by Dinah Muloch]

'Nathaniel Hawthorne', *National Review*, 11 (October 1860), 453–81

'Ethical and Dogmatic Fiction: Miss Yonge', *National Review*, 12 (January 1861), 211–30 [reviews five novels by Charlotte Yonge]

'*Great Expectations*', *Spectator*, 20 July 1861, 784–5

'Unctuous Sentiment', *Spectator*, 12 April 1862, 406 [on Dickens]

'Thackeray's Place in English Literature', *Spectator*, 2 January 1864, 9–11

'Can You Forgive Her?', *Spectator*, 2 September 1865, 978–9

'*Nina Balatka*', *Spectator*, 23 March 1867, 329–30

'Mr. Dickens's Moral Services to Literature', *Spectator*, 17 April 1869, 474–5

'The *Memoir* of Miss Austen', *Spectator*, 25 December 1869, 1533–5

'Mr. Thackeray's Satire', *Spectator*, 30 November 1871, 1313–14

'*David Copperfield* and Charles Dickens', *Spectator*, 9 December 1871, 1490–1

'*Far From the Madding Crowd*', *Spectator*, 19 December 1874, 1597–9

'Mr. Trollope on the Moral Effects of Novel Reading', *Spectator*, 4 January 1879, 9–10

'*The Return of the Native*', *Spectator*, 8 February 1879, 181–2

'The American Ideal of Character', *Spectator*, 19 April 1879, 1504–6 [on Henry James]

'Mr. Trollope's *Orley Farm*', *Spectator*, 11 October 1882, 1336–8

'Mr. Anthony Trollope', *Spectator*, 9 December 1882, 1573–4

'From Miss Austen to Mr. Trollope', *Spectator*, 16 December 1882, 1609–11

'Thin Pessimism', *Spectator*, 2 June 1883, 702–3 [on Henry James]

'Mr. Trollope as Critic', *Spectator*, 27 October 1883, 1373–4

'The Journal of Sir Walter Scott', *Spectator*, 8 November 1890, 648–9

'Was Thackeray Most Moralist or Satirist?', *Spectator*, 28 February 1891, 303–4

'Mr. Hardy's *Tess of the D'Urbervilles*', *Spectator*, 23 January 1892, 121–2

'How Long Will Dickens Hold His Place in the Future?', *Spectator*, 31 December 1892, 950–1

'Great Characters in Fiction', *Spectator*, 1 July 1893, 11–12

'Sam Weller and the Irony of the Streets', *Spectator*, 29 July 1893, 139–40

'Sir Walter Scott', *Spectator*, 29 May 1897, 648–9

9. *Related essays: religion*

'The State of Protestantism in Germany', *Prospective Review*, 3 (May 1847), 254–89

'Atheism', *National Review*, 2 (January 1856), 97–123

'Strauss' *Life of Nicodemus Frischlin*', *Saturday Review*, 15 November 1856, 641–3

'Strauss and German Hellenism', *National Review*, 4 (January 1857), 181–211

'Civilization and Faith', *National Review*, 6 (January 1858), 198–288

'The Religion of the Working Classes', *National Review*, 8 (January 1859), 167–97

'Positivism', *Spectator*, 25 January 1862, 98–9

'M. Renan's *Vie de Jésus*', *Victoria Magazine*, 1 (September 1863), 385–96

'Professor Shairp on Culture and Religion', *Spectator*, 24 December 1870, 1547

'The Debts of Theology to Secular Movements', *Spectator*, 14 January 1871, 37–9

'Mr. Herbert Spencer on Moral Intuitions and Moral Sentiments', *Contemporary Review*, 17 (July 1871), 463–72

'Realism in Unbelief', *Spectator*, 7 April 1877, 433–5

'A Modern "Symposium": The Influence upon Morality of a Decline in Religious Belief', *Nineteenth Century*, 1 (May 1877), 539–45

'The Magnanimity of Unbelief', *Spectator*, 27 October 1877, 1331–2

'Auguste Comte's Aspiration', *Spectator*, 17 November 1877, 1429–30

'*Is Life Worth Living?*', *Spectator*, 12 July 1879, 884–5 [review of W. H. Mallock]

'The Atheistic View of Life', *Fraser's Magazine*, NS 21 (May 1880) 652–67

'God and Ideas of God', *Spectator*, 14 August 1880, 1033–4

'Secularism', *Expositor*, NS 1 (January 1881), 457–72

'The Gospel for the Nineteenth Century', *Spectator*, 22 January 1881, 121–3

'Earthly Immortality', *Spectator*, 7 May 1881, 599

'The Worship of Humanity', *Spectator*, 7 January 1882, 9–11

'The Gospel of Divine Humanity', *Spectator*, 28 June 1884, 853–4

'The Service of Man', *Contemporary Review*, 51 (April 1887), 480–93

'What is Impartiality?', *Spectator*, 22 February 1890, 264–5

'The Extravagance of Altruism', *Spectator*, 14 May 1892, 671–2

'M. Renan and Christianity', *National Review*, 1883–1960, 20 (November 1892), 301–9

'Imagination and Faith', *Spectator*, 2 December 1893, 794–5

'Agnostic Morality', *Spectator*, 3 November 1894, 607–8

'Dual Consciousness', *Spectator*, 16 March 1895, 355–6

'Culture and Faith', *Spectator*, 21 December 1895, 891–2

2. Secondary sources

The following lists include books and articles cited in the text, and material directly related to the subject. The section is divided so as to include in the first list books by contemporaries of Hutton published in the first years of the twentieth century. The first list also includes modern editions of texts originally published in the nineteenth century. Essays by unidentified authors are entered under the title of the journal in which the piece first appeared.

(*a*) BOOKS AND ARTICLES PUBLISHED BEFORE 1912

Abbott, Edwin A., 'Illusion in Religion', *Contemporary Review*, 58 (November 1890), 721–42

—— *Newmanianism: A Preface to Philomythus*, second edition (London, 1891)

—— *Philomythus* (London, 1891)

—— 'The Early Life of Cardinal Newman', *Contemporary Review*, 59 (January 1891), 30–54

—— 'The Realities of Christianity', *Contemporary Review*, 59 (February 1891), 267–74

Academy, 'R. H. Hutton', 18 September 1897, 221–2

Academy, [R. H. Hutton's] '*Aspects of Religious and Scientific Thought*', 22 April 1899, 451–3

Arnold, Matthew, 'Wordsworth', *Macmillan's Magazine*, 40 (July 1879), 193–204

—— *Lectures and Essays in Criticism*, ed. R. H. Super, Prose Works of Matthew Arnold, 3 (Ann Arbor, 1962)

—— *Culture and Anarchy*, ed. R. H. Super, Prose Works of Matthew Arnold, 5 (Ann Arbor, 1965)

—— *Dissent and Dogma*, ed. R. H. Super, Prose Works of Matthew Arnold, 6 (Ann Arbor, 1968)

—— *English Literature and Irish Politics*, ed. R. H. Super, Prose Works of Matthew Arnold, 9 (Ann Arbor, 1973)

—— *Letters, 1848–1888*, ed. G. W. E. Russell, 2 vols. (London, 1889)

—— *Letters of Matthew Arnold to A. H. Clough*, ed. H. F. Lowry (London, 1932)

—— *Poems*, ed. Kenneth Allott (London, 1965)

—— *Unpublished Letters of Matthew Arnold*, ed. Arnold Whitridge (New Haven, 1923)

Athenaeum, [R. H. Hutton's] '*Cardinal Newman*', 18 October 1890, 507–8

Athenaeum, [R. H. Hutton's] *'Criticisms on Contemporary Thought and Thinkers'*, 2 June 1894, 704

Athenaeum, 'Richard Holt Hutton', 18 September 1897, 389–90

Athenaeum, [R. H. Hutton's] *'Aspects of Religious and Scientific Thought'*, 22 April 1899, 489–90

Austin, Alfred, *The Poetry of the Period* (London, 1870)

Bagehot, Walter, 'Tennyson's *Idylls'*, *National Review*, 9 (October 1859), 368–94

Bellot, H. H., *'Aspects of Religious and Scientific Thought'* [by R. H. Hutton[, *Westminster Review*, 151 (May 1899), 579–83

Besant, Walter, *The Art of Fiction* (London, 1884)

Bradley, F. H., *Ethical Studies* (London, 1876)

Brimley, Charles, *Essays*, ed. W. G. Clark, third edition (London, 1882)

Caird, Edward, 'Wordsworth', *Fraser's Magazine*, NS 21 (February 1880), 205–21

—— *Essays in Literature and Philosophy*, 2 vols. (Glasgow, 1892)

Catholic World, 'Cardinal Newman, by R. H. Hutton', 52 (1891), 604–6

Church, Alfred John, [R. H. Hutton's] *'Aspects of Religious and Scientific Thought'*, *Critic*, 37 (1900), 269–73

—— *Memories of Men and Books* (London, 1908)

Church Quarterly Review, 'Hutton's Essays', 28 (April–July 1889), 478–500 [reviews *Theological Essays*, *Literary Essays*, and *Modern Guides*]

Collet, S. D., 'Mr. Hutton as Critic and Theologian', *Contemporary Review*, 16 (1871), 634–50

Cory, William, *Letters and Journals*, ed. F. W. Cornish (Oxford, 1897)

Dallas, Eneas Sweetland, *The Gay Science* (London, 1866)

Davies, John Llewelyn, 'Utilitarianism and Christianity', *Victoria Magazine*, 1 (May 1863), 142–56

De Morgan, S. E., *Memoir of Augustus De Morgan* (London, 1882)

Dial. [R. H. Hutton's] *'Criticisms on Contemporary Thought and Thinkers'*, 17 (1894), 17–18

Dicey, E., 'Journalism New and Old', *Fortnightly Review*, 83 (1905), 904–18

Dodds, Marcus, [R. H. Hutton's] *'Criticisms on Contemporary Thought and Thinkers'*, *Bookman*, 6 (June 1894), 85–6

Drummond, J., and C. B. Upton, eds., *The Life and Letters of James Martineau*, 2 vols. (London, 1902)

Eliot, George, 'Evangelical Teaching; Dr. Cumming', *Westminster Review*, 64 (October 1855), 436–62

—— *Middlemarch*, 4 vols. (London, 1871–2)

—— *Impressions of Theophrastus Such* (Edinburgh, 1879)

—— *Essays*, ed. Thomas Pinney (London, 1963)

Eliot, George *Letters*, ed. G. S. Haight, 9 vols. (London, 1954–78)

Escott, T. H. S., 'R. H. Hutton—An Estimate of his Life and Work', *Bookman*, 13 (October 1897), 5–6

—— *Masters of English Journalism* (London, 1911)

Feuerbach, Ludwig, *The Essence of Christianity*, trans. Marian Evans [i.e. George Eliot], (London, 1854)

Fox-Bourne, H. R., *English Newspapers*, 2 vols. (London, 1887)

Froude, James Anthony, 'Father Newman on "The Grammar of Assent" ', *Fraser's Magazine*, NS 1 (May 1870), 428–52

Grant, James, *The Newspaper Press: Its Origin, Progress, and Present Position*, 3 vols. (London, 1871–2)

Grew, E. S., 'The Physiognomy of Newspapers', *Anglo-Saxon Review*, 9 (1901), 222–31

Guardian, 'Richard Holt Hutton of the *Spectator*', 5 July 1899, 930

Hamilton, William, 'On the State of English Universities', *Edinburgh Review*, 53 (1831), no. 106

Hardy, Thomas, *Jude the Obscure*, new Wessex edition (London, 1974)

Hinton, James, *The Mystery of Pain: A Book for the Sorrowful* (London, 1866)

—— *Chapters on the Art of Thinking* (London, 1879)

Hogben, John, *Richard Holt Hutton of the 'Spectator'* (London, 1899)

Hunt, F. Knight, *The Fourth Estate: Contributions Towards a History of Newspapers, and of the Liberty of the Press*, 2 vols. (London, 1850)

Hutton, Joseph, *Personal Duties and Social Relations* (London, 1861)

Jackson, A. W., *James Martineau* (London, 1900)

James, Henry, '*Felix Holt*', *Nation*, 16 August 1866, 127–8

—— '*Middlemarch*', *Galaxy*, 15 (March 1873), 424–8

Jevons, W. S., *Letters and Journals*, ed. Harriet A. Jevons (London, 1886)

Kavanagh, Julia, *English Women of Letters*, 2 vols. (London, 1863)

Kingsley, Charles, 'Tennyson', *Fraser's Magazine*, 42 (Sept. 1850), 245–55

Lewes, G. H., *The Life and Works of Goethe*, 2 vols. (London, 1855)

—— 'The Novels of Jane Austen', *Blackwood's Magazine*, 86 (July 1859), 99–113

—— 'Principles of Success in Literature: Of Vision in Art', *Fortnightly Review*, 1 (1865), 572–89

—— 'The Principles of Success in Literature: The Principle of Sincerity', *Fortnightly Review*, 1 (1865), 696–709

—— 'Criticism in Relation to Novels', *Fortnightly Review*, 3 (1866), 352–61

Linton, E. L., *My Literary Life* (London, 1899)

Macmillan, Alexander, *Letters*, ed. G. A. Macmillan (London, 1908)

Mallock, W. H., *Is Life Worth Living?* (London, 1879)

—— 'The Impressions of Theophrastus Such', Edinburgh Review, 150 (October 1879), 557–86

—— 'Are Scott, Dickens and Thackeray Obsolete?', Forum (New York), 14 (1893), 503–13

Martineau, James, 'Professional Religion', National Review, 7 (1858), 487–515 [reviews Scenes from Clerical Life]

—— Types of Ethical Theory, 2 vols. (London, 1885)

Massey, Gerald, 'The Poetry of Alfred Tennyson', Hogg's Instructor, 5 (July 1855), 1–14

Maurice, Frederick Denison, Theological Essays (London, 1853)

—— The Conscience: Lectures on Casuistry (London, 1868)

—— 'Dr. Newman's Grammar of Assent', Contemporary Review, 14 (May 1870), 151–72

Meliora, 'Tennyson and his Poetry', 7 (October 1859), 225–48

Morley, John, Critical Miscellanies, 3 vols. (London, 1886)

Mozley, J. B., 'An Essay in Aid of A Grammar of Assent', Quarterly Review, 129 (July 1870), 130–50

Myers, F. W., 'Tennyson as Prophet', Nineteenth Century, 25 (March 1889), 381–96

Nation, [R. H. Hutton's] 'Criticisms on Contemporary Thought and Thinkers', 17 January 1895, 57

Nation, [R. H. Hutton's] 'Cardinal Newman', 19 March 1891, 245–6

Newman, John Henry, Loss and Gain (London, 1848)

—— Parochial and Plain Sermons, new edition, 8 vols. (London, 1868)

—— Essays Critical and Historical, 2 vols. (London, 1872)

—— An Essay In Aid of A Grammar of Assent, new impression (London, 1973)

—— The Idea of a University, ed. Martin Svaglic (New York, 1960)

—— Letters and Diaries, ed. C. S. Dessain, T. Gornald, and others, vols. xii–xxx (London, 1962–76)

Nicoll, W. R., The Day Book of Claudius Clear (London, 1905)

—— The Key to the Blue Closet (London, 1907)

Pater, Walter, 'Coleridge's Writings', Westminster Review, NS 29 (January 1866), 107–32

—— 'On Wordsworth', Fortnightly Review, NS 15 (April 1874), 455–65

—— Appreciations (London, 1889)

Robertson, John Mackinnon, Culture and Action (London, 1887)

—— Essays Towards A Critical Method (London, 1889)

—— New Essays Towards A Critical Method (London, 1897)

Roscoe, William Caldwell, 'Tennyson's Maud', National Review, 1 (October 1855), 377–410

Ruskin, John, Modern Painters, new edition, 5 vols. (London, 1873)

Sidgwick, A., *Henry Sidgwick: A Memoir* (London, 1906)

Sidgwick, Henry, 'The Prophet of Culture', *Macmillan's Magazine*, 16 (August 1867), 271–80

—— '*The Poems and Prose Remains of Arthur Hugh Clough*', *Westminster Review*, 92 (October 1869), 363–87

—— 'Verification of Beliefs', *Contemporary Review*, 17 (July 1871), 582–90

—— '*Essays Theological and Literary*' [by R. H. Hutton], *Academy*, 1 July 1871, 326

Simpson, Richard, 'Jane Austen', *North British Review*, 52 (April 1870) 129–52

—— 'Dr. Newman's *Grammar of Assent*', *North British Review*, 52 (July 1870), 428–52

Solly, Henry, *These Eighty Years, or the Story of an Unfinished Life*, 2 vols. (London, 1893)

Speaker, 'The Modern Press: the *Spectator*', 4 March 1893, 242.

Spencer, Herbert, *An Autobiography*, 2 vols. (London, 1904)

Stebbing, William, *Charles Henry Pearson* (London, 1900)

Stephen, Leslie, *'The Times' on the American Civil War: An Historical Study* (London, 1865)

—— 'R. H. Hutton's Essays', *Saturday Review*, 18 February 1871, 214–15

—— 'Wordsworth's Ethics', *Cornhill Magazine*, 34 (August 1876), 206–26

—— 'Dr. Newman's Theory of Belief', *Fortnightly Review*, NS 22 (November 1877), 680–97, 792–810

—— 'Newman's Scepticism', *Nineteenth Century*, 29 (February 1891), 179–201

—— *What is Materialism?* (London, 1886)

—— *George Eliot* (London, 1902)

Sully, James, 'The Aesthetics of Human Character', *Fortnightly Review*, NS 9 (April 1871), 505–20

Swinburne, A. C., 'L'Année Terrible', *Fortnightly Review*, NS 12 (September 1872), 243–67

—— *Swinburne Replies*, ed. C. K. Hyder (Syracuse, 1966)

Synthetic Society, *Papers Read Before the Synthetic Society, 1896–1908* (London, 1909)

Tennyson, Hallam, ed., *Tennyson and his Friends* (London, 1911)

Thom, J. H., 'Newman's *Grammar of Assent*', *Theological Review*, 7 (July 1870), 354–77

Trollope, Anthony, *Autobiography*, second edition, 2 vols. (Edinburgh, 1883)

Tulloch, John, 'Dr. Newman's *Grammar of Assent*', *Edinburgh Review*, 132 (1870), 382–414

Waddington, Samuel, *A. H. Clough: A Monograph* (London, 1883)

Walker, Hugh, 'Living Critics IV: Mr. R. H. Hutton', *Bookman*, 9 (January 1896), 118–20

Ward, J. H., 'Frederick Maurice in Present Thought', *Andover Review*, 1 (1884), 612–31

Ward, Wilfred Philip, 'Mr. R. H. Hutton as Religious Thinker', *Dublin Review*, third series, 20 (1888), 1–21

Wedgwood, Julia, 'Richard Holt Hutton', *Contemporary Review*, 72 (1897), 457–69

Wordsworth, William, *Prose Works*, ed. W. J. B. Owen and J. W. Smyser, 3 vols. (Oxford, 1974)

Wordsworth Society, *Transactions Nos 1–8* (1882–7), reprinted facsimile, 2 vols. (London, 1966)

(*b*) BOOKS AND ARTICLES PUBLISHED AFTER 1912

Adamson, John W., *English Education, 1789–1902* (Cambridge, 1930)

Allon, Henry, *Letters to a Victorian Editor*, ed. Albert Peel (London, 1929)

Andrews, Alexander, *The History of British Journalism*, 2 vols. (London, 1959)

Annan, Noel, *Leslie Stephen: His Thought and Character in Relation to his Time* (London, 1951)

Appleman, Philip, ed., *1859: Entering an Age of Crisis* (Bloomington, 1959)

Armytage, W. H. G., *The German Influence on English Education* (London, 1969)

—— 'Newly Discovered Letters of R. H. Hutton', *Journal of English and Germanic Philology*, 49 (1956), 566–9

Ashton, Rosemary, *The German Idea: Four English Writers and the Reception of German Thought, 1800–1860*, (Cambridge, 1980)

Atkins, J. B., 'Reminiscences of the *Spectator* office', *Spectator*, centenary supplement, 3 November 1928, 12–20

Barrington, E. I., *The Servant of All: Pages from the Life of James Wilson*, 2 vols. (London, 1927)

Barrington, Mrs Russell, *The Life of Walter Bagehot* (London, 1914)

Bastable, J., 'The Germination of Belief within Probability According to Newman', *Philosophical Studies*, 11 (1961), 81–111

Bauer, N. S., *William Wordsworth: A Reference Guide to British Criticism, 1793–1899* (Boston, 1978)

Bellot, H. H., *University College London, 1826–1926* (London, 1929)

Bentley, James, *Ritualism and Politics in Victorian Britain: the Attempt to Legislate for Belief* (Oxford, 1978)

Bevington, Merl M., *The 'Saturday Review', 1855–1868: Representative Educated Opinion in Victorian England* (New York, 1951)

Blehl, V., and F. Connolly, eds. *Newman's Apologia: A Classic Reconsidered* (New York, 1964)

Boekraad, A. J., and H. Tristram, *The Argument from Conscience to the Existence of God According to J. H. Newman* (Louvain, 1961)

Boyce, George, *Newspaper History: from the Seventeenth Century to the Present Day* (London, 1979)

Brown, A. W., *The Metaphysical Society: Victorian Minds in Crisis, 1869–1880* (New York, 1947)

Brown, David, *Walter Scott and the Historical Imagination* (London, 1979)

Butts, Denis, 'Newman's Influence on Matthew Arnold's Theory of Poetry', *Notes and Queries*, NS 5 (1958), 225–6

Cameron, J. M., *The Night Battle* (London, 1962)

Cannon, Carl L., *Journalism: A Bibliography* (London, 1924)

Carswell, D., and C. Carswell, 'The Crisis in Criticism', *Nineteenth Century and After*, 113 (1933), 107–17

Casson, T. E., 'Wordsworth and the *Spectator*', *Review of English Studies*, 3 (1927), 157–61

Chadwick, Owen, *The Victorian Church*, 2 vols. (London, 1966–70)

—— *The Secularization of the European Mind in the Nineteenth Century* (London, 1975)

Chew, S. C., 'Swinburne's Contributions to the *Spectator* in 1862', *Modern Language Notes*, 35 (1920), 118–19

Clough, A. H., *Correspondence*, ed. F. L. Mulhauser, 2 vols. (London, 1957)

Colby, Robert A., 'As It Strikes a Contemporary: the *Spectator* as Critic', *Nineteenth Century Fiction*, 9 (1956), 182–206

Collini, Stefan, *Liberalism and Sociology: L. T. Hobhouse and Political Argument in England, 1880–1914* (Cambridge, 1979)

Collins, K. K., 'G. H. Lewes Revised: George Eliot and the Moral Sense', *Victorian Studies*, 21, No. 4 (1978), 463–92

Coulling, S. M. B., *Matthew Arnold and his Critics* (Athens, Ohio, 1974)

—— 'Matthew Arnold's 1853 Preface: its Origin and Aftermath', *Victorian Studies*, 7 (1964) 233–63

Coulson, John, and A. M. Allchin, eds., *The Rediscovery of Newman: An Oxford Symposium* (London, 1967)

—— *Newman and the Common Tradition: A Study in the Language of Church and Society* (London, 1970)

—— *Religion and Imagination* (London, 1981)

Cox, R. G., 'Nineteenth Century Periodical Criticism, 1800–1860' (unpublished Ph.D. dissertation, Cambridge University, 1940)

—— 'Victorian Critics of Poetry: The Minority Tradition', *Scrutiny*, 18 (1951), 2–17

Cranfield, Geoffrey Alan, *The Press and Society* (London, 1978)

Crawford, C., 'The Novel that Occasioned *Loss and Gain*', *Modern Language Notes*, 65 (1950), 414–18

Creevey, Patrick, 'Richard Holt Hutton on Matthew Arnold', *Victorian Poetry*, 16 (1978), 134–46

Crook, D. P., 'Portent of War: English Opinion on Secession', *Journal of American Studies*, 4 (1970–1), 163–79

Daiches, David, *Some Late Victorian Attitudes* (London, 1969)

Davis, Philip, *Memory and Writing from Wordsworth to Lawrence* (Liverpool, 1983)

De Baun, V. C., '*Temple Bar*: Index of Victorian Middle-Class Thought' *Journal of the Library of Rutgers University*, 19 (December 1955), 6–16

de Groot, H. B., 'The *British and Foreign Review*: An Account of its Publishing History, its Political Attitudes and its Contribution to Literary Criticism' (unpublished Ph.D. dissertation, London University, 1969)

DeLaura, D. J., 'The "Wordsworth" of Pater and Arnold: the Supreme, Artistic View of Life', *Studies in English Literature*, 6 (Autumn 1966), 651–67

—— *Hebrew and Hellene in Victorian England* (London, 1969)

De Ruggiero, Guido, *The History of European Liberalism*, trans. R. G. Collingwood (London, 1927)

Dessain, C. S., 'Cardinal Newman on the Laity', *Louvain Studies*, 16 (1961) 51–62

Dommett, Alfred, *Diary, 1872–1885*, ed. E. A. Horsman (Oxford, 1953)

Eliot, T. S., *The Use of Poetry and the Use of Criticism* (London, 1933)

—— *Selected Essays*, 3rd edition (London, 1951)

—— *Selected Prose*, ed. John Hayward (London, 1953)

Ellegard, Alvar, *The Readership of the Periodical Press in mid-Victorian Britain* (Göteborg, 1957)

Evans, G., 'Science and Mathematics in Newman's Thought', *Downside Review*, 96 (October 1978), 247–66

Everett, E. M., *The Party of Humanity: The 'Fortnightly Review' and its Contributors* (London, 1939)

Farrell, J. P., *Revolution as Tragedy: The Dilemma of the Moderate from Scott to Arnold* (London, 1980)

Femiano, S., *The Infallibility of the Laity* (New York, 1967)

Ferreira, M. J., *Doubt and Religious Commitment* (Oxford, 1980)

Ford, George H., *Dickens and His Readers: Aspects of Novel Criticism Since 1836* (Princeton, 1955)

Friedman, Norman, 'Newman, Aristotle and the New Criticism: On the Modern Element in Newman's Poetics', *PMLA* 81 (1966), 261–71

Frykman, Erik, *'Bitter Knowledge' and 'Unconquerable Hope': A Thematic Study of Attitudes Towards Life in Matthew Arnold's Poetry, 1849–1853*, Göteborg Studies in English, 18 (Göteborg, 1966)

Fryckstedt, Monica, *Elizabeth Gaskell's 'Mary Barton' and 'Ruth': A Challenge to Christian England* (Uppsala, 1982)

Galland, René, *George Meredith and British Criticism: 1851–1909* (Paris, 1923)

Gilbert, J., 'Histoire de la publication de *l'Apologie* dans ses éditions successives', *Études anglaises*, 27 (1973), 262–74

Gohdes, Clarence, *American Literature in Nineteenth-Century England* (London, 1944)

Goyne, G. C., 'Browning and the Higher Criticism' (unpublished Ph.D. thesis, Cambridge University, 1967)

Graham, Kenneth, *English Criticism of the Novel, 1865–1900* (Oxford, 1965)

Graham, Walter, *English Literary Periodicals* (London, 1930)

Gray, J. M., *Thro' the Vision of the Night* (Edinburgh, 1980)

Greenhunt, M., 'G. H. Lewes as a Critic of the Novel', *Studies in Philology*, 45 (1948), 491–511

Gregory, T. S., 'Newman and Liberalism', in *A Tribute to Newman: Essays on Aspects of His Life and Thought*, ed. Michael Tierney (Dublin, 1945)

Gross, John, *The Rise and Fall of the Man of Letters* (London, 1969)

Haight, Gordon S., *George Eliot: A Biography* (London, 1969)

Haines, G., *The German Influence on English Education and Science, 1800–1886* (London, 1957)

Hardy, Florence Emily, *The Life of Thomas Hardy* (London, 1962)

Hardy, Thomas, *Collected Letters*, ed. R. L. Purdy and M. Millgate (London, 1979)

Harold, C. F., *John Henry Newman: An Expository Study of His Mind, Thought and Art* (London, 1948)

Harper, C., ed., *Cardinal Newman and William Froude: A Correspondence* (Baltimore, 1933)

Hillhouse, James T., *The Waverley Novels and Their Critics* (London, 1936)

Hinton, Thomas, 'German Intellectuals on the Eve of 1848', *German Life and Letters*, NS 2 (1948–9), 13–21

Holmes, John, *More Roman than Rome: English Catholicism in the Nineteenth Century* (London, 1978)

—— 'Newman's Attitude Towards Historical Criticism and Biblical Inspiration', *Downside Review*, 89 (1971), 22–37

—— 'John Henry Newman: History, Liberalism and the Dogmatic Principle', *Philosophical Studies*, 23 (1974), 86–106

—— 'Newman's Relation to the Development of Scientific and Historical Criticism in England', *Clergy Review*, 64 (1979), 28–90

Houghton, Walter, ed., *Wellesley Index to Victorian Periodicals, 1824–1900*, 3 vols. (Toronto, 1966–79)

Jay, Elizabeth, *The Religion of the Heart: Anglican Evangelicism and the Nineteenth-Century Novel* (Oxford, 1979)

Jordan, H. D., 'The Daily and Weekly Press in England in 1861', *South Atlantic Quarterly*, 28 (1929), 302–17

Jump, J. D., 'Matthew Arnold and the *Spectator*', *Review of English Studies*, 25 (1949), 61–4

—— 'Matthew Arnold and the *Saturday Review*', *Review of English Studies*, 22 (1946), 322–4

—— 'Weekly Reviewing in the 1850s', *Review of English Studies*, 24 (1948), 42–57

—— 'Weekly Reviewing in the 1860s', *Review of English Studies*, 28 (1952), 244–62

Kaminsky, Alice R., *George Henry Lewes as Literary Critic* (Syracuse, 1978)

Kent, Christopher, 'Higher Journalism and the mid-Victorian Clerisy', *Victorian Studies*, 13, No. 2 (1969–70), 181–98

—— 'Periodical Criticism of Drama, Music and Art, 1830–1914', *Victorian Periodicals Review*, 13 (1980), 31–54

Khattab, E. A., *The Critical Reception of Browning's 'The Ring and the Book', 1868–1889 and 1951–1968* (Salzburg, 1977)

Knelman, Judith, 'Trollope's Experiment with Anonymity', *Victorian Periodicals Review*, 14, No. 1 (Spring 1981), 21–3

Knights, Ben, *The Idea of the Clerisy in the Nineteenth Century* (London, 1978)

Knoepflmacher, U. C., 'George Eliot, Feuerbach and the Question of Criticism', *Victorian Studies*, 7, No. 3 (1963–64), 306–9

Lamm, W., 'Newman on the Imagination', *Modern Language Notes*, 68 (1953), 73–80

Lash, Nicholas, 'The Notion of Implicit and Explicit Reason in Newman's University Sermons: A Difficulty', *Heythrop Journal*, 11 (1970), 48–54

Lee, Alan J., *The Growth of the Popular Press in England, 1855–1914* (London, 1976)

Litzinger, Boyd, *Time's Revenges: Browning's Reputation as a Thinker, 1889–1962* (Knoxville, Tennessee, 1964)

Livingstone, James C., *The Ethics of Belief* (Florida, 1974)

Logan, J. V., *Wordsworthian Criticism: A Guide and Bibliography* (New York, 1974)

Lorimer, Douglas A., 'The Role of Anti-Slavery Sentiment in English Reaction to the American Civil War', *Historical Journal*, 19 (1976), 405–20

Lovelace, R. E., 'Wordsworth and the Early Victorians: A Study of his Influence and Reputation, 1830–1860' (unpublished Ph.D. dissertation, Cambridge University, 1951)

MacColl, Malcolm, *Memoirs and Correspondence*, ed. G. W. E. Russell (London, 1914)

MacIntyre, Alasdair, *After Virtue: A Study in Moral Theory* (London, 1981)

Mackinnon, Donald, *A Study In Ethical Theory* (London, 1957)

—— *The Borderlands of Theology* (Cambridge, 1961)

McLachlan, H., *The Unitarian Movement in the Religious Life of England: Its Contribution to Thought and Learning, 1700–1900* (London, 1934)

McSweeney, T., 'Swinburne's Tennyson', *Victorian Studies*, 22, No. 1 (1978), 5–28

Madden, Lionel, and Diana Dixon, *The Nineteenth-Century Periodical Press in Britain: A Bibliography of Modern Studies* (New York, 1976)

Madden, W. A., *Matthew Arnold: A Study of the Aesthetic Temperament in Victorian England*, Indiana University Humanities Series, 63 (Bloomington, Ind., 1967)

Manning, D. J., *Liberalism* (London, 1976)

Marchand, Leslie A., *The 'Athenaeum': A Mirror of Victorian Culture* (London, 1941)

Martin, Robert, *The Dust of Combat: A Life of Charles Kingsley* (London, 1952)

Maurer, O., 'Leslie Stephen and the *Cornhill Magazine*, 1871–1882', *University of Texas Studies in English*, 32 (1953), 67–95

Mendel, S., 'Metaphor and Rhetoric in Newman's *Apologia*', *Essays in Criticism*, 23 (1973), 357–71

Metcalf, Priscilla, *James Knowles: Victorian Editor and Architect* (London, 1980)

Miller, D. A., *Narrative and its Discontents: Problems of Closure in the Traditional Novel* (Princeton, 1981)

Moran, Benjamin, *Journal*, ed. S. A. Wallace and F. E. Gillespie, 2 vols. (Chicago, 1948)

Munby, F. A., *Publishing and Bookselling* (London, 1930)

Murry, John Middleton, 'Newman and Sidgwick', *Adelphi*, 2 (February 1925), 731–42

Naulty, R., 'Newman's Dispute with Locke', *Journal of the History of Philosophy*, 11 (1973), 453–7

Nesbitt, George L., *Benthamite Reviewing: The First Twelve Years of the Westminster Review, 1824–1836* (New York, 1934)

Newton, K. M., *George Eliot, Romantic Humanist: A Study of the Philosophical Structure of her Novels* (Totowa, N. J., 1981)

Olive, M., 'Le Problème de la *Grammaire de l'assentiment* d'après la correspondence entre Newman et William Froude', *Bulletin de litérature ecclésiastique*, 37 (1936), 217–40

Ong, Walter J., 'Newman's *Essay on Development* in its Intellectual Milieu', *Theological Studies*, 7 (March 1946), 3–45

Pacey, Desmond, 'Flaubert and his Victorian Critics', *University of Toronto Quarterly*, 16 (1946), 74–84

Pailin, D. A., *The Way to Faith: An Examination of Newman's 'Grammar of Assent'* (London, 1969)

Parlett, Mathilde, 'The Influence of Contemporary Criticism on George Eliot', *Studies in Philology*, 30 (1930), 103–32

Pattison, Robert, *Tennyson and Tradition* (Cambridge, Mass., 1979)

Peterson, W. S., 'Gladstone's Review of *Robert Elsmere*', *Review of English Studies*, 21 (1971), 442–61

Pickering, S., *The Moral Tradition in English Fiction, 1785–1850* (Hanover, New Hampshire, 1976)

Price, W. C., *The Literature of Journalism: An Annotated Bibliography* (London, 1959)

Prickett, Stephen, *Romanticism and Religion* (Cambridge, 1976)

Pykett, L., 'The Real vs the Ideal: Theories of Fiction in Periodicals, 1850–1870', *Victorian Periodicals Review*, 15, No. 2 (Summer 1982), 63–74

Raleigh, J. H., 'What Scott Meant to the Victorians', *Victorian Studies*, 7, No. 1 (1963–4), 7–34

Reardon, B., 'Newman and the Psychology of Belief', *Church Quarterly Review*, 158 (1959), 315–32

Redinger, Ruby, *George Eliot: The Emergent Self* (London, 1975)

Robbins, William, *The Arnoldian Principle of Flexibility*, University of Victoria English Literary Studies, 15 (Victoria, B.C., 1979)

Robertson, Priscilla, 'Students on the Barricades': Germany and Austria, 1848', *Political Science Quarterly*, 84 (June 1969), 367–79

Roll-Hansen, D., 'Matthew Arnold and the *Academy*: A Note on English Criticism in the 1870s', *PMLA* 118 (1953), 384–96

—— *The 'Academy', 1868–1879: Victorian Intellectuals in Revolt* (London, 1957)

Rowell, Geoffrey, *Hell and the Victorians: A Study of Nineteenth-Century Theological Controversies Concerning Eternal Punishment and the Future Life* (Oxford, 1974)

Saunders, J. W., *The Profession of English Letters* (London, 1964)

Selby, Robin C., *The Principle of Reserve in the Writings of John Henry Cardinal Newman* (London, 1975)

Scott, J. D. Robertson, *The Story of the 'Pall Mall Gazette'* (London, 1950)

Shannon, Edgar Finley, *Tennyson and the Reviewers: A Study of his Literary Reputation and of the Influence of the Critics on his Poetry, 1827–1851* (Cambridge, Mass., 1952)

Shattock, Joanne, and Michael Woolf, eds., *The Victorian Periodical Press: Samplings and Soundings* (Leicester, 1982)

Simonis, H., *The Street of Ink: An Intimate History of Journalism* (London, 1917)

Simpson, James, *Matthew Arnold and Goethe*, MHRA Texts and Dissertations 11 (London, 1979)

Stang, Richard, *The Theory of the Novel in England, 1850–1870* (London, 1959)

Stevens, Albert Kunnen, 'R. H. Hutton, Theologian and Critic' (unpublished Ph.D. dissertation, University of Michigan, 1949)

Strachey, John St Loe, *The Adventure of Living* (New York, 1922)

Strawson, P. F., *Individuals: An Essay in Descriptive Metaphysics* (London, 1959)

Tarrant, W. G., 'Some Chapters in the Story of the *Inquirer*', *Transactions of the Unitarian Historical Society*, 4 (1927), 35–44

Taylor, John Tinnon, *Early Opposition to the Novel, 1760–1830* (New York, 1943)

Tener, R. H., 'Richard Holt Hutton', *Times Literary Supplement*, 24 April 1959, 241

—— 'The *Spectator* Records', *Victorian Periodicals Newsletter*, 17 (Spring 1960), 33–6

—— 'Spectatorial Strachey', *Times Literary Supplement*, 31 December 1964, 1181

—— 'The Importance of Being Hutton', *Dalhousie Review*, 44 (Winter 1964–5), 418–27

—— 'Checklist of the Writings of R. H. Hutton', *Victorian Periodicals Newsletter*, special numbers 17 (September 1972), 20 (June 1973)

—— 'R. H. Hutton's Editorial Career', *Victorian Periodicals Newsletter*, 7, No. 2 (June 1974), 3–10; 7, No. 4 (December 1974), 6–13; 8, No. 1 (March 1975), 6–17

Thomas, G. N., 'R. H. Hutton, a Biographical and Critical Study' (unpublished Ph.D. dissertation, University of Illinois, 1949)

Thomas, Roger, 'The *Inquirer*', *Inquirer*, 25 July 1942, 211

Thomas, William Beach, *The Story of the 'Spectator', 1828–1928* (London, 1928)

Thompson, D., 'A Hundred Years of Higher Journalism', *Scrutiny*, 4 (1935), 25–34

Tillotson, Kathleen, *Mid-Victorian Studies* (London, 1965)

Tjoa, Hock Guan, *G. H. Lewes: A Victorian Mind* (London, 1977)

Townsend, F., 'Newman and the Problem of Critical Pose', *Victorian Notes*, 14 (May 1956), 22–5

Tristram, Henry, 'J. H. Möhler and J. H. Newman: la Pensée allemande et la Renaissance catholique en Angleterre', *Revue des sciences philosophiques et théologiques*, 27 (1938), 184–204

Tyrrel, George, *Lèttres à Henri Bremond*, ed. Anne Louis-David (Paris, 1971)

Vann, J. D., and R. T. Van Arsdel, eds., *Victorian Periodicals: A Guide to Research* (New York, 1978)

Vogeler, M., 'George Eliot and the Positivists', *Nineteenth-Century Fiction*, 35 (1980), 406–31

Ward, Wilfred Philip, *The Life of Cardinal Newman*, 2 vols. (London, 1913)

Wartofsky, Mark, *Feuerbach* (London, 1977)

Watson, M. R., 'The *Spectator* Tradition and the Development of the Familiar Essay', *Journal of English Literary History*, 13 (1946), 189–215

Weatherby, H. L., 'Newman and Victorian Liberalism: A Study in the Failure of Influence', *Critical Quarterly*, 13, No. 3 (Autumn 1970), 205–15

White, Robert B., *The English Literary Journal to 1900: A Guide to Information Sources* (Detroit, 1977)

Whitridge, Arnold, 'British Liberals and the American Civil War', *History Today*, 12, No. 10 (October 1962), 688–95

Wigmore-Beddoes, Dennis G., *Yesterday's Radicals: A Study of the Affinity Between Unitarianism and Broad Church Anglicanism in the Nineteenth Century* (Cambridge, 1971)

Wilbur, Earl Morse, *A History of Unitarianism* (Cambridge, Mass., 1952)

Wilkins, C. T., *The English Reputation of Matthew Arnold, 1840–1877* (Urbana, Ill., 1959)

Wilkinson, A. B., 'The Principles of Criticism of Fiction in Quarterlies, 1850–1860' (unpublished Ph.D. thesis, University of Cambridge, 1959)

Wilson, John Dover, *Leslie Stephen and Matthew Arnold as Critics of Wordsworth* (Cambridge, 1939)

Wright, T. R., 'George Eliot and Positivism: A Reassessment', *Modern Language Review*, 76 (1981), 257–72

Yearly, L. H., *The Ideas of Newman: Christianity and Human Religiosity* (Pennsylvania, 1978)

Index

INDEX